Easy

and

Economical

A HEALTHY EXCHANGES® COOKBOOK

JoAnna M. Lund

HELPing Others HELP Themselves
the **Healthy Exchanges® Way™**

A Perigee Book

D1275409

A Perigee Book
Published by The Berkley Publishing Group
375 Hudson Street
New York, New York 10014

For more information about Healthy Exchanges products, contact:
Healthy Exchanges, Inc.
P.O. Box 80
DeWitt, Iowa 52742-0080
(563) 659-8324
Fax: (563) 659-2126

Perigee Special Sales edition: August 2003
ISBN 0-399-52979-9

The Penguin Group (USA) Inc. World Wide Web site address is
http://www.penguin.com

Printed in the United States of America

10   9   8   7   6   5   4   3   2   1

Contents

What Takes Almost No Time, Costs Very Little, and Couldn't Be Simpler?

At the heart of Healthy Exchanges has been my determined philosophy, "If it takes longer to cook it than eat it, forget it!" I've always been interested in the three themes of this book, even before I began creating healthy recipes, and I know my readers share my feelings. There isn't a mom or dad or working single person around who has tons of extra time on his or her hands, hours and hours to spend in the kitchen preparing fancy meals. But you still deserve to eat healthy, *and* to eat well. That doesn't mean spending a fortune at gourmet shops or driving for miles and miles to an out-of-the-way health food store for exotic, high-priced items. You want tasty foods that you can prepare quickly from handy ingredients and using cooking methods that don't take time or special skills.

You've come to the right place! I want to make eating healthy as pleasurable as possible, and I want to make it fit into your busy lifestyle as easily as you'll soon be slipping into those slacks that are currently just a little too snug.

Let's talk about what you can do to make food preparation **FAST**:

- Do you often have to remove three other saucepans from your cabinet to get to the one you need for a favorite recipe? Do you have five mixing bowls but you always use the same one—and it's the one on the bottom of the pile? Are you constantly "spinning your wheels" looking for spices or extracts you've stored on those revolving shelves?

The solution here is a simple one: Reorganize your kitchen, *just a little*, and place the items you use every day close at hand. Donate small appliances you never use to your church's rummage sale. Give your beat-up kitchen spoons to your grandbaby to use as drumsticks. The goal here is to "streamline"—not just your body, but also your work space. It'll make stirring up my healthy recipes a real breeze!

My recipes use ingredients you can easily find in just about any supermarket or grocery store, but as the prices of everything seem headed UP, UP, UP, I try to figure out smart ways to keep costs DOWN, DOWN, DOWN! What can you do to make healthy eating **CHEAP?**

- Collect the sale circulars of your favorite markets before the start of the week (if they're not in your Sunday paper, pick one up at the store—but don't start shopping just yet!), sit down with a cup of tea, and think about meal planning based on whatever's on special that week. If chicken breasts are amazingly cheap, buy double or triple your usual order. What you don't cook right away, you can freeze. If an item is shelf-stable and can last a long time, buy as much as you can afford, and stack it on shelves in the basement. (One of my readers told me about her aunt, who always bought tomato juice ten large cans at a time because it "made her feel rich"!) But don't get carried away by giant-size items unless you're sure you're really saving money—check the unit cost, and estimate how much of it you can use in the next few weeks or months.

Buying in quantity is usually a money saver, and can be an energy saver too (fewer trips to the store save gas). But don't try to cram those extras in your kitchen cabinets or even your pantry, if you're lucky enough to have one. Create a "stock list" of what you have stored elsewhere (the basement, the attic, under your bed) so you always know what you have and *where it is.*

Now, what else can I suggest to make living a healthy lifestyle **EASY?**

One of my favorite suggestions is what I call a "cooking marathon." It's a technique that worked for me when I first began creating Healthy Exchanges recipes, and it's still the best way I know to stick with what helped me lose 130 pounds and keep it off. I didn't have much time to cook back then; I worked full-time in insurance, I was raising three children, and I was finishing my college degree at night. These days, between radio interviews, tours of the "House That Recipes Built," speaking engagements, appearances on QVC, and testing recipes for my new books, I still don't have time to cook. At least, most of the time I don't.

But what I did then, and often still do now, is choose an afternoon or evening for a cooking marathon. I plan for it by shopping for the ingredients I need for three or four main dishes, a couple of sweet salads, a few vegetable side dishes, and at least two or three desserts. I figure, as long as I'm going to dirty a few pots and pans, why not dirty a few more—and really fill my refrigerator and freezer with tasty, healthy food I can heat up in seconds. Most of my casseroles cook at 350 degrees, so you can bake more than one at once. The salads and desserts stir up quickly, and can be easily divided and frozen or refrigerated. Just invest in some sturdy plastic containers, clear off your counters, put on your favorite music, and you're on your way!

Did you ever think living healthy could be this **fast, cheap, and easy?**

Dear Friends,

People often ask me why I include the same general information at the beginning of all my cookbooks. If you've seen any of my other books, you'll know that my "common folk" recipes are just one part of the Healthy Exchanges picture. You know that I firmly believe—and say so whenever and wherever I can— that *Healthy Exchanges is not a diet, it's a way of life!* That's why I include the story of Healthy Exchanges in every book, because I know that the tale of my struggle to lose weight and regain my health is one that speaks to the hearts of many thousands of people. And because Healthy Exchanges is not just a collection of recipes, I always include the wisdom that I've learned from my own experiences and the knowledge of the health and cooking professionals I meet. Whether it's learning about nutrition or making shopping and cooking easier, no Healthy Exchanges book would be complete without features like "A Peek into My Pantry" or "JoAnna's Ten Commandments of Successful Cooking."

Even if you've read my other books, you might still want to skim the following chapters—you never know when I'll slip in a new bit of wisdom or suggest a new product that will make your journey to health an easier and tastier one. If you're sharing this book with a friend or family member, you'll want to make sure they read the following pages before they start stirring up the recipes.

If this is the first book of mine that you've read, I want to welcome you with all my heart to the Healthy Exchanges Family. (And, of course, I'd love to hear your comments or questions. See the back of the book for my mailing address . . . or come visit if you happen to find yourself in DeWitt, Iowa—just ask anybody for directions to Healthy Exchanges!)

JoAnna M. Lund
and Healthy
Exchanges

Food is the first invited guest to every special occasion in every family's memory scrapbook. From baptism to graduation, from weddings to wakes, food brings us together.

It wasn't always that way at our house. I used to eat alone, even when my family was there, because while they were dining on real food, I was nibbling at whatever my newest diet called for. In fact, for twenty-eight years, I called myself the diet queen of DeWitt, Iowa.

I tried every diet I ever came across, every one I could afford, and every one that found its way to my small town in eastern Iowa. I was willing to try anything that promised to "melt off the pounds," determined to deprive my body in every possible way in order to become thin at last.

I sent away for expensive "miracle" diet pills. I starved myself on the Cambridge Diet and the Bahama Diet. I gobbled diet candies, took thyroid pills, fiber pills, prescription and over-the-counter diet pills. I went to endless weight-loss support group meetings—but I somehow managed to turn healthy programs such as Overeaters Anonymous, Weight Watchers, and TOPS into unhealthy diets . . . diets I could never follow for more than a few months.

I was determined to discover something that worked long-term, but each new failure increased my desperation that I'd never find it.

I ate strange concoctions and rubbed on even stranger potions. I tried liquid diets. I agreed to be hypnotized. I tried reflexology and even had an acupressure device stuck in my ear!

Does my story sound a lot like yours? I'm not surprised. No wonder the weight-loss business is a billion-dollar industry!

Every new thing I tried seemed to work—at least at first. And losing that first five or ten pounds would get me so excited, I'd believe that this new miracle diet would, finally, get my weight off for keeps.

Inevitably, though, the initial excitement wore off. The diet's routine and boredom set in, and I quit. I shoved the pills to the back of the medicine chest; pushed the cans of powdered shake mix to the rear of the kitchen cabinets; slid all the program materials out of sight under my bed; and once more I felt like a failure.

Like most dieters, I quickly gained back the weight I'd lost each time, along with a few extra "souvenir" pounds that seemed always to settle around my hips. I'd done the diet-lose-weight-gain-it-all-back "yo-yo" on the average of once a year. It's no exaggeration to say that over the years I've lost 1,000 pounds—and gained back 1,150 pounds.

Finally, at the age of forty-six, I weighed more than I'd ever imagined possible. I'd stopped believing that any diet could work for me. I drowned my sorrows in sacks of cake doughnuts and wondered if I'd live long enough to watch my grandchildren grow up.

Something had to change.

I had to change.

Finally, I did.

I'm just over fifty now—and I'm 130 pounds less than my all-time high of close to 300 pounds. I've kept the weight off for more than six years. I'd like to lose another ten pounds, but I'm not obsessed about it. If it takes me two or three years to accomplish it, that's okay.

What I *do* care about is never saying hello again to any of those unwanted pounds I said good-bye to!

How did I jump off the roller coaster I was on? For one thing, I finally stopped looking to food to solve my emotional problems. But what really shook me up—and got me started on the path that changed my life—was Operation Desert Storm in early 1991. I sent three children off to the Persian Gulf War—my son-in-law, Matt, a medic in Special Forces; my daughter, Becky, a full-time college student and member of a medical unit in the Army Reserve; and my son, James, a member of the Inactive Army Reserve, reactivated as a chemicals expert.

Somehow, knowing that my children were putting their lives on the line got me thinking about my own mortality—and I knew in my heart the last thing they needed while they were overseas was to get a letter from home saying that their mother was ill because of a food-related problem.

The day I drove the third child to the airport to leave for Saudi Arabia, something happened to me that would change my life for the better—and forever. I stopped praying my constant prayer as a professional dieter, which was simply "Please, God, let me lose ten pounds by Friday." Instead, I began praying, "God, please help me not to be a burden to my kids and my family." I quit praying for what I wanted and started praying for what I needed—and in the process my prayers were answered. I couldn't keep the kids safe—that was out of my hands—but I could try to get healthier to better handle the stress of it. It was the least I could do on the homefront.

That quiet prayer was the beginning of the new JoAnna Lund. My initial goal was not to lose weight or create healthy recipes. I only wanted to become healthier for my kids, my husband, and myself.

Each of my children returned safely from the Persian Gulf War. But something didn't come back—the 130 extra pounds I'd been lugging around for far too long. I'd finally accepted the truth after all those agonizing years of suffering through on-again, off-again dieting.

There are no "magic" cures in life.

No "miracle" potion, pill, or diet will make unwanted pounds disappear.

I found something better than magic, if you can believe it. When I turned my weight and health dilemma over to God for guidance, a new JoAnna Lund and Healthy Exchanges were born.

I discovered a new way to live my life—and uncovered an unexpected talent for creating easy "common folk" healthy recipes and sharing my commonsense approach to healthy living. I learned that I could motivate others to change their lives and adopt a positive outlook. I began publishing cookbooks and a monthly food newsletter, and speaking to groups all over the country.

I like to say, *"When life handed me a lemon, not only did I make healthy, tasty lemonade, I wrote the recipe down!"*

What I finally found was not a quick fix or a short-term diet, but a great way to live well for a lifetime.

I want to share it with you.

Food Exchanges and Weight Loss Choices™

If you've ever been on one of the national weight-loss programs like Weight Watchers or Diet Center, you've already been introduced to the concept of measured portions of different food groups that make up your daily food plan. If you are not familiar with such a system of weight-loss choices or exchanges, here's a brief explanation. (If you want or need more detailed information, you can write to the American Dietetic Association or the American Diabetes Association for comprehensive explanations.)

The idea of food exchanges is to divide foods into basic food groups. The foods in each group are measured in servings that have comparable values. These groups include Proteins/Meats, Breads/ Starches, Fruits, Skim Milk, Vegetables, Fats, Free Foods, and Optional Calories.

Each choice or exchange included in a particular group has about the same number of calories and a similar carbohydrate, protein, and fat content as the other foods in that group. Because any food on a particular list can be "exchanged" for any other food in that group, it makes sense to call the food groups *exchanges* or *choices*.

I like to think we are also "exchanging" bad habits and food choices for good ones!

By using Weight Loss Choices™ or exchanges, you can choose from a variety of foods without having to calculate the nutrient value of each one. This makes it easier to include a wide variety of foods in your daily menus and gives you the opportunity to tailor your choices to your unique appetite.

If you want to lose weight, you should consult your physician or other weight-control expert regarding the number of servings that would be best for you from each food group. Since men generally require more calories than women, and since the requirements for growing children and teenagers differ from those of adults, the right number of exchanges for any one person is a personal decision.

I have included a suggested plan of Weight Loss Choices in the pages following the exchange lists. It's a program I used to lose 130 pounds, and it's the one I still follow today.

(If you are a diabetic or have been diagnosed with heart problems, it is best to meet with your physician before using this or any other food program or recipe collection.)

Food Group Weight Loss Choices™/Exchanges

Not all food group exchanges are alike. The ones that follow are for anyone who's interested in weight loss or maintenance. If you are a diabetic, you should check with your health-care provider or dietitian to get the information you need to help you plan your diet. Diabetic exchanges are calculated by the American Diabetic Association, and information about them is provided in *The Diabetic's Healthy Exchanges Cookbook* (Perigee Books).

Every Healthy Exchanges recipe provides calculations in three ways:

- Weight Loss Choices/Exchanges

- Calories; Fat, Protein, Carbohydrates, and Fiber grams; and Sodium and Calcium milligrams

- Diabetic Exchanges calculated for me by a registered dietitian

Healthy Exchanges recipes can help you eat well and recover your health, whatever your health concerns may be. Please take a few minutes to review the exchange lists and the suggestions that follow on how to count them. You have lots of great eating in store for you!

Proteins

Meat, poultry, seafood, eggs, cheese, and legumes. One exchange of Protein is approximately 60 calories. Examples of one Protein choice or exchange:

1 ounce cooked weight of lean meat, poultry, or seafood
2 ounces white fish
1½ ounces 97% fat-free ham
1 egg (limit to no more than 4 per week)
¼ cup egg substitute
3 egg whites

¾ ounce reduced-fat cheese
½ cup fat-free cottage cheese
2 ounces cooked or ¾ ounce uncooked dry beans
1 tablespoon peanut butter (also count 1 fat exchange)

Breads

Breads, crackers, cereals, grains, and starchy vegetables. One exchange of Bread is approximately 80 calories. Examples of one Bread choice or exchange:

1 slice bread or 2 slices reduced-calorie bread (40 calories or less)
1 roll, any type (1 ounce)
½ cup cooked pasta or ¾ ounce uncooked (scant ½ cup)
½ cup cooked rice or 1 ounce uncooked (⅓ cup)
3 tablespoons flour
¾ ounce cold cereal
½ cup cooked hot cereal or ¾ ounce uncooked (2 tablespoons)
½ cup corn (kernels or cream-style) or peas
4 ounces white potato, cooked, or 5 ounces uncooked
3 ounces sweet potato, cooked, or 4 ounces uncooked
3 cups air-popped popcorn
7 fat-free crackers (¾ ounce)
3 (2½-inch squares) graham crackers
2 (¾-ounce) rice cakes or 6 mini
1 tortilla, any type (6-inch diameter)

Fruits

All fruits and fruit juices. One exchange of Fruit is approximately 60 calories. Examples of one Fruit choice or exchange:

1 small apple or ½ cup slices
1 small orange
½ medium banana
¾ cup berries (except strawberries and cranberries)
1 cup strawberries or cranberries
½ cup canned fruit, packed in fruit juice or rinsed well
2 tablespoons raisins

1 tablespoon spreadable fruit spread
½ cup apple juice (4 fluid ounces)
½ cup orange juice (4 fluid ounces)
½ cup applesauce

Skim Milk

Milk, buttermilk, and yogurt. One exchange of Skim Milk is approximately 90 calories. Examples of one Skim Milk choice or exchange:

1 cup skim milk
½ cup evaporated skim milk
1 cup low-fat buttermilk
¾ cup plain fat-free yogurt
⅓ cup nonfat dry milk powder

Vegetables

All fresh, canned, or frozen vegetables other than the starchy vegetables. One exchange of Vegetable is approximately 30 calories. Examples of one Vegetable choice or exchange:

½ cup vegetable
¼ cup tomato sauce
1 medium fresh tomato
½ cup vegetable juice

Fats

Margarine, mayonnaise, vegetable oils, salad dressings, olives, and nuts. One exchange of Fat is approximately 40 calories. Examples of one Fat choice or exchange:

1 teaspoon margarine or 2 teaspoons reduced-calorie margarine
1 teaspoon butter
1 teaspoon vegetable oil
1 teaspoon mayonnaise or 2 teaspoons reduced-calorie mayonnaise

1 teaspoon peanut butter
1 ounce olives
¼ ounce pecans or walnuts

Free Foods

Foods that do not provide nutritional value but are used to enhance the taste of foods are included in the Free Foods group. Examples of these are spices, herbs, extracts, vinegar, lemon juice, mustard, Worcestershire sauce, and soy sauce. Cooking sprays and artificial sweeteners used in moderation are also included in this group. However, you'll see that I include the caloric value of artificial sweeteners in the Optional Calories of the recipes.

You may occasionally see a recipe that lists "free food" as part of the portion. According to the published exchange lists, a free food contains fewer than 20 calories per serving. Two or three servings per day of free foods/drinks are usually allowed in a meal plan.

Optional Calories

Foods that do not fit into any other group but are used in moderation in recipes are included in Optional Calories. Foods that are counted in this way include sugar-free gelatin and puddings, fat-free mayonnaise and dressings, reduced-calorie whipped toppings, reduced-calorie syrups and jams, chocolate chips, coconut, and canned broth.

Sliders ™

These are 80 Optional Calorie increments that do not fit into any particular category. You can choose which food group to *slide* these into. It is wise to limit this selection to approximately three to four per day to ensure the best possible nutrition for your body while still enjoying an occasional treat.

Sliders may be used in either of the following ways:

1. If you have consumed all your Protein, Bread, Fruit, or Skim Milk Weight Loss Choices for the day and you want to eat additional foods from those food groups, you simply use a Slider. It's what I call "healthy horse trading." Remember that Sliders may not be traded for choices in the Vegetables or Fats food groups.

2. Sliders may also be deducted from your Optional Calories for the day or week. ¼ Slider equals 20 Optional Calories; ½ Slider equals 40 Optional Calories; ¾ Slider equals 60 Optional Calories; and 1 Slider equals 80 Optional Calories.

Healthy Exchanges® Weight Loss Choices™

My original Healthy Exchanges program of Weight Loss Choices was based on an average daily total of 1,400 to 1,600 calories per day. That was what I determined was right for my needs, and for those of most women. Because men require additional calories (about 1,600 to 1,900), here are my suggested plans for women and men. (*If you require more or fewer calories, please revise this plan to meet your individual needs.*)

Each day, women should plan to eat:

2 Skim Milk servings, 90 calories each
2 Fat servings, 40 calories each
3 Fruit servings, 60 calories each
4 Vegetable servings, or more, 30 calories each
5 Protein servings, 60 calories each
5 Bread servings, 80 calories each

Each day, men should plan to eat:

2 Skim Milk servings, 90 calories each
4 Fat servings, 40 calories each
3 Fruit servings, 60 calories each
4 Vegetable servings, or more, 30 calories each
6 Protein servings, 60 calories each
7 Bread servings, 80 calories each

Young people should follow the program for men but add 1 Skim Milk serving for a total of 3 servings.

You may also choose to add up to 100 Optional Calories per day, and up to 21 to 28 Sliders per week at 80 calories each. If you choose to include more Sliders in your daily or weekly totals, deduct those 80 calories from your Optional Calorie "bank."

A word about **Sliders**: These are to be counted toward your totals after you have used your allotment of choices of Skim Milk, Protein, Bread, and Fruit for the day. By "sliding" an additional choice into one of these groups, you can meet your individual needs for that day. Sliders are especially helpful when traveling, stressed-out, eating out, or for special events. I often use mine so I can enjoy my favorite Healthy Exchanges desserts. Vegetables are not to be counted as Sliders. 0Enjoy as many Vegetable choices as you need to feel satisfied. Because we want to limit our fat intake to moderate amounts, additional Fat choices should not be counted as Sliders. If you choose to include more fat on an *occasional* basis, count the extra choices as Optional Calories.

Keep a daily food diary of your Weight Loss Choices, checking off what you eat as you go. If, at the end of the day, your required selections are not 100 percent accounted for, but you have done the best you can, go to bed with a clear conscience. There will be days when you have ¼ Fruit or ½ Bread left over. What are you going to do—eat two slices of an orange or half a slice of bread and throw the rest out? I always say, "Nothing in life comes out exact." Just do the best you can . . . *the best you can.*

Try to drink at least eight 8-ounce glasses of water a day. Water truly is the "nectar" of good health.

As a little added insurance, I take a multivitamin each day. It's not essential, but if my day's worth of well-planned meals "bites the dust" when unexpected events intrude on my regular routine, my body still gets its vital nutrients.

The calories listed in each group of choices are averages. Some choices within each group may be higher or lower, so it's important to select a variety of different foods instead of eating the same three or four all the time.

Use your Optional Calories! They are what I call "life's little extras." They make all the difference in how you enjoy your food and appreciate the variety available to you. Yes, we can get by without them, but do you really want to? Keep in mind that you should be using all your daily Weight Loss Choices first to ensure you are getting the basics of good nutrition. But I guarantee that Optional Calories will keep you from feeling deprived—and help you reach your weight-loss goals.

Sodium, Fat, Cholesterol, and Processed Foods

A re Healthy Exchanges ingredients really healthy?

When I first created Healthy Exchanges, many people asked about sodium; about whether it was necessary to calculate the percentage of fat, saturated fat, and cholesterol in a healthy diet; and about my use of processed foods in many recipes. I researched these questions as I was developing my program, so you can feel confident about using the recipes and food plan.

Sodium

Most people consume more sodium than their bodies need. The American Heart Association and the American Diabetes Association recommend limiting daily sodium intake to no more than 3,000 milligrams per day. If your doctor suggests you limit your sodium even more, then *you really must read labels.*

Sodium is an essential nutrient and should not be completely eliminated. It helps to regulate blood volume and is needed for normal daily muscle and nerve functions. Most of us, however, have no trouble getting "all we need" and then some.

As with everything else, moderation is my approach. I rarely ever have salt on my list as an added ingredient. But if you're especially sodium-sensitive, make the right choices for you—and save high-sodium foods such as sauerkraut for an occasional treat.

I use lots of spices to enhance flavors, so you won't notice the absence of salt. In the few cases where it is used, salt is vital for the success of the recipe, so please don't omit it.

When I do use an ingredient high in sodium, I try to compensate by using low-sodium products in the remainder of the recipe. Many fat-free products are a little higher in sodium to make up for any loss of flavor that disappeared along with the fat. But when I take advantage of these fat-free, higher-sodium products, I stretch that ingredient within the recipe, lowering the amount of sodium per serving. A good example is my use of fat-free and reduced-sodium canned soups. While the suggested number of servings per can is two, I make sure my final creation serves at least four and sometimes six. So the soup's sodium has been "watered down" from one-third to one-half of the original amount.

Even if you don't have to watch your sodium intake for medical reasons, using moderation is another "healthy exchange" to make on your own journey to good health.

Fat Percentages

We've been told that 30 percent is the magic number—that we should limit fat intake to 30 percent or less of our total calories. It's good advice, and I try to have a weekly average of 15 percent to 25 percent myself. I believe any less than 15 percent is really just another restrictive diet that won't last. And more than 25 percent on a regular basis is too much of a good thing.

When I started listing fat grams along with calories in my recipes, I was tempted to include the percentage of calories from fat. After all, in the vast majority of my recipes, that percentage is well below 30 percent. This even includes my pie recipes that allow you a realistic serving instead of many "diet" recipes that tell you a serving is 1/12 of a pie.

Figuring fat grams is easy enough. Each gram of fat equals 9 calories. Multiply fat grams by 9, then divide that number by the total calories to get the percentage of calories from fat.

So why don't I do it? After consulting four registered dietitians for advice, I decided to omit this information. They felt that it's too easy for people to become obsessed by that 30 percent figure, which is after all supposed to be a percentage of total calories over the course of a day or a week. We mustn't feel we can't include a healthy ingredient such as pecans or olives in one recipe just because, on its own, it has more than 30 percent of its calories from fat.

An example of this would be a casserole made with 90 percent lean red meat. Most of us benefit from eating red meat in moderation, as it provides iron and niacin in our diets, and it also makes life more enjoyable for us and those who eat with us. If we *only* look at the percentage of calories from fat in a serving of this one dish, which might be as high as 40 to 45 percent, we might choose not to include this recipe in our weekly food plan.

The dietitians suggested that it's important to consider the total picture when making such decisions. As long as your overall food plan keeps fat calories to 30 percent, it's all right to enjoy an occasional dish that is somewhat higher in fat content. Healthy foods I include in **MODERATION** include 90 percent lean red meat, olives, and nuts. I don't eat these foods every day, and you may not either. But occasionally, in a good recipe, they make all the difference in the world between just getting by (deprivation) and truly enjoying your food.

Remember, the goal is eating in a healthy way so you can enjoy and live well the rest of your life.

Saturated Fats and Cholesterol

You'll see that I don't provide calculations for saturated fats or cholesterol amounts in my recipes. It's for the simple and yet not so simple reason that accurate, up-to-date, brand-specific information can be difficult to obtain from food manufacturers, especially since the way in which they produce food keeps changing rapidly. But once more I've consulted with registered dietitians and other professionals and found that, because I use only a few products that are high in saturated fat, and use them in such limited quantities, my recipes are suitable for patients concerned about controlling or lowering cholesterol. You'll also find that whenever I do use one of these ingredients *in moderation*, everything else in the recipe, and in the meals my family and I enjoy, is low in fat.

Processed Foods

Just what *is* processed food, anyway? What do I mean by the term "processed foods," and why do I use them, when the "purest" recipe developers in Recipe Land consider them "pedestrian" and won't ever use something from a box, container, or can? A letter I received and a passing statement from a stranger made me reflect on what I mean when I refer to processed foods, and helped me reaffirm why I use them in my "common folk" healthy recipes.

If you are like the vast millions who agree with me, then I'm not sharing anything new with you. And if you happen to disagree, that's okay, too.

A few months ago, a woman sent me several articles from various "whole food" publications and wrote that she was wary of processed foods, and wondered why I used them in my recipes. She then scribbled on the bottom of her note, "Just how healthy *is* Healthy Exchanges?" Then, a few weeks later, during a chance visit at a public food event with a very pleasant woman, I was struck by how we all have our own definitions of what processed foods are. She shared with me, in a somewhat self-righteous manner, that she *never* uses processed foods. She only cooked with fresh fruits and vegetables, she told me. Then later she said that she used canned reduced-fat soups all the time! Was her definition different than mine, I wondered? Soup in a can, whether it's reduced in fat or not, still meets my definition of a processed food.

So I got out a copy of my book *HELP: Healthy Exchanges Lifetime Plan* and reread what I had written back then about processed foods. Nothing in my definition had changed since I wrote that section. I still believe that healthy processed foods, such as canned soups, prepared piecrusts, sugar-free instant puddings, fat-free sour cream, and frozen whipped topping, when used properly, all have a place as ingredients in healthy recipes.

I never use an ingredient that hasn't been approved by either the American Diabetic Association, the American Dietetic Association, or the American Heart Association. Whenever I'm in doubt, I send for their position papers, then ask knowledgeable registered dietitians to explain those papers to me in layman's language. I've been assured by all of them that the sugar- and fat-free products I use in my recipes are indeed safe.

If you don't agree, nothing I can say or write will convince you otherwise. But, if you've been using the healthy processed foods and have been concerned about the almost daily hoopla you hear about yet another product that's going to be the doom of all of us, then just stick with reason. For every product on the grocery shelves, there are those who want you to buy it and there are those who don't, *because they want you to buy their products instead.* So we have to learn to sift the fact from the fiction. Let's take sugar substitutes, for example. In making your own evaluations, you should be skeptical about any information provided by the sugar substitute manufacturers, because they have a vested interest in our buying their products. Likewise, ignore any information provided by the sugar industry, because they have a vested interest in our *not* buying sugar substitutes. Then, if you aren't sure if you can really trust the government or any of its agencies, toss out their data, too. That leaves the three associations I mentioned earlier. Do you think any of them would say a product is safe if it isn't? Or say a product isn't safe when it is? They have nothing to gain or lose, *other than their integrity*, if they intentionally try to mislead us. That's why I only go to these associations for information concerning healthy processed foods.

I certainly don't recommend that everything we eat should come from a can, box, or jar. I think the best of all possible worlds is to start with the basics: grains such as rice, pasta, or corn. Then, for example, add some raw vegetables and extra-lean meat such as poultry, fish, beef, or pork. Stir in some healthy canned soup or tomato sauce, and you'll end up with something that is not only healthy but tastes so good, everyone from toddlers to great-grandparents will want to eat it!

I've never been in favor of spraying everything we eat with chemicals, and I don't believe that all our foods should come out of packages. But I do think we should use the best available healthy processed foods to make cooking easier and food taste better. I take advantage of the good-tasting low-fat and low-sugar products found in any grocery store. My recipes are created for busy people like me, people who want to eat healthily and economically but who still want the food to satisfy their tastebuds. I don't expect anyone to visit out-of-the-way health food stores or find the time to cook beans from scratch—*because I don't!* Most of you can't grow fresh food in the backyard and many of you may not have access to farmers' markets or large supermarkets. I want to help you figure out realistic ways to make healthy eating a reality *wherever you live,* or you will not stick to a healthy lifestyle for long.

So if you've been swayed (by individuals or companies with vested interests or hidden agendas) into thinking that all processed foods are bad for you, you may want to reconsider your position. Or if you've been fooling yourself into believing that you *never* use processed foods but regularly reach for that healthy canned soup, stop playing games with yourself—you are using processed foods in a healthy way. And, if you're like me and use healthy processed foods in *moderation,* don't let anyone make you feel ashamed about including these products in your healthy lifestyle. Only *you* can decide what's best for *you* and your family's needs.

Part of living a healthy lifestyle is making those decisions and then getting on with life. Congratulations on choosing to live a healthy lifestyle, and let's celebrate together by sharing a piece of Healthy Exchanges pie that I've garnished with Cool Whip Lite!

JoAnna's Ten Commandments of Successful Cooking

A very important part of any journey is knowing where you are going and the best way to get there. If you plan and prepare before you start to cook, you should reach mealtime with foods to write home about!

1. **Read the entire recipe from start to finish** and be sure you understand the process involved. Check that you have all the equipment you will need *before* you begin.

2. **Check the ingredient list** and be sure you have *everything* and in the amounts required. Keep cooking sprays handy—while they're not listed as ingredients, I use them all the time (just a quick squirt!).

3. **Set out *all* the ingredients and equipment needed** to prepare the recipe on the counter near you *before* you start. Remember that old saying *A stitch in time saves nine*? It applies in the kitchen, too.

4. **Do as much advance preparation as possible** before actually cooking. Chop, cut, grate, or do whatever is needed to prepare the ingredients and have them ready before you start to mix. Turn the oven on at least ten minutes before putting food in to bake, to allow the oven to preheat to the proper temperature.

5. **Use a kitchen timer** to tell you when the cooking or baking time is up. Because stove temperatures vary slightly by manufacturer, you may want to set your timer for five minutes less than the suggested time just to prevent overcooking. Check the progress of your dish at that time, then decide if you need the additional minutes or not.

6. **Measure carefully.** Use glass measures for liquids and metal or plastic cups for dry ingredients. My recipes are based on standard measurements. Unless I tell you it's a scant or full cup, measure the cup level.

7. **For best results, follow the recipe instructions exactly.** Feel free to substitute ingredients that *don't tamper* with the basic chemistry of the recipe, but be sure to leave key ingredients alone. For example, you could substitute sugar-free instant chocolate pudding for sugar-free instant butterscotch pudding, but if you use a six-serving package when a four-serving package is listed in the ingredients, or you use instant when cook-and-serve is required, you won't get the right result.

8. **Clean up as you go.** It is much easier to wash a few items at a time than to face a whole counter of dirty dishes later. The same is true for spills on the counter or floor.

9. **Be careful about doubling or halving a recipe.** Though many recipes can be altered successfully to serve more or fewer people, *many cannot.* This is especially true when it comes to spices and liquids. If you try to double a recipe that calls for 1 teaspoon pumpkin pie spice, for example, and you double the spice, you may end up with a too-spicy taste. I usually suggest increasing spices or liquid by 1½ times when doubling a recipe. If it tastes a little bland to you, you can increase the spice to 1¾ times the original amount the next time you prepare the dish. Remember: You can always add more, but you can't take it out after it's stirred in.

    The same is true with liquid ingredients. If you wanted to **triple** a recipe like my **Tex Mex Fiesta Casserole** because you were planning to serve a crowd, you might think you should use three times as much of every ingredient. Don't, or you could end up with Tex Mex Fiesta Casserole Soup! The original recipe calls for 1¾ cups tomato sauce, so I'd suggest using 3½ cups when you **triple** the recipe (or 2¾ cups if you **double** it). You'll still have a good-tasting dish that won't run all over the plate.

10. **Write your reactions next to each recipe once you've served it.** Yes, that's right, I'm giving you permission to write in this book. It's yours, after all. Ask yourself: Did everyone like it? Did you have to add another half teaspoon of chili seasoning to please your family, who like to live on the spicier side of the street? You may even want to rate the recipe on a scale of 1☆ to 4☆, depending on what you thought of it. (Four stars would be the top rating—and I hope you'll feel that way about many of my recipes.) Jotting down your comments while they are fresh in your mind will help you personalize the recipe to your own taste the next time you prepare it.

My Best Healthy Exchanges Tips and Tidbits

Measurements, General Cooking Tips, and Basic Ingredients

Sugar Substitutes

The word **moderation** best describes **my use of fats, sugar substitutes,** and **sodium** in these recipes. Wherever possible, I've used cooking spray for sautéing and for browning meats and vegetables. I also use reduced-calorie margarine and fat-free mayonnaise and salad dressings. Lean ground turkey *or* ground beef can be used in the recipes. Just be sure whatever you choose is at least *90 percent lean.*

I've also included **small amounts of sugar substitutes as the sweetening agent** in many of the recipes. I don't drink a hundred cans of soda a day or eat enough artificially sweetened foods in a 24-hour time period to be troubled by sugar substitutes. But if this is a concern of yours and you *do not* need to watch your sugar intake, you can always replace the sugar substitutes with processed sugar and the sugar-free products with regular ones.

I created my recipes knowing they would also be used by hypoglycemics, diabetics, and those concerned about triglycerides. If you choose to use sugar instead, be sure to count the additional calories.

A word of caution when cooking with **sugar substitutes:** Use **saccharin**-based sweeteners when **heating or baking.** In recipes that **don't require heat, aspartame** (known as NutraSweet) works well in uncooked dishes but leaves an aftertaste in baked products.

Sugar Twin is my first choice for a sugar substitute. If you can't find that, use

22

Sprinkle Sweet. They measure like sugar, you can cook and bake with them, they're inexpensive, and they are easily poured from their boxes.

Many of my recipes for quick breads, muffins, and cakes include a package of sugar-free instant pudding mix, which is sweetened with NutraSweet Yet we've been told that NutraSweet breaks down under heat. I've tested my recipes again and again, and here's what I've found: Baking with a NutraSweet product sold for home sweetening doesn't work, but baking with NutraSweet-sweetened instant pudding mixes turns out great. I choose not to question why this is, but continue to use these products in creating my Healthy Exchanges recipes.

How much sweetener is the right amount? I use pourable Sugar Twin, Brown Sugar Twin, and Sprinkle Sweet in my recipes because they measure just like sugar. What could be easier? I also use them because they work wonderfully in cooked and baked products.

If you are using a brand other than these, you need to check the package to figure out how much of your sweetener will equal what's called for in the recipe.

If you choose to use real sugar or brown sugar, then you would use the same amount the recipe lists for pourable Sugar Twin or Brown Sugar Twin.

You'll see that I list specific brands only when the recipe preparation involves heat. In a salad or other recipe that doesn't require cooking, I will list the ingredient as "sugar substitute to equal 2 tablespoons sugar." You can then use any sweetener you choose—Equal, Sweet'n Low, Sweet Ten, or any other aspartame-based sugar substitute. Just check the label so you'll be using the right amount to equal those 2 tablespoons of sugar. Or if you choose, you can use regular sugar.

With Healthy Exchanges recipes, the "sweet life" is the only life for me!

Pan Sizes

I'm often asked why I use an **8-by-8-inch baking dish** in my recipes. It's for portion control. If the recipe says it serves 4, just cut down the center, turn the dish, and cut again. Like magic, there's your serving. Also, if this is the only recipe you are preparing requiring an oven, the square dish fits into a tabletop toaster oven easily and energy can be conserved.

While many of my recipes call for an 8-by-8-inch baking dish, others ask for a 9-by-9-inch cake pan. If you don't have a 9-inch-square pan, is it all right to use your 8-inch dish instead? In most cases, the small difference in the size of these two pans won't significantly affect the finished product, so until you can get your hands on the right-size pan, go ahead and use your baking dish.

However, since the 8-inch dish is usually made of glass, and the 9-inch cake pan is made of metal, you will want to adjust the baking temperature. If you're using a glass baking dish in a recipe that calls for a 9-inch pan, be sure to lower your baking temperature by 15 degrees *or* check your finished product at least 6 to 8 minutes before the specified baking time is over.

But it really is worthwhile to add a 9-by-9-inch pan to your collection, and if you're going to be baking lots of my Healthy Exchanges cakes, you'll definitely use it a lot. A cake baked in this pan will have a better texture, and the servings will be a little larger. Just think of it—an 8-by-8-inch pan produces 64 square inches of dessert, while a 9-by-9-inch pan delivers 81 square inches. Those 17 extra inches are too tasty to lose!

To make life even easier, **whenever a recipe calls for ounce measurements** (other than raw meats) I've included the closest cup equivalent. I need to use my scale daily when creating recipes, so I've measured for you at the same time.

Freezing Leftovers

Most of the recipes are for **4 to 8 servings.** If you don't have that many to feed, do what I do: freeze individual portions. Then all you have to do is choose something from the freezer and take it to work for lunch or have your evening meals prepared in advance for the week. In this way, I always have something on hand that is both good to eat and good for me.

Unless a recipe includes hard-boiled eggs, cream cheese, mayonnaise, or a raw vegetable or fruit, **the leftovers should freeze well.** (I've marked recipes that freeze well with the symbol of a **snowflake❄.**) This includes most of the cream pies. Divide any recipe into individual servings and freeze for your own TV dinners.

Another good idea is **cutting leftover pie into individual pieces and freezing each one separately** in a small Ziploc freezer bag. Once you've cut the pie into portions, place them on a cookie sheet and put it in the freezer for 15 minutes. That way, the creamy topping won't get smashed and your pie will keep its shape.

When you want to thaw a piece of pie for yourself, you don't have to thaw the whole pie. You can practice portion control at the same time, and it works really well for brown-bag lunches. Just pull a piece out of the freezer on your way to work and by lunchtime you will have a wonderful dessert waiting for you.

Why do I so often recommend freezing leftover desserts? One reason is that if you leave baked goods made with sugar substitute out on the counter for more than a day or two, they get moldy. Sugar is a preservative and retards the molding process. It's actually what's called an antimicrobial agent, meaning it works against microbes such as molds, bacteria, fungi, and yeasts that grow in foods and can cause food poisoning. Both sugar and salt work as antimicrobial agents to withdraw water from food. Since microbes can't grow without water, food protected in this way doesn't spoil.

So what do we do if we don't want our muffins to turn moldy, but we also don't want to use sugar because of the excess carbohydrates and calories? Freeze them! Just place each muffin or individually sliced bread serving into a Ziploc sandwich bag, seal, and toss into your freezer. Then, whenever you want one for a snack or a meal, you can choose to let it thaw naturally or "zap" it in the microwave.

If you know that baked goods will be eaten within a day or two, packaging them in a sealed plastic container and storing in the refrigerator will do the trick.

Unless I specify **"covered" for simmering or baking**, prepare my recipes **uncovered**. Occasionally you will read a recipe that asks you to cover a dish for a time, then to uncover, so read the directions carefully to avoid confusion—and to get the best results.

Cooking Spray

Low-fat cooking spray is another blessing in a Healthy Exchanges kitchen. It's currently available in three flavors . . .

- **OLIVE OIL–FLAVORED** when cooking Mexican, Italian, or Greek dishes

- **BUTTER-FLAVORED** when the hint of butter is desired

- **REGULAR** for everything else.

A quick spray of butter-flavored makes air-popped popcorn a low-fat taste treat, or try it as a butter substitute on steaming hot corn on the cob. One light spray of the skillet when browning meat will convince you that you're using "old-fashioned fat," and a quick coating of the casserole dish before you add the ingredients will make serving easier and cleanup quicker.

Baking Times

Sometimes I give you a range as a **baking time**, such as 22 to 28 minutes. Why? Because every kitchen, every stove, and every chef's cooking technique are slightly different. On a hot and humid day in Iowa, the optimum cooking time won't be the same as on a cold, dry day. Some stoves bake hotter than the temperature setting indicates; other stoves bake cooler. Electric ovens are usually more temperamental than gas ovens. If you place your baking pan on a lower shelf, the temperature is warmer than if you place it on a higher shelf. If you stir the mixture more vigorously than I do, you could affect the required baking time by a minute or more.

The best way to gauge the heat of your particular oven is to purchase an oven temperature gauge that hangs in the oven. These can be found in any discount store or kitchen equipment store, and if you're going to be cooking and baking regularly, it's a good idea to own one. Set the oven to 350 degrees and when the oven indicates that it has reached that temperature, check the reading on the gauge. If it's less than 350 degrees, you know your oven cooks cooler, and you need to add a few minutes to the cooking time *or* set your oven at a higher temperature. If it's more than 350 degrees, then your oven is warmer and you need to subtract a few minutes from the cooking time. In any event, always treat the suggested baking time as approximate. Check on your baked product at the earliest suggested time.

You can always continue baking a few minutes more if needed, but you can't unbake it once you've cooked it too long.

Miscellaneous Ingredients/Tips

I use reduced-sodium **canned chicken broth** in place of dry bouillon to lower the sodium content. The intended flavor is still present in the prepared dish. As a reduced-sodium beef broth is not currently available (at least not in DeWitt, Iowa), I use the canned regular beef broth. The sodium content is still lower than regular dry bouillon.

Whenever **cooked rice or pasta** is an ingredient, follow the package directions, but eliminate the salt and/or margarine called for. This helps lower the sodium and fat content. It tastes just fine; trust me on this.

Here's another tip: When **cooking rice or noodles**, why not cook extra "for the pot"? After you use what you need, store leftover rice in a covered container (where it will keep for a couple of days). With noodles like spaghetti or macaroni, first rinse and drain as usual, then measure out what you need. Put the leftovers in a bowl covered with water, then store in the refrigerator, covered, until they're needed. Then, measure out what you need, rinse and drain them, and they're ready to go.

Does your **pita bread** often tear before you can make a sandwich? Here's my tip to make them open easily: cut the bread in half, put the halves in the microwave for about 15 seconds, and they will open up by themselves. *Voilà!*

When **chunky salsa** is listed as an ingredient, I leave the degree of "heat" up to your personal taste. In our house, I'm considered a wimp. I go for the "mild" while Cliff prefers "extra-hot." How do we compromise? I prepare the recipe with mild salsa because he can always add a spoonful or two of the hotter version to his serving, but I can't enjoy the dish if it's too spicy for me.

Milk, Yogurt, and More

Take it from me—nonfat dry milk powder is great! I *do not* use it for drinking, but I *do* use it for cooking. Three good reasons why:

(1) It is very **inexpensive**.

(2) It does not **sour** because you use it only as needed. Store the box in your refrigerator or freezer and it will keep almost forever.

(3) You can easily **add extra calcium** to just about any recipe without added liquid.

I consider nonfat dry milk powder one of Mother Nature's modern-day miracles of convenience. But do purchase a good national name brand (I like Carnation) and keep it fresh by proper storage.

I've said many times, "Give me my mixing bowl, my wire whisk, and a box of nonfat dry milk powder, and I can conquer the world!" Here are some of my favorite ways to use dry milk powder:

1. You can make a **pudding** with the nutrients of 2 cups of skim milk, but the liquid of only 1¼ to 1½ cups by using ⅔ cup nonfat dry milk powder, a 4-serving package of sugar-free instant pudding, and the lesser amount of water. This makes the pudding taste much creamier and more like homemade. Also, pie filling made my way will set up in minutes. If company is knocking at your door, you can prepare a pie for them almost as fast as you can open the door and invite them in. And if by chance you have leftovers, the filling will not separate the way it does when you use the 2 cups of skim milk suggested on the package. (If you absolutely refuse to use this handy powdered milk, you can substitute skim milk in the amount of water I call for. Your pie won't be as creamy, and will likely get runny if you have leftovers.)

2. You can make your own "**sour cream**" by combining ¾ cup plain fat-free yogurt with ⅓ cup nonfat dry milk powder. What you did by doing this is fourfold: (1) The dry milk stabilizes the yogurt and keeps the whey from separating. (2) The dry milk slightly helps to cut the tartness of the yogurt. (3) It's still virtually fat-free. (4) The calcium has been increased by 100 percent. Isn't it great how we can make that distant relative of sour cream a first kissin' cousin by adding the nonfat dry milk powder? Or, if you place 1 cup plain fat-free yogurt in a sieve lined with a coffee filter, and place the sieve over a small bowl and refrigerate for about 6 hours, you will end up with a very good alternative for sour cream. To **stabilize yogurt** when cooking or baking with it, just add 1 teaspoon cornstarch to every ¾ cup yogurt.

3. You can make **evaporated skim milk** by using ⅓ cup nonfat dry milk powder and ½ cup water for every ½ cup evaporated skim milk you need. This is handy to know when you want to prepare a recipe calling for evaporated skim milk and you don't have any in the cupboard. And if you are using a recipe that requires only 1 cup evaporated skim milk, you don't have to worry about what to do with the leftover milk in the can.

4. You can make **sugar-free and fat-free sweetened condensed milk** by using 1⅓ cups nonfat dry milk powder mixed with ½ cup cold water and microwaving on HIGH until the mixture is hot but not boiling. Then stir

in ½ cup Sprinkle Sweet or pourable Sugar Twin. Cover and chill at least 4 hours.

5. For any recipe that calls for **buttermilk**, you might want to try **JO's Buttermilk**: Blend 1 cup water and ⅔ cup nonfat dry milk powder (the nutrients of 2 cups of skim milk). It'll be thicker than this mixed-up milk usually is, because it's doubled. Add 1 teaspoon white vinegar and stir, then let it sit for at least ten minutes.

What else? Nonfat dry milk powder adds calcium without fuss to many recipes, and it can be stored for months in your refrigerator or freezer.

Soup Substitutes

One of my subscribers was looking for a way to further restrict salt intake and needed a substitute for **cream of mushroom soup**. For many of my recipes, I use Healthy Request Cream of Mushroom Soup, as it is a reduced-sodium product. The label suggests two servings per can, but I usually incorporate the soup into a recipe serving at least four. By doing this, I've reduced the sodium in the soup by half again.

But if you must restrict your sodium even more, try making my Healthy Exchanges **Creamy Mushroom Sauce.** Place 1½ cups evaporated skim milk and 3 tablespoons flour in a covered jar. Shake well and pour the mixture into a medium saucepan sprayed with butter-flavored cooking spray. Add ½ cup canned sliced mushrooms, rinsed and drained. Cook over medium heat, stirring often, until the mixture thickens. Add any seasonings of your choice. You can use this sauce in any recipe that calls for one 10¾-ounce can of cream of mushroom soup.

Why did I choose these proportions and ingredients?

- 1½ cups evaporated skim milk is the amount in one can.

- It's equal to three Skim Milk choices or exchanges.

- It's the perfect amount of liquid and flour for a medium cream sauce.

- 3 tablespoons flour is equal to one Bread/Starch choice or exchange.

- Any leftovers will reheat beautifully with a flour-based sauce, but not with a cornstarch base.

- The mushrooms are one Vegetable choice or exchange.

- This sauce is virtually fat-free, sugar-free, and sodium-free.

Proteins

Eggs

I use eggs in moderation. I enjoy the real thing on an average of three to four times a week. So, my recipes are calculated on using whole eggs. However, if you choose to use egg substitute in place of the egg, the finished product will turn out just fine and the fat grams per serving will be even lower than those listed.

If you like the look, taste, and feel of **hard-boiled eggs** in salads but haven't been using them because of the cholesterol in the yolk, I have a couple of alternatives for you. (1) Pour an 8-ounce carton of egg substitute into a medium skillet sprayed with cooking spray. Cover the skillet tightly and cook over low heat until the substitute is just set, about 10 minutes. Remove from heat and let set, still covered, for 10 minutes more. Uncover and cool completely. Chop the set mixture. This will make about 1 cup of chopped egg. (2) Even easier is to hard-boil "real eggs," toss the yolk away, and chop the white. Either way, you don't deprive yourself of the pleasure of egg in your salad.

In most recipes calling for **egg substitutes**, you can use 2 egg whites in place of the equivalent of 1 egg substitute. Just break the eggs open and toss the yolks away. I can hear some of you already saying, "But that's wasteful!" Well, take a look at the price on the egg substitute package (which usually has the equivalent of 4 eggs in it), then look at the price of a dozen eggs, from which you'd get the equivalent of 6 egg substitutes. Now, what's wasteful about that?

Meats

Whenever I include **cooked chicken** in a recipe, I use roasted white meat without skin. Whenever I include **roast beef or pork** in a recipe, I use the loin cuts because they are much leaner. However, most of the time, I do my roasting of all these meats at the local deli. I just ask for a chunk of their lean roasted meat, 6 or 8 ounces, and ask them not to slice it. When I get home, I cube or dice the meat and am ready to use it in my recipe. The reason I do this is threefold: (1) I'm getting just the amount I need without leftovers; (2) I don't have the expense of heating the oven; and (3) I'm not throwing away the bone, gristle, and fat I'd be cutting off the meat. Overall, it is probably cheaper to "roast" it the way I do.

Did you know that you can make an acceptable meatloaf without using egg for the binding? Just replace every egg with ¼ cup of liquid. You could use beef broth, tomato sauce, even applesauce, to name just a few. For a meatloaf to serve 6, I always use 1 pound of extra-lean ground beef or turkey, 6 tablespoons of dried fine bread crumbs, and ¼ cup of the liquid, plus anything else healthy that strikes my fancy at the time. I mix well and place the mixture in an 8-by-8-inch baking dish or 9-by-5-inch loaf pan sprayed with cooking spray. Bake uncovered at 350 degrees for 35 to 50 minutes (depending on the added ingredients). You will never miss the egg.

Any time you are **browning ground meat** for a casserole and want to get rid of almost all the excess fat, just place the uncooked meat loosely in a plastic colander. Set the colander in a glass pie plate. Place in the microwave and cook on HIGH for 3 to 6 minutes (depending on the amount being browned), stirring often. Use as you would for any casserole. You can also chop up onions and brown them with the meat if you want.

Gravy

For **gravy** with all the "old time" flavor but without the extra fat, try this almost effortless way to prepare it. (It's almost as easy as opening up a store-bought jar.) Pour the juice off your roasted meat, then set the roast aside to "rest" for about 20 minutes. Place the juice in an uncovered cake pan or other large flat pan (we want the large air surface to speed up the cooling process) and put in the freezer until the fat congeals on top and you can skim it off. Or, if you prefer, use a skimming pitcher purchased at your kitchen gadget store. Either way, measure about 1½ cups skimmed broth and pour into a medium saucepan. Cook over medium heat until heated through, about 5 minutes. In a covered jar, combine ½ cup water or cooled potato broth with 3 tablespoons flour. Shake well. Pour the flour mixture into the warmed juice. Combine well using a wire whisk. Continue cooking until the gravy thickens, about 5 minutes. Season with salt and pepper to taste.

Why did I use flour instead of cornstarch? Because any leftovers will reheat nicely with the flour base and would not with a cornstarch base. Also, 3 tablespoons of flour works out to 1 Bread/Starch exchange. This virtually fat-free gravy makes about 2 cups, so you could spoon about ½ cup gravy on your low-fat mashed potatoes and only have to count your gravy as ¼ Bread/Starch exchange.

Fruits and Vegetables

If you want to enjoy a **"fruit shake"** with some pizzazz, just combine soda water and unsweetened fruit juice in a blender. Add crushed ice. Blend on HIGH until thick. Refreshment without guilt.

You'll see that many recipes use ordinary **canned vegetables.** They're much cheaper than reduced-sodium versions, and once you rinse and drain them, the sodium is reduced anyway. I believe in saving money wherever possible so we can afford the best fat-free and sugar-free products as they come onto the market.

All three kinds of **vegetables—fresh, frozen, and canned—**have their place in a healthy diet. My husband, Cliff, hates the taste of frozen or fresh green beans, thinks the texture is all wrong, so I use canned green beans instead. In this case, canned vegetables have their proper place when I'm feeding my husband. If someone in your family has a similar concern, it's important to respond to it so everyone can be happy and enjoy the meal.

When I use **fruits or vegetables** like apples, cucumbers, and zucchini, I wash them really well and **leave the skin on.** It provides added color, fiber, and attractiveness to any dish. And, because I use processed flour in my cooking, I like to increase the fiber in my diet by eating my fruits and vegetables in their closest-to-natural state.

To help keep **fresh fruits and veggies fresh**, just give them a quick "shower" with lemon juice. The easiest way to do this is to pour purchased lemon juice into a kitchen spray bottle and store in the refrigerator. Then, every time you use fresh fruits or vegetables in a salad or dessert, simply give them a quick spray with your "lemon spritzer." You just might be amazed by how this little trick keeps your produce from turning brown so fast.

The next time you warm canned vegetables such as carrots or green beans, drain and heat the vegetables in ¼ cup beef or chicken broth. It gives a nice variation to an old standby. Here's a simple **white sauce** for vegetables and casseroles without added fat that can be made by spraying a medium saucepan with butter-flavored cooking spray. Place 1½ cups evaporated skim milk and 3 tablespoons flour in a covered jar. Shake well. Pour into the sprayed saucepan and cook over medium heat until thick, stirring constantly. Add salt and pepper to taste. You can also add ½ cup canned drained mushrooms and/or 3 ounces (¾ cup) shredded reduced-fat cheese. Continue cooking until the cheese melts.

Zip up canned or frozen green beans with **chunky salsa**: ½ cup salsa to 2 cups beans. Heat thoroughly. Chunky salsa also makes a wonderful dressing on lettuce salads. It only counts as a vegetable, so enjoy.

Another wonderful **South of the Border** dressing can be stirred up by using ½ cup of chunky salsa and ¼ cup fat-free ranch dressing. Cover and store in your refrigerator. Use as a dressing for salads or as a topping for baked potatoes.

Delightful Dessert Ideas

For a special treat that tastes anything but "diet," try placing **spreadable fruit** in a container and microwave for about 15 seconds. Then pour the melted fruit spread over a serving of nonfat ice cream or frozen yogurt. One tablespoon of spreadable fruit is equal to 1 Fruit choice or exchange. Some combinations to get you started are apricot over chocolate ice cream, strawberry over strawberry ice cream, or any flavor over vanilla.

Another way I use spreadable fruit is to make a delicious **topping for a cheesecake or angel food cake**. I take ½ cup fruit and ½ cup Cool Whip Lite and blend the two together with a teaspoon of coconut extract.

Here's a really **good topping** for the fall of the year. Place 1½ cups unsweetened applesauce in a medium saucepan or 4-cup glass measure. Stir in 2 tablespoons raisins, 1 teaspoon apple pie spice, and 2 tablespoons Cary's Sugar Free Maple Syrup. Cook over medium heat on the stovetop or microwave on HIGH until warm. Then spoon about ½ cup of the warm mixture over pancakes, French toast, or sugar- and fat-free vanilla ice cream. It's as close as you will get to guilt-free apple pie!

Do you love hot fudge sundaes as much as I do? Here's my secret for making **Almost Sinless Hot Fudge Sauce.** Just combine the contents of a 4-serving package of JELL-O sugar-free chocolate cook-and-serve pudding with ⅔ cup Carnation Nonfat Dry Milk Powder in a medium saucepan. Add 1¼ cups water. Cook over medium heat, stirring constantly with a wire whisk, until the mixture thickens and starts to boil. Remove from heat and stir in 1 teaspoon vanilla extract, 2 teaspoons reduced-calorie margarine, and ½ cup miniature marshmallows. This makes six ¼-cup servings. Any leftovers can be refrigerated and reheated later in the microwave. Yes, you can buy fat-free chocolate syrup nowadays, but have you checked the sugar content? For a ¼-cup serving of store-bought syrup (and you show me any true hot fudge sundae lover who would settle for less than ¼ cup) it clocks in at over 150 calories with 39 grams of sugar! Hershey's Lite Syrup, while better, still has 100 calories and 10 grams of sugar. But this "homemade" version costs you only 60 calories, less than ½ gram of fat, and just 6 grams of sugar for the same ¼-cup serving. For an occasional squirt on something where 1 teaspoon is enough, I'll use Hershey's Lite Syrup. But when I crave a hot fudge sundae, I scoop out some sugar- and fat-free ice cream, then spoon my Almost Sinless Hot Fudge Sauce over the top and smile with pleasure.

A quick yet tasty way to prepare **strawberries for shortcake** is to place about ¾ cup sliced strawberries, 2 tablespoons Diet Mountain Dew, and sugar substitute to equal ¼ cup sugar in a blender container. Process on BLEND until the mixture is smooth. Pour the mixture into a bowl. Add 1¼ cups sliced strawberries and mix well. Cover and refrigerate until ready to serve with shortcakes. This tastes just like the strawberry sauce I remember my mother making when I was a child.

Have you tried **thawing Cool Whip Lite** by stirring it? Don't! You'll get a runny mess and ruin the look and taste of your dessert. You can *never* treat Cool Whip Lite the same way you did regular Cool Whip because the "lite" version just doesn't contain enough fat. Thaw your Cool Whip Lite by placing it in your refrigerator at least two hours before you need to use it. When they took the excess fat out of Cool Whip to make it "lite," they replaced it with air. When you stir the living daylights out of it to hurry up the thawing, you also stir out the air. You also can't thaw your Cool Whip Lite in the microwave, or you'll end up with Cool Whip Soup!

Always have a thawed container of Cool Whip Lite in your refrigerator, as it keeps well for up to two weeks. It actually freezes and thaws and freezes and thaws again quite well, so if you won't be using it soon, you could refreeze your leftovers. Just remember to take it out a few hours before you need it, so it'll be creamy and soft and ready to use.

Remember, anytime you see the words "fat-free" or "reduced-fat" on the labels of cream cheese, sour cream, or whipped topping, handle them gently. The fat has been replaced by air or water, and the product has to be treated with special care.

How can you **frost an entire pie with just ½ cup of whipped topping?** First, don't use an inexpensive brand. I use Cool Whip Lite or La Creme Lite. Make sure the topping is fully thawed. Always spread from the center to the sides using a rubber spatula. This way, ½ cup topping will cover an entire pie. Remember, the operative word is *frost,* not pile the entire container on top of the pie!

Another trick I often use is to include tiny amounts of "real people" food, such as coconut, but extend the flavor by using extracts. Try it—you will be surprised by how little of the real thing you can use and still feel you are not being deprived.

If you are preparing a pie filling that has ample moisture, just line the bottom of a 9-by-9-inch cake pan with **graham crackers**. Pour the filling over the top of the crackers. Cover and refrigerate until the moisture has enough time to soften the crackers. Overnight is best. This eliminates the added **fats and sugars of a piecrust.**

One of my readers provided a smart and easy way to enjoy a **two-crust pie** without all the fat that usually comes along with those two crusts. Just use one Pillsbury refrigerated piecrust. Let it set at room temperature for about 20 minutes. Cut the crust in half on the folded line. Gently roll each half into a ball. Wipe your counter with a wet cloth and place a sheet of wax paper on it. Put one of the balls on the wax paper, then cover with another piece of wax paper, and roll it out with your rolling pin. Carefully remove the wax paper on one side and place that side into your 8- or 9-inch pie plate. Fill with your usual pie filling, then repeat the process for the top crust. Bake as usual. Enjoy!

When you are preparing a pie that uses a purchased piecrust, simply tear out the paper label on the plastic cover (but do check it for a coupon good on a future purchase) and turn the cover upside down over the prepared pie. You now have a cover that protects your beautifully garnished pie from having anything fall on top of it. It makes the pie very portable when it's your turn to bring dessert to a get-together.

Did you know you can make your own **fruit-flavored yogurt?** Mix 1 tablespoon of any flavor of spreadable fruit spread with ¾ cup plain yogurt. It's every bit as tasty and much cheaper. You can also make your own **lemon yogurt** by combining 3 cups plain fat-free yogurt with 1 tub Crystal Light lemonade powder. Mix well, cover, and store in the refrigerator. I think you will be pleasantly surprised by the ease, cost, and flavor of this "made from scratch" calcium-rich treat. P.S.: You can make any flavor you like by using any of the Crystal Light mixes— Cranberry? Iced Tea? You decide.

Other Smart Substitutions

Many people have inquired about **substituting applesauce and artificial sweetener for butter and sugar**, but what if you aren't satisfied with the result? One woman wrote to me about a recipe for her grandmother's cookies that called for 1 cup of butter and 1½ cups of sugar. Well, any recipe that depends on as much butter and sugar as this one does is generally not a good candidate for "healthy exchanges." The original recipe needed a large quantity of fat to produce a crisp cookie just like Grandma made.

Applesauce can often be used instead of vegetable oil, but generally doesn't work well as a replacement for butter, margarine, or lard. If a recipe calls for ½ cup vegetable oil or less and your recipe is for a bar cookie, quick bread, muffin, or cake mix, you can try substituting an equal amount of unsweetened applesauce. If the recipe calls for more, try using ½ cup applesauce and the rest oil. You're cutting down the fat but shouldn't end up with a taste disaster! This "applesauce shortening" works great in many recipes, but so far I haven't been able to figure out a way to deep-fat fry with it!

Another rule for healthy substitution: Up to ½ cup sugar or less can be replaced by *an artificial sweetener that can withstand the heat of baking*, like pourable Sugar Twin or Sprinkle Sweet. If it requires more than ½ cup sugar, cut the amount needed by 75 percent and use ½ cup sugar substitute and sugar for the rest. Other options: Reduce the butter and sugar by 25 percent and see if the finished product still satisfies you in taste and appearance. Or, make the cookies just like Grandma did, realizing they are part of your family's holiday tradition. Enjoy a *moderate* serving of a couple of cookies once or twice during the season, and just forget about them the rest of the year.

Did you know that you can replace the fat in many quick breads, muffins, and shortcakes with **fat-free mayonnaise** or **fat-free sour cream?** This can work if the original recipe doesn't call for a lot of fat *and* sugar. If the recipe is truly fat and sugar dependent, such as traditional sugar cookies, cupcakes, or pastries, it won't work. Those recipes require the large amounts of sugar and fat to make love in the dark of the oven to produce a tender finished product. But if you have a favorite quick bread that doesn't call for a lot of sugar or fat, why don't you give one of these substitutes a try?

If you enjoy beverage mixes like those from Alba, here are my Healthy Exchanges versions:

For **chocolate flavored,** use ⅓ cup nonfat dry milk powder and 2 tablespoons Nestlé Sugar-Free Chocolate Flavored Quik. Mix well and use as usual. Or, use ⅓ cup nonfat dry milk powder, 1 teaspoon unsweetened cocoa, and sugar substitute to equal 3 tablespoons sugar. Mix well and use as usual.

For **vanilla flavored,** use ⅓ cup nonfat dry milk powder, sugar substitute to equal 2 tablespoons sugar, and add 1 teaspoon vanilla extract when adding liquid.

For **strawberry flavored,** use ⅓ cup nonfat dry milk powder, sugar substitute to equal 2 tablespoons sugar, and add 1 teaspoon strawberry extract and 3–4 drops red food coloring when adding liquid.

Each of these makes one packet of drink mix. If you need to double the recipe, double everything but the extract. Use 1½ teaspoons of extract or it will be too strong. Use 1 cup cold water with one recipe mix to make a glass of flavored milk. If you want to make a shake, combine the mix, water, and 3–4 ice cubes in your blender, then process on BLEND till smooth.

A handy tip when making **healthy punch** for a party: Prepare a few extra cups of your chosen drink, freeze it in cubes in a couple of ice trays, then keep your punch from "watering down" by cooling it with punch cubes instead.

What should you do if you can't find the product listed in a Healthy Exchanges recipe? You can substitute in some cases—use Lemon JELL-O if you can't find Hawaiian Pineapple, for example. But if you're determined to track down the product you need, and your own store manager hasn't been able to order it for you, why not use one of the new online grocers and order exactly what you need, no matter where you live. Try **http://www.netgrocer.com**.

Not all low-fat cooking products are interchangeable, as one of my readers recently discovered when she tried to cook pancakes on her griddle using I Can't Believe It's Not Butter! spray—and they stuck! This butter-flavored spray is wonderful for a quick squirt on air-popped popcorn or corn on the cob, and it's great for topping your pancakes once they're cooked. In fact, my tastebuds have to check twice because it tastes so much like real butter! (And this is high praise from someone who once thought butter was the most perfect food ever created.)

But I Can't Believe It's Not Butter! doesn't work well for sautéing or browning. After trying to fry an egg with it and cooking up a disaster, I knew this product had its limitations. So I decided to continue using Pam or Weight Watchers butter-flavored cooking spray whenever I'm browning anything in a skillet or on a griddle.

Many of my readers have reported difficulty finding a product I use in many recipes: JELL-O cook-and-serve puddings. I have three suggestions for those of you with this problem:

1. **Work with your grocery store manager to get this product into your store**, and then make sure you and everyone you know buy it by the bagful! Products that sell well are reordered and kept in stock, especially with today's computerized cash registers that record what's purchased. You may also want to write or call Kraft General Foods and ask for their help. They can be reached at (800) 431-1001 weekdays from 9 A.M. to 4 P.M. (EST).

2. **You can prepare the recipe that calls for cook-and-serve pudding by using instant pudding of the same flavor.** Yes, that's right, you **can** cook with the instant when making my recipes. The finished product won't be quite as wonderful, but still at least a 9 on a 10-star scale. You can never do the opposite—never use cook-and-serve in a recipe that calls for instant! One time at a cooking demonstration, I could not understand why my Blueberry Mountain Cheesecake never did set up. Then I spotted the box in the trash and noticed I'd picked the wrong type of pudding mix. Be careful—the boxes are both blue, but the instant has pudding on a silver spoon, and the cook-and-serve has a stream of milk running down the front into a bowl with a wooden spoon.

3. **You can make JO's Sugar-Free Vanilla Cook-and-Serve Pudding Mix instead of using JELL-O's.** Here's my recipe: 2 tablespoons cornstarch, ½ cup pourable Sugar Twin or Sprinkle Sweet, ⅔ cup Carnation Nonfat Dry Milk Powder, 1½ cups water, 2 teaspoons vanilla extract, and 4 to 5 drops yellow food coloring. Combine all this in a medium saucepan and cook over medium heat, stirring constantly, until the mixture comes to a full boil and thickens. This is for basic cooked sugar-free vanilla pudding. For a chocolate version, the recipe is 2 tablespoons cornstarch, ¼ cup pourable Sugar Twin or Sprinkle Sweet, 2 tablespoons Nestlé's Sugar-Free Chocolate Flavored Quik, 1½ cups water, and 1 teaspoon vanilla extract. Follow the same cooking instructions as for the vanilla.

If you're preparing this as part of a recipe that also calls for adding a package of gelatin, just stir that into the mix.

Adapting a favorite family cake recipe? Here's something to try: Replace an egg and oil in the original with ⅓ cup plain fat-free yogurt and ¼ cup fat-free mayonnaise. Blend these two ingredients with your liquids in a separate bowl, then add the yogurt mixture to the flour mixture and mix gently just to combine. (You don't want to overmix or you'll release the gluten in the batter and end up with a tough batter.)

Want a tasty coffee creamer without all the fat? You could use Carnation's Fat Free Coffee-mate, which is 10 calories per teaspoon, but if you drink several cups a day with several teaspoons each, that adds up quickly to nearly 100 calories a day! Why not try my version? It's not quite as creamy, but it *is* good. Simply combine ⅓ cup Carnation Nonfat Dry Milk Powder and ¼ cup pourable Sugar Twin. Cover and store in your cupboard or refrigerator. At 3 calories per teaspoon, you can enjoy three teaspoons for less than the calories of one teaspoon of the purchased variety.

Some Helpful Hints

Sugar-free puddings and gelatins are important to many of my recipes, but if you prefer to avoid sugar substitutes, you could still prepare the recipes with regular puddings or gelatins. The calories would be higher, but you would still be cooking low-fat.

When a recipe calls for **chopped nuts** (and you only have whole ones), who wants to dirty the food processor just for a couple of tablespoonsful? You could try to chop them using your cutting board, but be prepared for bits and pieces to fly all over the kitchen. I use "Grandma's food processor." I take the biggest nuts I can find, put them in a small glass bowl, and chop them into chunks just the right size using a metal biscuit cutter.

A quick hint about **reduced-fat peanut butter:** Don't store it in the refrigerator. Because the fat has been reduced, it won't spread as easily when it's cold. Keep it in your cupboard and a little will spread a lot further.

Crushing **graham crackers** for topping? A self-seal sandwich bag works great!

If you have a **leftover muffin** and are looking for something a little different for breakfast, you can make a **"breakfast sundae."** Crumble the muffin into a cereal bowl. Sprinkle a serving of fresh fruit over it and top with a couple of tablespoons of plain fat-free yogurt sweetened with sugar substitute and your choice of extract. The thought of it just might make you jump out of bed with a smile on your face. (Speaking of muffins, did you know that if you fill the unused muffin wells with water when baking muffins, you help ensure more even baking and protect the muffin pan at the same time?) Another muffin hint: Lightly spray the inside of paper baking cups with butter-flavored cooking spray before spooning the muffin batter into them. Then you won't end up with paper clinging to your fresh-baked muffins.

The secret of making **good meringues** without sugar is to use 1 tablespoon of Sprinkle Sweet or pourable Sugar Twin for every egg white, and a small amount of extract. Use ½ to 1 teaspoon for the batch. Almond, vanilla, and coconut are all good choices. Use the same amount of cream of tartar you usually do. Bake the meringue in the same old way. Even if you can't eat sugar, you can enjoy a healthy meringue pie when it's prepared the *Healthy Exchanges Way*. (Remember that egg whites whip up best at room temperature.)

Try **storing your Bisquick Reduced Fat Baking Mix** in the freezer. It won't freeze, and it *will* stay fresh much longer. (It works for coffee, doesn't it?)

If you lightly **spray the inside of paper baking cups** with butter-flavored cooking spray before spooning the muffin batter into them, you won't end up with "clinging paper" on your fresh baked muffins. If you love muffins as much as I do, but hate washing muffin tins as much as I do, you'll agree this idea is worth its weight in muffin batter!

If you've ever wondered about **changing ingredients** in one of my recipes, the answer is that some things can be changed to suit your family's tastes, but others should not be tampered with. **Don't change** the amount of flour, bread crumbs, reduced-fat baking mix, baking soda, baking powder, liquid, or dry milk powder. And if I include a small amount of salt, it's necessary for the recipe to turn out correctly. **What you can change:** an extract flavor (if you don't like coconut, choose vanilla or almond instead); a spreadable fruit flavor; the type of fruit in a pie filling (but be careful about substituting fresh for frozen and vice versa—sometimes it works but it may not); the flavor of pudding or gelatin. As long as package sizes and amounts are the same, go for it. It will never hurt my feelings if you change a recipe, so please your family—don't worry about me!

Because I always say that "good enough" isn't good enough for me anymore, here's a way to make your cup of **fat-free and sugar-free hot cocoa** more special. After combining the hot chocolate mix and hot water, stir in ½ teaspoon vanilla extract and a light sprinkle of cinnamon. If you really want to feel decadent, add a tablespoon of Cool Whip Lite. Isn't life grand?

If you must limit your sugar intake, but you love the idea of sprinkling **powdered sugar** on dessert crepes or burritos, here's a pretty good substitute: Place 1 cup Sprinkle Sweet or pourable Sugar Twin and 1 teaspoon cornstarch in a blender container, then cover and process on HIGH until the mixture resembles powdered sugar in texture, about 45 to 60 seconds. Store in an airtight container and use whenever you want a dusting of "powdered sugar" on any dessert.

Want my "almost instant" pies to set up even more quickly? Do as one of my readers does: freeze your Keebler piecrusts. Then, when you stir up one of my pies and pour the filling into the frozen crust, it sets up within seconds.

Some of my "island-inspired" recipes call for **rum or brandy extracts**, which provide the "essence" of liquor without the real thing. I'm a teetotaler by choice, so I choose not to include real liquor in any of my recipes. They're cheaper than liquor and you won't feel the need to shoo your kids away from the goodies. If you prefer not to use liquor extracts in your cooking, you can always substitute vanilla extract.

Some Healthy Cooking Challenges and How I Solved 'Em

When you stir up one of my pie fillings, do you ever have a problem with **lumps?** Here's an easy solution for all you "careful" cooks out there. Lumps occur when the pudding starts to set up before you can get the dry milk powder incorporated into the mixture. I always advise you to dump, pour, and stir fast with that wire whisk, letting no more than 30 seconds elapse from beginning to end.

But if you are still having problems, you can always combine the dry milk powder and the water in a separate bowl before adding the pudding mix and whisking quickly. Why don't I suggest this right from the beginning? Because that would mean an extra dish to wash every time—and you know I hate to wash dishes!

With a little practice and a light touch, you should soon get the hang of my original method. But now you've got an alternative way to lose those lumps!

I love the chemistry of foods and so I've gotten great pleasure from analyzing what makes fat-free products tick. By dissecting these "miracle" products, I've learned how to make them work best. They require different handling than the high-fat products we're used to, but if treated properly, these slimmed-down versions can produce delicious results!

Fat-free sour cream: This product is wonderful on a hot baked potato, but have you noticed that it tends to be much gummier than regular sour cream? If you want to use it in a stroganoff dish or baked product, you must stir a tablespoon or two of skim milk into the fat-free sour cream before adding it to other ingredients.

Cool Whip Free: When the fat went out of the formula, air was stirred in to fill the void. So, if you stir it too vigorously, you release the air and *decrease* the volume. Handle it with kid gloves—gently. Since the manufacturer forgot to ask for my input, I'll share with you how to make it taste almost the same as it used to. Let the container thaw in the refrigerator, then ever so gently stir in 1 teaspoon vanilla extract. Now, put the lid back on and enjoy it a tablespoon at a time, the same way you did Cool Whip Lite.

Fat-free cream cheese: When the fat was removed from this product, water replaced it. So don't ever use an electric mixer on the fat-free version, or you risk releasing the water and having your finished product look more like dip than cheesecake! Stirring it gently with a sturdy spoon in a glass bowl with a handle will soften it just as much as it needs to be. And don't be alarmed if the cream cheese gets caught in your wire whisk when you start combining the pudding mix and other ingredients. Just keep knocking it back down into the bowl by hitting the whisk against the rim of the bowl, and as you continue blending, it will soften even more and drop off the whisk. When it's time to pour the filling into your crust, your whisk shouldn't have anything much clinging to it.

Reduced-fat margarine: Again, the fat was replaced by water. If you try to use the reduced-fat kind in your cookie recipe spoon for spoon, you will end up with a cake-like cookie instead of the crisp kind most of us enjoy. You have to take into consideration that some water will be released as the product bakes. Use less liquid than the recipe calls for (when re-creating family recipes *only*—I've figured this into Healthy Exchanges recipes). And never, never, never use fat-*free* margarine and expect anyone to ask for seconds!

Homemade or Store-Bought?

I've been asked which is better for you: homemade from scratch, or purchased foods. My answer is *both!* Each has a place in a healthy lifestyle, and what that place is has everything to do with you.

Take **piecrusts**, for instance. If you love spending your spare time in the kitchen preparing foods, and you're using low-fat, low-sugar, and reasonably low-sodium ingredients, go for it! But if, like so many people, your time is limited and you've learned to read labels, you could be better off using purchased foods.

I know that when I prepare a pie (and I experiment with a couple of pies each week, because this is Cliff's favorite dessert), I use a purchased crust. Why? Mainly because I can't make a good-tasting piecrust that is lower in fat than the brands I use. Also, purchased piecrusts fit my rule of "If it takes longer to fix than to eat, forget it!"

I've checked the nutrient information for the purchased piecrusts against recipes for traditional and "diet" piecrusts, using my computer software program. The purchased crust calculated lower in both fat and calories! I have tried some low-fat and low-sugar recipes, but they just didn't spark my tastebuds, or were so complicated you needed an engineering degree just to get the crust in the pie plate.

I'm very happy with the purchased piecrusts in my recipes, because the finished product rarely, if ever, has more than 30 percent of total calories coming from fats. I also believe that we have to prepare foods our families and friends will eat with us on a regular basis and not feel deprived, or we've wasted time, energy, and money.

I could use a purchased "lite" **pie filling**, but instead I make my own. Here I can save both fat and sugar, and still make the filling almost as fast as opening a can. The bottom line: Know what you have to spend when it comes to both time and fat/sugar calories, then make the best decision you can for you and your family. And don't go without an occasional piece of pie because you think it isn't *necessary*. A delicious pie prepared in a healthy way is one of the simple pleasures of life. It's a little thing, but it can make all the difference between just getting by with the bare minimum and living a full and healthy lifestyle.

I'm sure you'll add to this list of cooking tips as you begin preparing Healthy Exchanges recipes and discover how easy it can be to adapt your own favorite recipes using these ideas and your own common sense.

A Peek into My Pantry

and My Favorite Brands

Everyone asks me what foods I keep on hand and what brands I use. There are lots of good products on the grocery shelves today—many more than we dreamed about even a year or two ago. And I can't wait to see what's out there twelve months from now. The following are my staples and, where appropriate, my favorites *at this time*. I feel these products are healthier, tastier, easy to get—and deliver the most flavor for the least amount of fat, sugar, or calories. If you find others you like as well *or better,* please use them. This is only a guide to make your grocery shopping and cooking easier. (You'll note that I've supplied you with my entire current list of favorites, even though some products are not used in any of my recipes. I hope this makes your shopping easier.)

Fat-free plain yogurt (Yoplait or Dannon)
Nonfat dry milk powder (Carnation)
Evaporated skim milk (Carnation)
Skim milk
Fat-free cottage cheese
Fat-free cream cheese (Philadelphia)
Fat-free mayonnaise (Kraft)
Fat-free salad dressings (Kraft)
Fat-free sour cream (Land O Lakes)
Reduced-calorie margarine (Weight Watchers, Promise, or Smart Beat)
Cooking spray
   Olive oil–flavored and regular (Pam)
   Butter-flavored for sautéing (Pam or Weight Watchers)
   Butter-flavored for spritzing after cooking (I Can't Believe It's Not Butter!)
Vegetable oil (Puritan Canola Oil)
Reduced-calorie whipped topping (Cool Whip Lite or Cool Whip Free)
Sugar substitute
   if no heating is involved (Equal)

if heating is required

    white (pourable Sugar Twin or Sprinkle Sweet)

    brown (Brown Sugar Twin)

Sugar-free gelatin and pudding mixes (JELL-O)

Baking mix (Bisquick Reduced Fat)

Pancake mix (Aunt Jemima Reduced Calorie)

Reduced-calorie pancake syrup (Cary's Sugar Free)

Parmesan cheese (Kraft fat-free)

Reduced-fat cheese (Kraft 2% Reduced Fat)

Shredded frozen potatoes (Mr. Dell's)

Spreadable fruit spread (Smucker's, Welch's, or Knott's Berry Farm)

Peanut butter (Peter Pan reduced-fat, Jif reduced-fat, or Skippy reduced-fat)

Chicken broth (Healthy Request)

Beef broth (Swanson)

Tomato sauce (Hunt's—plain, Italian, or chili)

Canned soups (Healthy Request)

Tomato juice (Campbell's Reduced-Sodium)

Ketchup (Heinz Light Harvest or Healthy Choice)

Purchased piecrust

    unbaked (Pillsbury—from dairy case)

    graham cracker, butter flavored, or chocolate flavored (Keebler)

Crescent rolls (Pillsbury Reduced Fat)

Pastrami and corned beef (Carl Buddig Lean)

Luncheon meats (Healthy Choice or Oscar Mayer)

Ham (Dubuque 97% fat-free and reduced-sodium or Healthy Choice)

Frankfurters and kielbasa sausage (Healthy Choice)

Canned white chicken, packed in water (Swanson)

Canned tuna, packed in water (Starkist or Chicken of the Sea)

90–95 percent lean ground turkey and beef

Soda crackers (Nabisco Fat-Free)

Reduced-calorie bread—40 calories per slice or less

Hamburger buns—80 calories each (Less)

Rice—instant, regular, brown, and wild

Instant potato flakes (Betty Crocker Potato Buds)

Noodles, spaghetti, and macaroni

Salsa (Chi-Chi's Mild Chunky)

Pickle relish—dill, sweet, and hot dog

Mustard—Dijon, prepared, and spicy

Unsweetened apple juice

Unsweetened applesauce

Fruit—fresh, frozen (no sugar added), or canned in juice

Vegetables—fresh, frozen, or canned
Spices—JO's Spices
*Lemon and lime juice (in small plastic fruit-shaped bottles found in the produce
    section)*
Instant fruit beverage mixes (Crystal Light)
Dry dairy beverage mixes (Nestlé Quik)
"Ice cream" (Wells' Blue Bunny sugar- and fat-free)

The items on my shopping list are everyday foods found in just about any grocery store in America. But all are as low in fat, sugar, calories, and sodium as I can find—and still taste good! I can make any recipe in my cookbooks and newsletters as long as I have my cupboards and refrigerator stocked with these items. Whenever I use the last of any one item, I just make sure I pick up another supply the next time I'm at the store.

If your grocer does not stock these items, why not ask if they can be ordered on a trial basis? If the store agrees to do so, be sure to tell your friends to stop by, so that sales are good enough to warrant restocking the new products. Competition for shelf space is fierce, so only products that sell well stay around.

Shopping the

Healthy Exchanges Way

Sometimes, as part of a cooking demonstration, I take the group on a field trip to the nearest supermarket. There's no better place to share my discoveries about which healthy products taste best, which are best for you, and which healthy products don't deliver enough taste to include in my recipes.

While I'd certainly enjoy accompanying you to your neighborhood store, we'll have to settle for a field trip *on paper*. I've tasted and tried just about every fat- and sugar-free product on the market, but so many new ones keep coming all the time, you're going to have to learn to play detective on your own. I've turned label reading into an art, but often the label doesn't tell me everything I need to know.

Sometimes you'll find, as I have, that the product with *no* fat doesn't provide the taste satisfaction you require; other times, a no-fat or low-fat product just doesn't cook up the same way as the original product. And some foods, including even the leanest meats, can't eliminate *all* the fat. That's okay, though—a healthy diet should include anywhere from 15 to 25 percent of total calories from fat on any given day.

Take my word for it—your supermarket is filled with lots of delicious foods that can and should be part of your healthy diet for life. Come, join me as we check it out on the way to the checkout!

Before I buy anything at the store, I read the label carefully: I check the total fat plus the saturated fat; I look to see how many calories are in a realistic serving, and I say to myself, Would I eat that much—or would I eat more? I look at the sodium and I look at the total carbohydrates. I like to check those ingredients because I'm cooking for diabetics and heart patients too. And I check the total calories from fat.

Remember that 1 fat gram equals 9 calories, while 1 protein or 1 carbohydrate gram equals 4 calories.

A wonderful new product is I Can't Believe It's Not Butter! spray, with zero calories and zero grams of fat in five squirts. It's great for your air-popped popcorn. As for **light margarine spread**, beware—most of the fat-free brands don't melt on toast, and they don't taste very good either, so I just leave them on the shelf. For the few times I do use a light margarine I tend to buy Smart Beat Ultra, Promise Ultra, or Weight Watchers Light Ultra. The number-one ingredient in them is water. I occasionally use the light margarine in cooking, but I don't really put margarine on my toast anymore. I use apple butter or make a spread with fat-free cream cheese mixed with a little spreadable fruit instead.

So far, Pillsbury hasn't released a reduced-fat **crescent roll**, so you'll only get one crescent roll per serving from me. I usually make eight of the rolls serve twelve by using them for a crust. The house brands may be lower in fat but they're usually not as good flavorwise—and they don't quite cover the pan when you use them to make a crust. If you're going to use crescent rolls with lots of other stuff on top, then a house brand might be fine.

The Pillsbury French Loaf makes a wonderful **pizza crust** and fills a giant jelly-roll pan. One-fifth of this package "costs" you only 1 gram of fat (and I don't even let you have that much!). Once you use this for your pizza crust, you will never go back to anything else instead. I use it to make calzones too.

I use only Philadelphia fat-free **cream cheese** because it has the best consistency. I've tried other brands, but I wasn't happy with them. Healthy Choice makes lots of great products, but their cream cheese just doesn't work as well with my recipes.

Let's move to the **cheese** aisle. My preferred brand is Kraft 2% Reduced Fat Shredded Cheeses. I will not use the fat-free versions because *they don't melt.* I would gladly give up sugar and fat, but I will not give up flavor. This is a happy compromise. I use the reduced-fat version, I use less, and I use it where your eyes "eat" it, on top of the recipe. So you walk away satisfied and with a finished product that's very low in fat. If you want to make grilled cheese sandwiches for your kids, use the Kraft reduced-fat cheese slices, and they'll taste exactly like the ones they're used to. The fat-free will not.

Dubuque's Extra-Lean Reduced-Sodium **ham** tastes wonderful, reduces the sodium as well as the fat, and gives you a larger serving. Don't be fooled by products called turkey ham; they may *not* be lower in fat than a very lean pork product. Here's one label as an example: I checked a brand of turkey ham called Genoa. It gives you a 2-ounce serving for 70 calories and 3½ grams of fat. The Dubuque extra-lean ham, made from pork, gives you a 3-ounce serving for 90 calories, but only 2½ grams of fat. *You get more food and less fat.*

Frozen dinners can be expensive and high in sodium, but it's smart to have two or three in the freezer as a backup when your best-laid plans go awry and you need to grab something on the run. It's not a good idea to rely on them too much—what if you can't get to the store to get them, or you're short on cash? The sodium can be high in some of them because they often replace the fat with salt, so be sure to read the labels. Also ask yourself if the serving is enough to satisfy you; for many of us, it's not.

Egg substitute is expensive, and probably not necessary unless you're cooking for someone who has to worry about every bit of cholesterol in his or her diet. If you occasionally have a fried egg or an omelet, *use the real egg.* For cooking, you can usually substitute two egg whites for one whole egg. Most of the time it won't make any difference, but check your recipe carefully.

Healthy frozen desserts are hard to find except for the Weight Watchers brands. I've always felt that their portions are so small, and for their size still pretty high in fat and sugar. (This is one of the reasons I think I'll be successful marketing my frozen desserts someday. After Cliff tasted one of my earliest healthy pies—and licked the plate clean—he remarked that if I ever opened a restaurant, people would keep coming back for my desserts alone!) Keep an eye out for fat-free or very low-fat frozen yogurt or sorbet products. Even Häagen-Dazs, which makes some of the highest-fat-content ice cream, now has a fat-free fruit sorbet pop out that's pretty good. I'm sure there will be more before too long.

You have to be realistic: What are you willing to do, and what are you *not* willing to do? Let's take **bread,** for example. Some people just have to have the real thing—rye bread with caraway seeds or a whole-wheat version with bits of bran in it.

I prefer to use reduced-calorie bread because I like a *real* sandwich. This way, I can have two slices of bread and it counts as only one Bread/Starch exchange.

How I Shop for Myself

I always keep my kitchen stocked with my basic staples; that way, I can go to the cupboard and create new recipes anytime I'm inspired. I hope you will take the time (and allot the money) to stock your cupboards with items from the staples list, so you can enjoy developing your own healthy versions of family favorites without making extra trips to the market.

I'm always on the lookout for new products sitting on the grocery shelf. When I spot something I haven't seen before, I'll usually grab it, glance at the front, then turn it around and read the label carefully. I call it looking at the "promises" (the "come-on" on the front of the package) and then at the "warranty" (the ingredients list and the label on the back).

If it looks as good on the back as it does on the front, I'll say okay and either create a recipe on the spot or take it home for when I do think of something to do with it. Picking up a new product is just about the only time I buy something not on my list.

The items on my shopping list are normal, everyday foods, but as low-fat and low-sugar (*while still tasting good*) as I can find. I can make any recipe in this book as long as these staples are on my shelves. After using these products for a couple of weeks, you will find it becomes routine to have them on hand. And I promise you, I really don't spend any more at the store now than I did a few years ago when I told myself I couldn't afford some of these items. Back then, of course, plenty of unhealthy, high-priced snacks I really didn't need somehow made the magic leap from the grocery shelves into my cart. Who was I kidding?

Yes, you often have to pay a little more for fat-free or low-fat products, including meats. But since I frequently use a half pound of meat to serve four to six people, your cost per serving will be much lower.

Try adding up what you were spending before on chips and cookies, premium-brand ice cream, and fatty cuts of meat, and you'll soon see that we've *streamlined* your shopping cart, and taken the weight off your pocketbook as well as your hips!

Remember, your good health is *your* business—but it's big business too. Write to the manufacturers of products you and your family enjoy but feel are just too high in fat, sugar, or sodium to be part of your new healthy lifestyle. Companies are spending millions of dollars to respond to consumers' concerns about food products, and I bet that in the next few years, you'll discover fat-free and low-fat versions of nearly every product piled high on your supermarket shelves!

The Healthy Exchanges

Kitchen

You might be surprised to discover I still don't have a massive test kitchen stocked with every modern appliance and handy gadget ever made. The tiny galley kitchen where I first launched Healthy Exchanges has room for only one person at a time, but it never stopped me from feeling the sky's the limit when it comes to seeking out great healthy taste!

Because storage is at such a premium in my kitchen, I don't waste space with equipment I don't really need. Here's a list of what I consider worth having. If you notice serious gaps in your equipment, you can probably find most of what you need at a local discount store or garage sale. If your kitchen is equipped with more sophisticated appliances, don't feel guilty about using them. Enjoy every appliance you can find room for or that you can afford. Just be assured that healthy, quick, and delicious food can be prepared with the "basics."

A Healthy Exchanges Kitchen Equipment List

Good-quality nonstick skillets (medium, large)
Good-quality saucepans (small, medium, large)
Glass mixing bowls (small, medium, large)
Glass measures (1-cup, 2-cup, 4-cup, 8-cup)
Sharp knives (paring, chef, butcher)
Rubber spatulas
Wire whisks
Measuring spoons
Measuring cups
Large mixing spoons
Egg separator
Covered jar
Vegetable parer
Grater

4-inch round custard dishes
Glass pie plates
8-by-8-inch glass baking dishes
Cake pans (9-by-9-inch, 9-by-13-inch)
10¾-by-7-by-1½-inch biscuit pan
Cookie sheets (good nonstick ones)
Jelly-roll pan
Muffin tins

Potato masher
Electric mixer
Electric blender
Electric skillet
Cooking timer
Slow cooker
Air popper for popcorn

5-by-9-inch bread pan
Plastic colander
Cutting board
Pie wedge server
Square-shaped server
Can opener (I prefer manual)
Rolling pin

Kitchen scales (unless you *always* use my recipes)
Wire racks for cooling baked goods
Electric toaster oven (to conserve energy for those times when only one item is being baked or for a recipe that requires a short baking time)

How to Read a Healthy Exchanges Recipe

The Healthy Exchanges Nutritional Analysis

Before using these recipes, you may wish to consult your physician or health-care provider to be sure they are appropriate for you. The information in this book is not intended to take the place of any medical advice. It reflects my experiences, studies, research, and opinions regarding healthy eating.

Each recipe includes nutritional information calculated in three ways:

Healthy Exchanges Weight Loss Choices™ or Exchanges
Calories, fiber, and fat grams
Diabetic exchanges

In every Healthy Exchanges recipe, the diabetic exchanges have been calculated by a Registered Dietitian. All the other calculations were done by computer, using the Food Processor II software. When the ingredient listing gives more than one choice, the first ingredient listed is the one used in the recipe analysis. Due to inevitable variations in the ingredients you choose to use, the nutritional values should be considered approximate.

The annotation "(limited)" following Protein counts in some recipes indicates that consumption of whole eggs should be limited to four per week.

Please note the following symbols:

☆ This star means read the recipe's directions carefully for special instructions about **division** of ingredients.

❋ This symbol indicates **FREEZES WELL.**

A Few Cooking Terms to Ease the Way

Everyone can learn to cook the *Healthy Exchanges Way*. It's simple, it's quick, and the results are delicious! If you've tended to avoid the kitchen because you find recipe instructions confusing or complicated, I hope I can help you feel more confident. I'm not offering a full cooking course here, just some terms I use often that I know you'll want to understand.

Bake: To cook food in the oven; sometimes called roasting

Beat: To mix very fast with a spoon, wire whisk, or electric mixer

Blend: To mix two or more ingredients together thoroughly so that the mixture is smooth

Boil: To cook in liquid until bubbles form

Brown: To cook at low to medium-low heat until ingredients turn brown

Chop: To cut food into small pieces with a knife, blender, or food processor

Combine: To mix ingredients together with a spoon

Cool: To let stand at room temperature until food is no longer hot to the touch

Dice: To chop into small, even-sized pieces

Drain: To pour off liquid; sometimes you will need to reserve the liquid to use in the recipe, so please read carefully

Drizzle: To sprinkle drops of liquid (for example, chocolate syrup) lightly over the top of food

Fold in: To combine delicate ingredients with other foods by using a gentle, circular motion (for example, adding Cool Whip Lite to an already stirred-up bowl of pudding)

Preheat: To heat your oven to the desired temperature, usually about 10 minutes before you put your food in to bake

Sauté: To cook in a skillet or frying pan until the food is soft

Simmer: To cook in a small amount of liquid over low heat; this lets the flavors blend without too much liquid evaporating

Whisk: To beat with a wire whisk until mixture is well mixed; don't worry about finesse here, just use some elbow grease!

How to Measure

I try to make it as easy as possible by providing more than one measurement for many ingredients in my recipes—both the weight in ounces and the amount measured by a measuring cup, for example. Just remember:

- You measure **solids** (flour, Cool Whip Lite, yogurt, nonfat dry milk powder) in your set of separate measuring cups (¼, ⅓, ½, 1 cup)

- You measure **liquids** (Diet Mountain Dew, water, juice) in the clear glass or plastic measuring cups that measure ounces, cups, and pints. Set the cup on a level surface and pour the liquid into it, or you may get too much.

- You can use your measuring spoon set for liquids or solids. **Note:** Don't pour a liquid like an extract into a measuring spoon held over the bowl in case you overpour; instead, do it over the sink.

Here are a few handy equivalents:

3 teaspoons	equals	1 tablespoon
4 tablespoons	equals	¼ cup
5⅓ tablespoons	equals	⅓ cup
8 tablespoons	equals	½ cup
10⅔ tablespoons	equals	⅔ cup
12 tablespoons	equals	¾ cup
16 tablespoons	equals	1 cup
2 cups	equals	1 pint
4 cups	equals	1 quart
8 ounces liquid	equals	1 fluid cup

That's it. Now, ready, set, cook!

The Recipes

Speedy Soups

Soup . . . Just the word makes you close your eyes and envision a steaming, thick bowl of goodness that can warm you all the way through. But is the only time you serve soup at home these days directly from a can? "It's too time-consuming," you say apologetically. "I would love to serve my family rich, homemade soup, but I haven't got the time it would take to do it right."

Do you feel that preparing soup has to take hours in order to be good? Do you suspect that only if you've invested lots of time will your family believe that you really love them? Well, it's "time" to stop believing that fairytale and start eating great soup prepared in a jiffy!

My goal is to keep the spirit of soup alive, to create recipes for soups that warm the heart and soul but don't keep you locked in the kitchen, chopping and stirring for an entire afternoon. Think of it this way—I love my grandmother's old-fashioned soup kettle, and I keep it as a wonderful symbol of the "good old days," but I prefer to cook (most of the time) in a sturdy nonstick pot for easy cleanup!

Just because it's fast doesn't mean that soup can't be fabulous as well! Wait till you ladle up bowls of my **Cheesy Garden Chowder**, so creamy-rich it's a satisfying, speedy supper. And I'll bet you'll win cheers for my **Magical Minestrone Stew**, a soup so full of goodness your tummy will feel delightfully full afterward. Whether your choice is a hearty chili (**Jackpot Ham Chili**) or a tangy veggie soup (**Southern California Gazpacho**), you'll find fast solutions for all occasions in this chapter!

Basil-Tomato Pasta Soup

Talk about tasty flavors that seem to make each other better than they could ever be alone! Here, the tomatoes and basil perform a kind of culinary magic—and with hardly an "Abracadabra" on your part, you've prepared a soup that's special enough to serve to company. ◗ Serves 4 (1 cup)

1 (10¾-ounce) can Healthy Request Tomato Soup

2 cups (one 16-ounce can) tomatoes, finely chopped and undrained

1 cup water

1 tablespoon pourable Sugar Twin

1½ teaspoons dried basil

1 cup hot cooked rotini pasta, rinsed and drained

¼ cup (¾ ounce) grated Kraft fat-free Parmesan cheese

In a large saucepan, combine tomato soup, undrained tomatoes, water, Sugar Twin, and basil. Stir in rotini pasta. Cook over medium heat for about 6 to 8 minutes, or until mixture is heated through, stirring often. When serving, sprinkle 1 tablespoon Parmesan cheese over top of each bowl.

HINT: ¾ cup uncooked rotini pasta usually cooks to about 1 cup.

Each serving equals:

HE: 1 Vegetable • ½ Bread • ¼ Protein • ½ Slider • 5 Optional Calories

133 Calories • 1 gm Fat • 4 gm Protein • 27 gm Carbohydrate • 506 mg Sodium • 54 mg Calcium • 3 gm Fiber

DIABETIC: 1 Vegetable • 1 Starch

Southern California Gazpacho

Some places you visit just seem to encourage a particular lifestyle, don't you think? Southern California is home to great fresh produce, and restaurant menus reflect this by featuring all kinds of lively recipes that use those veggies to real advantage. This cold soup is remarkably refreshing and will really give your taste-buds a wake-up call!   ☻   Serves 6 (1 cup)

3 cups Healthy Request tomato juice or any reduced-sodium tomato juice
½ cup Kraft Fat Free Catalina Dressing
½ cup finely chopped onion
½ cup finely chopped green bell pepper
1 cup finely chopped fresh tomato
1 cup finely chopped unpeeled cucumber
1 teaspoon dried basil

In a large bowl, combine tomato juice and Catalina dressing. Add onion, green pepper, tomato, cucumber, and basil. Mix well to combine. Cover and refrigerate for at least 15 minutes. Gently stir again just before serving.

Each serving equals:

HE: 2 Vegetable • ¼ Slider • 13 Optional Calories

64 Calories • 0 gm Fat • 2 gm Protein • 14 gm Carbohydrate •
301 mg Sodium •16 mg Calcium • 2 gm Fiber

DIABETIC: 2 Vegetable

Magical Minestrone Stew

This "kitchen sink" of stews combines an abundance of delicious ingredients, takes very little watching, and delivers a great, high-fiber, high-protein dish without any meat! That's gotta be some kind of magic! ☻ Serves 4 (1½ cups)

1½ cups hot water ☆
¾ cup chopped onion
¾ cup chopped celery
½ teaspoon dried minced garlic
2 cups (one 16-ounce can) tomatoes, finely chopped and undrained
1 cup (one 8-ounce can) Hunt's Tomato Sauce
⅓ cup (¾ ounce) uncooked macaroni
10 ounces (one 16-ounce can) red kidney beans, rinsed and drained
1 cup chopped fresh or frozen broccoli
1 cup diced fresh or frozen carrots
2 teaspoons dried parsley flakes
1 teaspoon Italian seasoning
⅛ teaspoon black pepper

In a large saucepan, combine ½ cup water, onion, celery, and garlic. Cook over medium heat for 5 minutes, stirring often. Add undrained tomatoes, tomato sauce, uncooked macaroni, kidney beans, remaining 1 cup water, broccoli, carrots, parsley flakes, Italian seasoning, and black pepper. Mix well to combine. Bring mixture to a boil. Lower heat and simmer for 20 to 25 minutes or until vegetables and macaroni are tender, stirring occasionally.

Each serving equals:

HE: 3¾ Vegetable • 1¼ Protein • ¼ Bread

169 Calories • 1 gm Fat • 8 gm Protein • 32 gm Carbohydrate • 611 mg Sodium • 98 mg Calcium • 9 gm Fiber

DIABETIC: 3 Vegetable • 1½ Starch • 1 Meat

Cheesy Garden Chowder

What's more delectable than a rich and creamy cheese soup? But the traditional recipe is so high in fat and calories, it's not something you dare enjoy very often, if at all. I took that as a challenge and came up with a thick, satisfying blend that's not only good for you but downright GOOD!   ☻   Serves 4 (1¼ cups)

> 2 cups (one 16-ounce can) Healthy Request Chicken Broth
>
> 1 cup frozen peas, thawed
>
> 1 cup frozen whole-kernel corn, thawed
>
> ½ cup chopped onion
>
> 1 cup finely diced celery
>
> 1 cup shredded carrots
>
> ⅔ cup Carnation Nonfat Dry Milk Powder
>
> 1 cup water
>
> 3 tablespoons all-purpose flour
>
> ¾ cup (3 ounces) shredded Kraft reduced-fat Cheddar cheese
>
> 2 teaspoons dried parsley flakes
>
> ⅛ teaspoon black pepper

In a large saucepan, combine chicken broth, peas, corn, onion, celery, and carrots. Bring mixture to a boil. Lower heat and simmer for 15 minutes, or until vegetables are tender. In a covered jar, combine dry milk powder, water, and flour. Shake well to blend. Pour milk mixture into vegetable mixture. Add Cheddar cheese, parsley flakes, and black pepper. Mix well to combine. Continue simmering for 5 minutes or until mixture starts to thicken and cheese melts, stirring often.

HINT: Thaw peas and corn by placing in a colander and rinsing under hot water for one minute.

Each serving equals:

HE: 1½ Vegetable • 1 Bread • 1 Protein • ½ Skim Milk •
8 Optional Calories

---

211 Calories • 3 gm Fat • 15 gm Protein • 31 gm Carbohydrate •
521 mg Sodium • 316 mg Calcium • 5 gm Fiber

DIABETIC: 1 Vegetable • 1 Starch • 1 Meat • 1 Skim Milk

Spinach-Chicken Soup

This may be one of the fastest soups I've ever created, but it doesn't taste as if you had no time to cook! Soups like this one really warm the soul as well as the tummy, and this one is so low in calories, you can still enjoy a hearty entree afterward.   ☻   Serves 4 (1 full cup)

> 4 cups (two 16-ounce cans) Healthy Request Chicken Broth
> 1½ cups (8 ounces) chopped cooked chicken breast
> 1 teaspoon lemon pepper
> 1½ cups shredded fresh spinach leaves

In a medium saucepan, combine chicken broth, chicken, and lemon pepper. Bring mixture to a boil. Stir in spinach leaves. Continue cooking for 2 to 3 minutes, stirring often and being careful not to overcook. Serve at once.

HINT: If you don't have leftovers, purchase a chunk of cooked chicken breast from your local deli.

Each serving equals:

HE: 2 Protein • ½ Vegetable • 16 Optional Calories

110 Calories • 2 gm Fat • 21 gm Protein • 2 gm Carbohydrate • 539 mg Sodium • 29 mg Calcium • 1 gm Fiber

DIABETIC: 2 Meat

Chicken Vegetable Noodle Soup

Here's a classic, family-pleasing soup that's very traditional in its ingredients. Just watch the smiles around the table as you ladle it from the pot, and if you've been clever enough to double the recipe so you'll have leftovers, I can guess what the kids will want for lunch tomorrow.　　☻　Serves 4 (1½ cups)

> 2 cups (one 16-ounce can) Healthy Request Chicken Broth
> 3 cups water
> ½ cup chopped onion
> 1½ cups diced celery
> 1 cup shredded carrots
> 2 cups (10 ounces) diced cooked chicken breast
> 2 tablespoons dried parsley flakes
> ⅛ teaspoon black pepper
> Scant 1 cup (1½ ounces) uncooked noodles

In a large saucepan, combine chicken broth, water, onion, celery, carrots, chicken, parsley flakes, and black pepper. Bring mixture to a boil. Lower heat and simmer for 15 minutes, stirring occasionally. Stir in uncooked noodles. Cover and continue simmering for 10 minutes or until vegetables and noodles are tender, stirring occasionally.

HINT:　If you don't have leftovers, purchase a chunk of cooked chicken breast from your local deli.

Each serving equals:

HE: 2½ Protein • 1½ Vegetable • ½ Bread • 8 Optional Calories

223 Calories • 3 gm Fat • 27 gm Protein • 22 gm Carbohydrate • 346 mg Sodium • 54 mg Calcium • 2 gm Fiber

DIABETIC: 2½ Meat • 1½ Starch • 1 Vegetable

Fast Turkey-Corn Chowder

No one's prouder of Iowa's heritage as a corn producer than I am, so I love coming up with fresh and flavorful ways to serve our "state vegetable." This creamy-rich chowder is just chock-full of flavor—and it delivers a nice wallop of calcium in every serving. ☺ Serves 6 (1½ cups)

2 cups (10 ounces) chopped unpeeled raw potatoes
1 cup sliced onion
1 cup chopped celery
2 cups (one 16-ounce can) Healthy Request Chicken Broth
1 teaspoon dried parsley flakes
⅛ teaspoon black pepper
1 cup skim milk
1½ cups (one 12-fluid-ounce can) Carnation Evaporated Skim Milk
1 cup (one 8-ounce can) cream-style corn
1 cup (one 8-ounce can) whole-kernel corn, rinsed and drained
2 full cups (12 ounces) diced cooked turkey breast
¼ cup (one 2-ounce jar) chopped pimiento, drained

In a large saucepan, combine potatoes, onion, celery, chicken broth, parsley flakes, and black pepper. Cook over medium heat for 10 minutes or until potatoes are tender. Add skim milk, evaporated skim milk, cream-style corn, whole-kernel corn, turkey, and pimiento. Mix well to combine. Lower heat and simmer for 10 to 15 minutes, stirring occasionally.

HINT: If you don't have leftovers, purchase a chunk of cooked turkey breast from your local deli.

Each serving equals:

HE: 2 Protein • 1 Bread • ⅔ Skim Milk • ⅔ Vegetable •
5 Optional Calories

234 Calories • 2 gm Fat • 27 gm Protein • 27 gm Carbohydrate •
440 mg Sodium • 263 mg Calcium • 2 gm Fiber

DIABETIC: 2 Meat • 1 Starch • 1 Skim Milk • ½ Vegetable

Diner-Style Burger Soup

Nothing's more all-American than diner food, and I thought this would be a perfect addition to the menu at your favorite diner! It's real 1950s-style soup, a mouth-watering dish for a cold and rainy evening when you want to get warm inside and out just as fast as you can!   ☻   Serves 4 (full 1½ cups)

  8 ounces ground 90% lean turkey or beef
  1 cup chopped onion
  1 (10¾-ounce) can Healthy Request Tomato Soup
  1 cup (one 8-ounce can) Hunt's Tomato Sauce
  1½ cups water
  ⅔ cup (2 ounces) uncooked Minute Rice
  1 cup (one 8-ounce can) sliced green beans, rinsed and drained
  2 teaspoons dried parsley flakes
  ⅛ teaspoon black pepper

In a large saucepan sprayed with butter-flavored cooking spray, brown meat and onion. Stir in tomato soup, tomato sauce, and water. Bring mixture to a boil. Add uncooked rice, green beans, parsley flakes, and black pepper. Mix well to combine. Lower heat, cover, and simmer for 15 minutes or until rice is tender, stirring occasionally.

Each serving equals:

HE: 2 Vegetable • 1½ Protein • ½ Bread • ½ Slider •
5 Optional Calories

202 Calories • 6 gm Fat • 13 gm Protein • 24 gm Carbohydrate •
657 mg Sodium • 39 mg Calcium • 3 gm Fiber

DIABETIC: 1½ Vegetable • 1½ Meat • 1 Starch

Cream of Mushroom Soup

Why would I create a recipe for this most beloved cream soup of all when you can already find it in a can? Well, my Healthy Exchanges version boasts more fresh mushrooms and a special blend of spices, but my best reason is a simple one: I think this is just the creamiest healthy soup I've ever tried!

☻ Serves 4 (1 cup)

> 2 cups chopped fresh mushrooms
> ½ cup chopped onion
> ½ teaspoon dried minced garlic
> 2 cups (one 16-ounce can) Healthy Request Chicken Broth
> 1 tablespoon reduced-sodium soy sauce
> ¼ teaspoon black pepper
> 1½ cups (one 12-fluid-ounce can) Carnation Evaporated Skim Milk
> 6 tablespoons all-purpose flour

In a large saucepan sprayed with butter-flavored cooking spray, sauté mushrooms, onion, and garlic for 5 minutes or until mushrooms start to turn limp. Add chicken broth. Mix well to combine. Bring mixture to a boil. Lower heat. Stir in soy sauce and black pepper. In a covered jar, combine evaporated skim milk and flour. Shake well to blend. Pour milk mixture into mushroom mixture. Continue simmering until mixture thickens, stirring often.

Each serving equals:

HE: 1¼ Vegetable • ¾ Skim Milk • ½ Bread • 8 Optional Calories

156 Calories • 0 gm Fat • 12 gm Protein • 27 gm Carbohydrate • 808 mg Sodium • 293 mg Calcium • 3 gm Fiber

DIABETIC: 1 Skim Milk • 1 Starch • ½ Vegetable

Cream of Tomato Soup

For those times when you don't feel like a heavy meal, soup makes terrifically nourishing and soothing lighter fare! You'll be astonished at how rich this home-made version of your childhood favorite tastes—and how simple it can be to fix it!

☻ Serves 4 (1½ cups)

> 3 cups (one 28-ounce can) tomatoes, coarsely chopped and undrained
> ½ cup chopped onion
> ½ cup chopped celery
> ¼ cup chopped fresh parsley
> 3 cups skim milk
> ¼ cup all-purpose flour
> 1 teaspoon dried parsley flakes
> ⅛ teaspoon black pepper

In a large covered saucepan, combine undrained tomatoes, onion, celery, and fresh parsley. Cook over medium-low heat for 10 minutes or until vegetables are tender. Pour hot mixture into a blender container. Cover and process on BLEND for 30 seconds or until smooth. In a large covered jar, combine skim milk and flour. Shake well to blend. Pour milk mixture into a large saucepan sprayed with butter-flavored cooking spray. Cook over medium heat until mixture starts to thicken, stirring constantly. Add blended tomato mixture, parsley flakes, and black pepper. Mix well to combine. Lower heat and simmer for 10 minutes or until mixture is heated through.

Each serving equals:

HE: 2 Vegetable • ¾ Skim Milk • ⅓ Bread

---

141 Calories • 1 gm Fat • 9 gm Protein • 24 gm Carbohydrate • 127 mg Sodium • 265 mg Calcium • 3 gm Fiber

---

DIABETIC: 2 Vegetable • 1 Skim Milk

Cream of Potato and Cabbage Soup

Hearty soups are a wonderful way to feed your family without spending a lot, but they won't notice your smart economy, just the cozy feeling that a big bowl of soup always delivers! If your kids love mashed potatoes as much as mine do, they'll look forward with glee to supper when it features this thick and appetizing creamy soup.

♥ Serves 4 (1¼ cups)

> 2 cups (one 16-ounce can) Healthy Request Chicken Broth
> ¼ teaspoon dried minced garlic
> ½ cup sliced green onion with tops
> 1 cup shredded carrots
> 2 cups shredded cabbage
> 1½ cups (one 12-fluid-ounce can) Carnation Evaporated Skim Milk
> 1 cup skim milk
> 1⅓ cups (3 ounces) instant potato flakes
> ¼ teaspoon black pepper
> 1 teaspoon dried parsley flakes

In a medium saucepan, combine chicken broth and garlic. Add onion, carrots, and cabbage. Mix well to combine. Cook over medium heat for 10 minutes or until vegetables are tender. Add evaporated skim milk, skim milk, potato flakes, black pepper, and parsley flakes. Mix well to combine. Lower heat and simmer for 5 minutes, or until mixture thickens and is heated through, stirring often.

Each serving equals:

HE: 1¾ Vegetable • 1 Skim Milk • 1 Bread • 8 Optional Calories

184 Calories • 0 gm Fat • 13 gm Protein • 33 gm Carbohydrate • 420 mg Sodium • 390 mg Calcium • 3 gm Fiber

DIABETIC: 1 Vegetable • 1 Skim Milk • 1 Starch

Italian Bean Soup

Maybe it's because their gardens produce such glorious produce, but there's a long tradition of main-dish soups in the Mediterranean countries, especially Italy. When you top a steaming bowl of beans and veggies with just a touch of fragrant Parmesan cheese, you've turned an ordinary meal into a banquet for the taste buds! ❂ Serves 4 (1½ cups)

½ cup chopped onion

2 cups (one 16-ounce can) tomatoes, coarsely chopped and undrained

10 ounces (one 16-ounce can) great northern beans, rinsed and drained

½ cup (one 2.5-ounce jar) sliced mushrooms, drained

2 cups (one 16-ounce can) cut green beans, rinsed and drained

1 (10¾-ounce) can Healthy Request Tomato Soup

½ cup water

1 teaspoon Italian seasoning

1 teaspoon Sugar Twin or Sprinkle Sweet

¼ cup (¾ ounce) grated Kraft fat-free Parmesan cheese

In a large saucepan sprayed with butter-flavored cooking spray, sauté onion for 5 minutes or just until tender. Meanwhile, place undrained tomatoes in a blender container, cover, and process on BLEND for 15 seconds or until smooth. Stir blended tomatoes into skillet with onion. Add great northern beans, mushrooms, green beans, tomato soup, water, Italian seasoning, and Sugar Twin. Mix well to combine. Bring mixture to a boil. Lower heat and simmer for 10 minutes, stirring occasionally. When serving, sprinkle 1 tablespoon Parmesan cheese over top of each bowl.

Each serving equals:

HE: 2½ Vegetable • 1½ Protein • ½ Slider • 6 Optional Calories

197 Calories • 1 gm Fat • 9 gm Protein • 38 gm Carbohydrate • 437 mg Sodium • 84 mg Calcium • 8 gm Fiber

DIABETIC: 2 Vegetable • 1½ Starch • 1 Meat

Peasant Vegetable Bean Soup

Even if you make your home in one of our big cities, there's no reason not to "live off the land" . . . just "harvest" your ingredients at the weekly farmers' market! The peasant tradition has always celebrated the ripest and best from the fields, and this soup will make your family smack their lips in delight.

● Serves 6 (1⅓ cups)

> 4 cups (two 16-ounce cans) tomatoes, coarsely chopped and undrained
> 2 cups water
> ½ cup finely chopped celery
> ½ cup chopped onion
> 2 cups shredded cabbage
> 2 teaspoons chili seasoning
> ⅛ teaspoon black pepper
> 1 teaspoon dried parsley flakes
> 10 ounces (one 16-ounce can) pinto beans, rinsed and drained
> 10 ounces (one 16-ounce can) red kidney beans, rinsed and drained

Place undrained tomatoes in a blender container. Cover and process on BLEND for 15 seconds or until smooth. Pour blended tomatoes into a large saucepan. Add water, celery, onion, cabbage, chili seasoning, black pepper, and parsley flakes. Mix well to combine. Stir in pinto beans and kidney beans. Bring mixture to a boil. Lower heat and simmer for 30 minutes, stirring occasionally.

Each serving equals:

HE: 2⅓ Vegetable • 1⅔ Protein

148 Calories • 0 gm Fat • 8 gm Protein • 29 gm Carbohydrate • 276 mg Sodium • 95 mg Calcium • 9 gm Fiber

DIABETIC: 1½ Vegetable • 1 Starch • 1 Meat

Heartland Beef and Noodle Soup

So many of our smartest, thriftiest recipes have come from the Midwest, most of them created by farm wives who often had to make do with less than they'd like! My own mother worked magic in the kitchen with leftover bits of this and that, instilling in me a desire to be just such a creative cook. This flavorful soup is a good example of doing a lot with just a little! ☻ Serves 4 (1½ cups)

> 1 full cup (6 ounces) diced cooked lean roast beef
> ½ cup chopped onion
> 1¾ cups (one 14½-ounce can) Swanson Beef Broth
> 2¼ cups water
> ⅛ teaspoon black pepper
> ¼ teaspoon dried minced garlic
> 1¾ cups (3 ounces) uncooked noodles
> ½ cup (one 2.5-ounce jar) sliced mushrooms, drained
> 1 teaspoon dried parsley flakes

In a large saucepan sprayed with butter-flavored cooking spray, sauté roast beef and onion for 5 minutes or until onion is tender. Add beef broth, water, black pepper, and garlic. Mix well to combine. Bring mixture to a boil. Lower heat and simmer for 10 minutes. Stir in uncooked noodles, mushrooms, and parsley flakes. Cover and continue simmering for 10 minutes or until noodles are tender, stirring occasionally.

HINT: If you don't have leftovers, purchase a chunk of cooked lean roast beef from your local deli.

Each serving equals:

HE: 1½ Protein • 1 Bread • ½ Vegetable • 8 Optional Calories

188 Calories • 4 gm Fat • 17 gm Protein • 21 gm Carbohydrate • 475 mg Sodium • 19 mg Calcium • 2 gm Fiber

DIABETIC: 1½ Meat • 1½ Starch/Carbohydrate

Chunky Chicken Soup

Here's a great example of how economizing on meat doesn't have to mean feeling deprived! By boosting the flavor content of this rich soup with so many tasty veggies, I can make six ounces of chicken feed a family of four—and nobody leaves the table hungry.   ☻   Serves 4 (1½ cups)

½ cup chopped onion

½ cup chopped green bell pepper

1 cup sliced celery

½ teaspoon dried minced garlic

1¾ cups (one 15-ounce can) Hunt's Chunky Tomato Sauce

2 cups (one 16-ounce can) Healthy Request Chicken Broth

1 full cup (6 ounces) diced cooked chicken breast

1 cup water

⅔ cup (2 ounces) uncooked Minute Rice

1 cup fresh or frozen whole-kernel corn

1 cup fresh or frozen cut green beans or okra

½ teaspoon Tabasco sauce

1 tablespoon Creole seasoning

⅛ teaspoon black pepper

In a large saucepan sprayed with butter-flavored cooking spray, sauté onion, green pepper, and celery for 10 minutes or until tender. Add garlic, tomato sauce, chicken broth, chicken, and water. Mix well to combine. Stir in uncooked rice, corn, and green beans. Add Tabasco sauce, Creole seasoning, and black pepper. Mix well to combine. Bring mixture to a boil. Lower heat and simmer for 25 to 30 minutes, stirring occasionally.

HINT: If you don't have leftovers, purchase a chunk of cooked chicken breast from your local deli.

Each serving equals:

HE: 3¼ Vegetable • 1½ Protein • 1 Bread • 8 Optional Calories

194 Calories • 2 gm Fat • 18 gm Protein • 26 gm Carbohydrate • 1,002 mg Sodium • 36 mg Calcium • 4 gm Fiber

DIABETIC: 3 Vegetable • 1½ Meat • 1 Starch

Tex-Mex Vegetable Soup

This spicy down-home veggie soup could almost be called a chili, it's so jam-packed with mouthwatering ingredients! Besides delivering a lot of nutrition and flavor, it's easily prepared in little more than a half hour. And it's so filling, it's perfect for satisfying a tableful of hungry kids! ☻   Serves 6 (1½ cups)

16 ounces ground 90% lean turkey or beef

1 cup chopped onion

1 cup chopped celery

1¾ cups (one 14½-ounce can) Swanson Beef Broth

2 cups Healthy Request tomato juice or any reduced-sodium tomato juice

6 ounces (one 8-ounce can) red kidney beans, rinsed and drained

2 cups (one 16-ounce can) tomatoes, coarsely chopped and undrained

1½ cups frozen whole-kernel corn

1 cup frozen sliced carrots

1 cup frozen cut green beans

½ teaspoon dried minced garlic

2 teaspoons chili seasoning

¼ teaspoon black pepper

In a large saucepan sprayed with olive oil–flavored cooking spray, brown meat and onion. Add celery, beef broth, tomato juice, kidney beans, undrained tomatoes, corn, carrots, and green beans. Mix well to combine. Stir in garlic, chili seasoning, and black pepper. Bring mixture to a boil. Lower heat, cover, and simmer for 30 minutes, stirring occasionally.

Each serving equals:

HE: 2⅔ Vegetable • 2½ Protein • ½ Bread • 6 Optional Calories

235 Calories • 7 gm Fat • 19 gm Protein • 24 gm Carbohydrate • 394 mg Sodium • 42 mg Calcium • 5 gm Fiber

DIABETIC: 2 Vegetable • 2 Meat • 1 Starch

Ham and Corn Chowder

Cliff loves a thick corn chowder, especially when it's chock-full of potatoes and little bits of ham like this one. When you can make something so delicious and satisfying so quickly, you'll never have to worry about what to serve for supper.

❂ Serves 4 (1½ cups)

> 1¼ cups water
>
> 1 cup (5 ounces) diced raw potatoes
>
> ½ cup chopped onion
>
> 1 full cup (6 ounces) diced Dubuque 97% fat-free ham or any extra-lean ham
>
> 2 cups (one 16-ounce can) cream-style corn
>
> 1 cup skim milk
>
> 1 (10¾-ounce) can Healthy Request Cream of Mushroom Soup
>
> 1 teaspoon dried parsley flakes
>
> ¼ teaspoon black pepper

In a medium saucepan, combine water, potatoes, and onion. Cook over medium heat until potatoes are just tender. Stir in ham, corn, skim milk, mushroom soup, parsley flakes, and black pepper. Lower heat and simmer for 15 minutes, stirring occasionally.

Each serving equals:

HE: 1¼ Bread • 1 Protein • ¼ Skim Milk • ¼ Vegetable •
½ Slider • 1 Optional Calorie

231 Calories • 3 gm Fat • 12 gm Protein • 39 gm Carbohydrate •
1,059 mg Sodium • 138 mg Calcium • 2 gm Fiber

DIABETIC: 2½ Starch/Carbohydrate • 1 Meat

Chunky Bean and Franks Soup

Tired of serving hot dogs the same old way, but can't seem to think of what else to do with this economical source of healthy protein? Why not stir up this fragrant and robust combination, then just enjoy the oohs and aahs of your family as they gobble it down?　　●　Serves 4 (1½ cups)

> 8 ounces Healthy Choice 97% fat-free frankfurters, diced
> 10 ounces (one 16-ounce can) great northern beans, rinsed and drained
> 2 cups (one 16-ounce can) French-style green beans, rinsed and drained
> 1 (10¾-ounce) can Healthy Request Tomato Soup
> 1¾ cups (one 14½-ounce can) Swanson Beef Broth
> ¼ teaspoon black pepper

In a medium saucepan, combine frankfurters, great northern beans, green beans, and tomato soup. Add beef broth and black pepper. Mix well to combine. Bring mixture to a boil. Lower heat and simmer for 15 minutes, stirring occasionally.

Each serving equals:

HE: 2½ Protein • 1 Vegetable • ½ Slider • 13 Optional Calories

219 Calories • 3 gm Fat • 16 gm Protein • 32 gm Carbohydrate • 1,166 mg Sodium • 74 mg Calcium • 5 gm Fiber

DIABETIC: 2 Meat • 1½ Starch • 1 Vegetable

Garden-Style Chili

There are as many recipes for chili as stars in the sky, or at least that's the way it seems sometimes! I wanted a hearty blend of meat with lots of different veggies, so that each bite you spooned up would make you smile with anticipation.

☻ Serves 6 (1½ cups)

16 ounces ground 90% lean turkey or beef
1 cup chopped onion
1 cup chopped green bell pepper
1 cup chopped celery
1¾ cups (one 14½-ounce can) Swanson Beef Broth
1 cup (one 8-ounce can) sliced carrots, rinsed and drained
2 cups (one 16-ounce can) French-style green beans, rinsed and drained
4 cups (two 16-ounce cans) tomatoes, coarsely chopped and undrained
2 teaspoons chili seasoning
⅛ teaspoon black pepper

In a large saucepan sprayed with butter-flavored cooking spray, brown meat, onion, green pepper, and celery. Add beef broth, carrots, green beans, and undrained tomatoes. Mix well to combine. Stir in chili seasoning and black pepper. Bring mixture to a boil. Lower heat, cover, and simmer for at least 15 minutes, stirring occasionally.

Each serving equals:

HE: 3 Vegetable • 2 Protein • 6 Optional Calories

---

179 Calories • 7 gm Fat • 16 gm Protein • 13 gm Carbohydrate •
351 mg Sodium • 39 mg Calcium • 3 gm Fiber

DIABETIC: 2 Vegetable • 2 Meat

Jackpot Ham Chili

The name for this recipe came when Cliff took his first bite and said, "JoAnna, you've really hit the jackpot with this one!" He got a kick out of finding ham in his chili, along with tangy olives and soothing rice. Don't wait to hit the lottery—serve this tonight, and you'll feel like a big winner!

● Serves 8 (1½ cups)

> 2 full cups (12 ounces) finely diced Dubuque 97% fat-free ham or
>   any extra-lean ham
> 1 cup chopped onion
> 1 cup chopped green bell pepper
> 1 cup (one 8-ounce can) Hunt's Tomato Sauce
> 5 cups Healthy Request tomato juice or any reduced-sodium tomato juice
> ¾ cup water
> 1 tablespoon chili seasoning
> 10 ounces (one 16-ounce can) red kidney beans, rinsed and drained
> 2 cups hot cooked rice
> ½ cup (2 ounces) sliced ripe olives
> ½ cup + 1 tablespoon (2.5 ounces) shredded Kraft reduced-fat
>   Cheddar cheese

In a large saucepan sprayed with olive oil–flavored cooking spray, sauté ham, onion, and green pepper for 5 minutes or until browned. Stir in tomato sauce, tomato juice, water, and chili seasoning. Bring mixture to a boil. Add kidney beans and rice. Mix well to combine. Stir in olives and Cheddar cheese. Lower heat and simmer for 10 minutes or until cheese melts, stirring often.

HINT: 1⅓ cups uncooked rice usually cooks to about 2 cups.

Each serving equals:

HE: 2¼ Vegetable • 2 Protein • ½ Bread • ¼ Fat

168 Calories • 4 gm Fat • 13 gm Protein • 20 gm Carbohydrate • 711 mg Sodium • 98 mg Calcium • 4 gm Fiber

DIABETIC: 2 Vegetable • 2 Meat • 1 Starch

Swift and Simple Salads

Salads are the little extras that fill up the plate when you're serving a healthy entree, and they really do make the difference between feeling deprived and feeling joyfully well nourished! Yet if you're rushed or on a tight schedule, they're often the first to go.

But just think how much pleasure a sweet or savory salad can add to any meal. They provide color (those vivid greens of broccoli and lettuce, the bright orange energy of fresh carrots), texture (a little cauliflower crunch will wake up your mouth and dazzle your senses), and intense flavors (those tiny morsels like bacon bits and sprinkles of Parmesan cheese provide plenty of pizzazz!).

Salads are also a wonderful way to increase the number of fruits and vegetables in your daily menu, and you can't read a newspaper these days without hearing that we all need to include more of them. If your kids tend to push their vegetables aside, you can "sneak" some good-for-you veggies into a tasty slaw, and if your husband usually ignores the bowl of fruit and heads for the cake donuts, you can cleverly make sure he's getting what he needs by presenting lively fruit salads as part of the meal.

Salads are a beloved and timeless tradition here in the Midwest, whether you dish up hearty potato and pasta salads (**Garden Potato Salad, Summer Rotini Salad**) or sprightly fresh and fruity gelatin blends (**Blueberry-Lemon Salad, Coconut Mandarin Orange Salad**) that appeal to the eyes as much as to your tastebuds! This is one corner you don't want to cut when you're busy, and with these delectable recipes, you won't have to anymore!

Harvest Cabbage Salad

Crunch and color and different textures, all wrapped up in a luscious dressing, make this quick mix a perfect choice for a summer night, especially if your tomato plants are hanging heavy with beautiful red spheres!   ☻   Serves 4 (1 cup)

> 3 cups chopped cabbage
> 1 cup chopped carrots
> 1 cup chopped tomato
> ½ cup chopped green bell pepper
> ⅓ cup Kraft Fat Free Thousand Island Dressing
> 2 tablespoons Kraft fat-free mayonnaise

In a medium bowl, combine cabbage, carrots, tomato, and green pepper. In a small bowl, combine Thousand Island dressing and mayonnaise. Add dressing mixture to cabbage mixture. Mix gently to combine. Cover and refrigerate for at least 15 minutes. Gently stir again just before serving.

Each serving equals:

HE: 2¾ Vegetable • ¼ Slider • 18 Optional Calories

68 Calories • 0 gm Fat • 2 gm Protein • 15 gm Carbohydrate • 273 mg Sodium • 36 mg Calcium • 3 gm Fiber

DIABETIC: 2 Vegetable

Country Time Slaw

Some like it tangy, some like it creamy, and some just like it as often as they can get it! This flavorful coleslaw offers a little extra zing when you add the horseradish to the creamy dressing. ☻ Serves 4 (1 cup)

 4 cups purchased coleslaw mix
 1 cup diced celery
 ½ cup finely diced onion
 ¾ cup Yoplait plain low-fat yogurt
 1 tablespoon prepared horseradish
 Sugar substitute to equal 2 tablespoons sugar
 2 tablespoons white or cider vinegar
 1 teaspoon celery seed
 ⅛ teaspoon black pepper

In a large bowl, combine coleslaw mix, celery, and onion. In a small bowl, combine yogurt, horseradish, sugar substitute, vinegar, celery seed, and black pepper. Add dressing mixture to cabbage mixture. Mix well to combine. Cover and refrigerate for at least 15 minutes. Gently stir again just before serving.

HINT: 3¼ cups shredded cabbage and ¾ cup shredded carrots may be used in place of purchased coleslaw mix.

Each serving equals:

HE: 2¾ Vegetable • ¼ Skim Milk • 3 Optional Calories

64 Calories • 0 gm Fat • 4 gm Protein • 12 gm Carbohydrate •
349 mg Sodium • 145 mg Calcium • 3 gm Fiber

DIABETIC: 1½ Vegetable • ½ Starch/Carbohydrate

Crunchy Cauliflower Salad

Here's a wonderful salad to serve alongside your next pasta meal. The combo of Parmesan and garlic complements whatever sauce you've chosen, and the texture of all those fresh vegetables provides a terrific contrast to that of the noodles (no matter how *al dente* they are!).   ♥   Serves 4 (¾ cup)

> 2 cups chopped fresh cauliflower
> ¾ cup shredded carrots
> ¼ cup chopped green or white onion
> ½ cup chopped celery
> ¼ cup Kraft Fat Free Ranch Dressing
> ¼ cup Kraft fat-free mayonnaise
> ¼ cup (¾ ounce) grated Kraft fat-free Parmesan cheese
> ½ teaspoon dried minced garlic
> 1 teaspoon dried parsley flakes

In a medium bowl, combine cauliflower, carrots, onion, and celery. In a small bowl, combine Ranch dressing, mayonnaise, Parmesan cheese, garlic, and parsley flakes. Add dressing mixture to vegetable mixture. Mix gently to combine. Cover and refrigerate for at least 15 minutes. Gently stir again just before serving.

Each serving equals:

HE: 1¾ Vegetable • ¼ Protein • ¼ Slider • 15 Optional Calories

76 Calories • 0 gm Fat • 2 gm Protein • 17 gm Carbohydrate • 404 mg Sodium • 32 mg Calcium • 3 gm Fiber

DIABETIC: 2 Vegetable • ½ Starch/Carbohydrate

French Quarter Confetti Salad

New Orleans is more than a city; it's a festive experience whether you're eating or dancing or viewing the sights! Even if you're not dining Cajun-style in a noisy club, you can still let the good times roll when you serve this colorful party salad.

◐ Serves 6 (¾ cup)

1 cup (one 8-ounce can) whole-kernel corn, rinsed and drained

2 cups (one 16-ounce can) peas, rinsed and drained

2 cups (one 16-ounce can) French-style green beans, rinsed and drained

¾ cup diced celery

¼ cup finely chopped onion

¼ cup (one 2-ounce jar) chopped pimiento, drained

¾ cup Kraft Fat Free French Dressing

1 teaspoon dried parsley flakes

In a large bowl, combine corn, peas, green beans, celery, onion, and pimiento. Add French dressing and parsley flakes. Mix gently to combine. Cover and refrigerate for at least 15 minutes. Gently stir again just before serving.

Each serving equals:

HE: 1 Bread • 1 Vegetable • ½ Slider • 10 Optional Calories

128 Calories • 0 gm Fat • 4 gm Protein • 28 gm Carbohydrate • 319 mg Sodium • 33 mg Calcium • 5 gm Fiber

DIABETIC: 1½ Starch • 1 Vegetable

Broccoli-Cheese Tossed Salad

Crunch, crunch, crunch, mmm—those are the sounds you're sure to hear when the guests at your next dinner party dig into this lively presentation! What's the *"mmm"*? Could be the cheese, could be the bits of bacon, or just a word from their tastebuds telling you how happy they feel!　　❂　　Serves 8 (½ cup)

> 2¼ cups chopped fresh broccoli
> 2¼ cups chopped fresh cauliflower
> ½ cup chopped onion
> 3 tablespoons Hormel Bacon Bits
> ¾ cup (3 ounces) shredded Kraft reduced-fat Cheddar cheese
> ½ cup Kraft fat-free mayonnaise
> 2 tablespoons pourable Sugar Twin
> 1 tablespoon white vinegar

In a large bowl, combine broccoli, cauliflower, onion, bacon bits, and Cheddar cheese. In a small bowl, combine mayonnaise, Sugar Twin, and vinegar. Add dressing mixture to vegetable mixture. Mix well to combine. Cover and refrigerate for at least 15 minutes. Gently stir again just before serving.

HINT: 1 (16-ounce) package California Blend, cooked to just tender, drained and cooled, may be used in place of fresh broccoli and cauliflower.

Each serving equals:

HE: 1¼ Vegetable • ½ Protein • ¼ Slider • 1 Optional Calorie

66 Calories • 2 gm Fat • 5 gm Protein • 7 gm Carbohydrate • 328 mg Sodium • 90 mg Calcium • 1 gm Fiber

DIABETIC: 1 Vegetable • ½ Meat

Grande Corn Salad

This is one of Cliff's favorite summer salads, and it's easy to guess why: the salsa! This would make a wonderful go-along with a traditional Mexican-style meal, because the textures contrast beautifully—soft and smooth versus chunky and crunchy!　　❂　　Serves 6 (½ cup)

2 cups frozen whole-kernel corn, thawed
¼ cup chopped red radishes
¼ cup chopped green or white onion
½ cup chopped green bell pepper
½ cup chunky salsa (mild, medium, or hot)
¼ cup Kraft Fat Free Ranch Dressing
¼ cup Kraft fat-free mayonnaise
2 teaspoons dried parsley flakes
⅛ teaspoon black pepper

In a large bowl, combine corn, radishes, onion, and green pepper. In a small bowl, combine salsa, Ranch dressing, mayonnaise, parsley flakes, and black pepper. Add dressing mixture to corn mixture. Mix gently to combine. Cover and refrigerate for at least 15 minutes. Gently stir again just before serving.

HINT: Thaw corn by placing in a colander and rinsing under hot water for one minute.

Each serving equals:

HE: ⅔ Bread • ½ Vegetable • ¼ Slider • 3 Optional Calories

72 Calories • 0 gm Fat • 1 gm Protein • 17 gm Carbohydrate • 185 mg Sodium • 33 mg Calcium • 2 gm Fiber

DIABETIC: 1 Starch • ½ Vegetable

Garden Potato Salad

Are you an adventurous potato salad eater, or have you been stuck in a kind of potato salad rut for a while? I think this variation on a classic theme will wake up your tummy and give it that happy, satisfied sensation.

● Serves 6 (¾ cup)

> 3 cups (16 ounces) diced cooked potatoes
> ¼ cup chopped onion
> ¾ cup chopped celery
> ½ cup diced unpeeled cucumber
> ½ cup shredded carrots
> 2 hard-boiled eggs, chopped
> ⅓ cup Kraft Fat Free French Dressing
> 2 tablespoons Kraft fat-free mayonnaise
> ⅛ teaspoon black pepper

In a large bowl, combine potatoes, onion, celery, cucumber, carrots, and eggs. Add French dressing, mayonnaise, and black pepper. Mix gently to combine. Cover and refrigerate for at least 15 minutes. Gently stir again just before serving.

HINT: If you want the look and feel of egg without the cholesterol, toss out the yolk and dice the white.

Each serving equals:

HE: ⅔ Bread • ⅔ Vegetable • ⅓ Protein (limited) •
17 Optional Calories

84 Calories • 0 gm Fat • 3 gm Protein • 18 gm Carbohydrate •
334 mg Sodium • 25 mg Calcium • 2 gm Fiber

DIABETIC: 1 Starch • ½ Vegetable

Summer Rotini Salad

There's no better July lunch than this festive pasta salad (a special favorite of my daughter-in-law Pam's), which I've created with rotini in mind (but you could certainly make it with your favorite pasta shape!). If you spot yellow peppers in your market, chop some in along with the red and green!   ☻   Serves 4 (1 cup)

> 2 cups cold cooked rotini pasta, rinsed and drained
> ½ cup chopped green bell pepper
> ½ cup chopped red bell pepper
> ¾ cup sliced fresh mushrooms
> ¼ cup sliced green onion
> ¼ cup (¾ ounce) grated Kraft fat-free Parmesan cheese
> 1 tablespoon + 1 teaspoon Hormel Bacon Bits
> ½ cup Kraft Fat Free Italian Dressing

In a large bowl, combine rotini pasta, green pepper, red pepper, mushrooms, and green onion. Add Parmesan cheese, bacon bits, and Italian dressing. Mix gently to combine. Cover and refrigerate for at least 15 minutes. Gently stir again just before serving.

HINT: 1½ cups uncooked rotini pasta usually cooks to about 2 cups.

Each serving equals:

HE: 1 Bread • 1 Vegetable • ¼ Protein • ¼ Slider •
4 Optional Calories
_____
181 Calories • 1 gm Fat • 7 gm Protein • 36 gm Carbohydrate •
807 mg Sodium • 12 mg Calcium • 5 gm Fiber
_____
DIABETIC: 1½ Starch • 1 Vegetable

Italian Macaroni Salad

Here's a great example of a fresh way to use the low-fat cold cuts that have turned up in the supermarket. Did you ever think that pepperoni could be part of a healthy summer salad? When you combine it with cheese, olives, and a tangy dressing, you've got a dish that deserves lots of Bravos!

❂ Serves 4 (1½ cups)

> 2 cups cold, cooked shell macaroni, rinsed and drained
>
> 1 cup diced fresh tomatoes
>
> 1 (3.5-ounce) package Hormel reduced-fat sliced pepperoni
>
> ⅔ cup (2¼ ounces) shredded Kraft reduced-fat Cheddar cheese
>
> ¼ cup (1 ounce) sliced ripe olives
>
> ½ cup chopped onion
>
> ½ cup chopped green bell pepper
>
> 1 cup chopped celery
>
> ¼ cup Kraft Fat Free Italian Dressing
>
> ⅛ teaspoon black pepper

In a large bowl, combine macaroni, tomatoes, pepperoni, Cheddar cheese, olives, onion, green pepper, and celery. Add Italian dressing and black pepper. Mix well to combine. Cover and refrigerate for at least 15 minutes. Gently stir again just before serving.

HINT: 1⅓ cups uncooked macaroni usually cooks to about 2 cups.

Each serving equals:

HE: 1⅔ Protein • 1½ Vegetable • 1 Bread • ¼ Fat • 8 Optional Calories

230 Calories • 6 gm Fat • 16 gm Protein • 28 gm Carbohydrate • 711 mg Sodium • 223 mg Calcium • 2 gm Fiber

DIABETIC: 1½ Meat • 1½ Starch • 1 Vegetable

Fantastic Potato Salad

This is a great way to serve potato salad for a family party or picnic. The recipe doubles or triples easily if you're expecting a crowd, and it'll appeal to your youngest guests as well as to anyone who remembers the good old days!

● Serves 6 (scant 1 cup)

⅔ cup Kraft fat-free mayonnaise

3 tablespoons skim milk

¼ cup Hormel Bacon Bits

1 teaspoon dried parsley flakes

¼ teaspoon lemon pepper

3½ cups (18 ounces) peeled and diced cooked potatoes

¾ cup finely chopped celery

¼ cup finely chopped onion

2 hard-boiled eggs, diced

⅓ cup (1½ ounces) sliced pimiento-stuffed green olives

In a small bowl, combine mayonnaise, skim milk, bacon bits, parsley flakes, and lemon pepper. Set aside. In a large bowl, combine potatoes, celery, and onion. Add eggs and olives. Mix gently to combine. Stir in mayonnaise mixture. Cover and refrigerate for at least 15 minutes. Gently stir again just before serving.

HINT: If you want the look and feel of egg without the cholesterol, toss out the yolk and dice the white.

Each serving equals:

HE: ¾ Bread • ⅓ Vegetable • ⅓ Protein (limited) • ¼ Fat • ¼ Slider • 17 Optional Calories

123 Calories • 3 gm Fat • 6 gm Protein • 18 gm Carbohydrate • 439 mg Sodium • 32 mg Calcium • 2 gm Fiber

DIABETIC: 1½ Starch

Boardinghouse Dilled-Pea Salad

My grandmother kept her boarders happy with many different vegetable salads, but this recipe is inspired by one of her best-loved dishes. There's just something wonderful and extra-special about peas in a creamy dressing touched with dill.

☻ Serves 4 (¾ cup)

2 cups frozen peas, thawed
¾ cup finely chopped celery
¼ cup finely chopped onion
¼ cup (one 2-ounce jar) chopped pimiento, drained
½ cup Kraft fat-free mayonnaise
2 tablespoons skim milk
Sugar substitute to equal 1 tablespoon sugar
½ teaspoon dried dill weed
⅛ teaspoon black pepper
1 hard-boiled egg, chopped

In a large bowl, combine peas, celery, onion, and pimiento. In a small bowl, combine mayonnaise, skim milk, sugar substitute, dill weed, and black pepper. Add mayonnaise mixture to pea mixture. Mix gently to combine. Fold in chopped egg. Cover and refrigerate for at least 15 minutes. Gently stir again just before serving.

HINTS: 1. Thaw peas by placing in a colander and rinsing under hot water for one minute.
2. If you want the look and feel of egg without the cholesterol, toss out the yolk and dice the white.

Each serving equals:

HE: 1 Bread • 1 Vegetable • ¼ Protein (limited) • ¼ Slider • 4 Optional Calories

114 Calories • 2 gm Fat • 6 gm Protein • 18 gm Carbohydrate • 305 mg Sodium • 48 mg Calcium • 5 gm Fiber

DIABETIC: 1½ Starch/Carbohydrate

Blueberry-Lemon Salad

Lemony and fruity, this delightful salad is as pretty to look at as it is luscious to eat! I think bananas and blueberries are a dazzling combination of flavors and textures, so that every spoonful you devour is both sweet and just a little tart. I tested this when my daughter-in-law Angie was visiting, and she declared it a hit!

☻ Serves 8 (½ cup)

1 (4-serving) package JELL-O sugar-free instant vanilla pudding mix
1 (4-serving) package JELL-O sugar-free lemon gelatin
⅓ cup Carnation Nonfat Dry Milk Powder
¾ cup Yoplait plain fat-free yogurt
1 cup (one 8-ounce can) crushed pineapple, packed in fruit juice, undrained
¾ cup water
¾ cup Cool Whip Free
2 cups (2 medium) diced bananas
1½ cups fresh blueberries

In a large bowl, combine dry pudding mix, dry gelatin, and dry milk powder. Add yogurt, undrained pineapple, and water. Mix well using a wire whisk. Fold in Cool Whip Free. Add bananas and blueberries. Mix gently to combine. Cover and refrigerate for at least 15 minutes. Gently stir again just before serving.

HINT: To prevent bananas from turning brown, mix with 1 teaspoon lemon juice or sprinkle with Fruit Fresh.

Each serving equals:

HE: 1 Fruit • ¼ Skim Milk • ¼ Slider • 9 Optional Calories

---

124 Calories • 0 gm Fat • 4 gm Protein • 27 gm Carbohydrate • 230 mg Sodium • 85 mg Calcium • 2 gm Fiber

---

DIABETIC: 1 Fruit • ½ Starch/Carbohydrate

Lemon Fluff Fruit Cocktail Salad

"Fluff" is always a big treat at our house, whether my grandsons, Zach and Josh, are visiting or I'm just preparing dinner for Cliff and me. This is especially good with a hearty, meaty entree, and it's even lovely enough to serve for a light dessert.

● Serves 6 (¾ cup)

1 (4-serving) package JELL-O sugar-free instant vanilla pudding mix
1 (4-serving) package JELL-O sugar-free lemon gelatin
⅔ cup Carnation Nonfat Dry Milk Powder
1 cup (one 8-ounce can) crushed pineapple, packed in fruit juice, undrained
2 cups (one 16-ounce can) fruit cocktail, packed in fruit juice, drained, and ⅓
    cup liquid reserved
⅔ cup water
¾ cup Cool Whip Free
¾ cup (1½ ounces) mini marshmallows

In a large bowl, combine dry pudding mix, dry gelatin, and dry milk powder. Add undrained pineapple, reserved fruit cocktail liquid, and water. Mix well using a wire whisk. Blend in Cool Whip Free. Add fruit cocktail and marshmallows. Mix gently to combine. Cover and refrigerate for at least 15 minutes. Gently stir again just before serving.

Each serving equals:

HE: 1 Fruit • ⅓ Skim Milk • ½ Slider • 11 Optional Calories

152 Calories • 0 gm Fat • 4 gm Protein • 34 gm Carbohydrate •
309 mg Sodium • 105 mg Calcium • 1 gm Fiber

DIABETIC: 1 Fruit • 1 Starch/Carbohydrate

Can't-Be-Easier Apple Salad

The name says it all: fast, simple, flavorful—and downright dazzling! I like this with Red Delicious apples, but if you find a special kind of apple at the farmers' market one fall morning, be inventive and try it with this!

☻ Serves 8 (⅔ cup)

> 3 cups (6 small) cored, unpeeled, and chopped Red Delicious apples
> 1 cup (6 ounces) seedless red grapes, halved
> 1 (6-ounce) container Yoplait sugar- and fat-free cherry vanilla yogurt

In a large bowl, combine apples and grapes. Add yogurt. Mix well to combine. Cover and refrigerate for at least 15 minutes. Gently stir again just before serving.

HINT: Any sugar- and fat-free yogurt flavor of your choice can be used.

Each serving equals:

HE: 1 Fruit • 13 Optional Calories

48 Calories • 0 gm Fat • 2 gm Protein • 10 gm Carbohydrate • 22 mg Sodium • 61 mg Calcium • 1 gm Fiber

DIABETIC: 1 Fruit

Delicious French Apple Salad

This nutty, crunchy, fruity dish is amazingly refreshing. Based on that splendid classic, the Waldorf salad, this Continental version deserves to be cheered as truly "*magnifique!*" ☻ Serves 4 (¾ cup)

¼ cup Kraft Fat Free French Dressing

1 tablespoon Kraft fat-free mayonnaise

1 teaspoon lemon juice

2 cups (4 small) cored, unpeeled, and diced Red Delicious apples

1 cup finely chopped celery

2 tablespoons (½ ounce) chopped walnuts

In a medium bowl, combine French dressing, mayonnaise, and lemon juice. Add apples, celery, and walnuts. Mix well to combine. Cover and refrigerate for at least 15 minutes. Gently stir again just before serving.

Each serving equals:

HE: 1 Fruit • ½ Vegetable • ¼ Fat • ¼ Slider •
11 Optional Calories

86 Calories • 2 gm Fat • 0 gm Protein • 17 gm Carbohydrate •
209 mg Sodium • 19 mg Calcium • 2 gm Fiber

DIABETIC: 1 Fruit

September Song Fruit Salad

If just the right recipe can awaken the sweetest old memories, then this pretty salad will surely take you back to the happiest of good times! I think the apple pie spice could whisk you back to childhood with just one whiff. . . .

♥ Serves 8 (½ cup)

1 cup (2 small) diced unpeeled pears
1 cup (2 small) cored, unpeeled, and chopped Red Delicious apples
1 cup (6 ounces) Thompson seedless green grapes, halved
¼ cup Kraft fat-free mayonnaise
1 teaspoon lemon juice
Sugar substitute to equal 2 tablespoons sugar
¼ teaspoon apple pie spice

In a large bowl, combine pears, apples, and grapes. In a small bowl, combine mayonnaise, lemon juice, sugar substitute, and apple pie spice. Add dressing mixture to fruit mixture. Mix gently to combine. Cover and refrigerate for at least 15 minutes. Gently stir again just before serving.

Each serving equals:

HE: ¾ Fruit • 7 Optional Calories

36 Calories • 0 gm Fat • 0 gm Protein • 9 gm Carbohydrate •
67 mg Sodium • 18 mg Calcium • 1 gm Fiber

DIABETIC: 1 Fruit

Orange Grove Waldorf Salad

I've never strolled through a Florida orange grove, but I've imagined how delicious the scent of all those fresh oranges might be! This appetizing new take on a favorite dish will surprise you with its truly luscious flavors.

☻ Serves 8 (½ cup)

> 1 (4-serving) package JELL-O sugar-free instant vanilla pudding mix
>
> 1 (4-serving) package JELL-O sugar-free orange gelatin
>
> ⅔ cup Carnation Nonfat Dry Milk Powder
>
> 1⅓ cups water
>
> ¾ cup Cool Whip Free
>
> 1 cup finely chopped celery
>
> 3 cups (6 small) cored, unpeeled, and chopped Red Delicious apples
>
> ¼ cup (1 ounce) chopped pecans

In a large bowl, combine dry pudding mix, dry gelatin, dry milk powder, and water. Mix well using a wire whisk. Blend in Cool Whip Free. Add celery, apples, and pecans. Mix gently to combine. Cover and refrigerate for at least 15 minutes. Gently stir again just before serving.

Each serving equals:

HE: ¾ Fruit • ½ Fat • ¼ Skim Milk • ¼ Vegetable • ¼ Slider • 9 Optional Calories

94 Calories • 2 gm Fat • 3 gm Protein • 16 gm Carbohydrate • 240 mg Sodium • 79 mg Calcium • 1 gm Fiber

DIABETIC: 1 Fruit • 1 Fat • ½ Starch/Carbohydrate

Coconut Mandarin Orange Salad

A spoonful of this pleasing dish is like an instant vacation in the tropics! Can't you just taste the sun and the soothing ocean breezes in every single bite? My grandchildren love everything made with mandarin oranges, so this is served often at our house. ☺ Serves 6 (⅔ cup)

1 (4-serving) package JELL-O sugar-free instant vanilla pudding mix
1 (4-serving) package JELL-O sugar-free orange gelatin
⅓ cup Carnation Nonfat Dry Milk Powder
¾ cup Yoplait plain fat-free yogurt
¾ cup water
¾ cup Cool Whip Free
1 teaspoon coconut extract
3 cups (three 11-ounce cans) mandarin oranges, rinsed and drained
2 tablespoons flaked coconut

In a large bowl, combine dry pudding mix, dry gelatin, and dry milk powder. Add yogurt and water. Mix well to combine. Fold in Cool Whip Free and coconut extract. Add mandarin oranges and coconut. Mix gently to combine. Cover and refrigerate for at least 15 minutes. Gently stir again just before serving.

Each serving equals:

HE: 1 Fruit • ⅓ Skim Milk • ½ Slider • 3 Optional Calories

120 Calories • 0 gm Fat • 5 gm Protein • 25 gm Carbohydrate •
313 mg Sodium • 117 mg Calcium • 1 gm Fiber

DIABETIC: 1 Fruit • 1 Skim Milk

On-the-Go Fruit Salad

Ready, set, and you're off! It's that easy, really—just run into the house, pour everything into one pretty bowl, and tuck it into the fridge while you take a quick shower and put on something festive. When you haven't got more than a minute, make this recipe your first choice! ☻ Serves 6 (⅔ cup)

¾ cup Yoplait plain fat-free yogurt
⅓ cup Carnation Nonfat Dry Milk Powder
Sugar substitute to equal 2 tablespoons sugar
1 (4-serving) package JELL-O sugar-free strawberry gelatin
¾ cup Cool Whip Free
1½ cups fat-free cottage cheese
2 cups sliced fresh strawberries

In a large bowl, combine yogurt, dry milk powder, and sugar substitute. Add dry gelatin. Mix well to combine. Gently stir in Cool Whip Free and cottage cheese. Fold in strawberries. Cover and refrigerate for at least 15 minutes. Gently stir again just before serving.

Each serving equals:

HE: ½ Protein • ⅓ Skim Milk • ⅓ Fruit • ¼ Slider •
4 Optional Calories

100 Calories • 0 gm Fat • 12 gm Protein • 13 gm Carbohydrate •
294 mg Sodium • 133 mg Calcium • 1 gm Fiber

DIABETIC: 1 Starch/Carbohydrate • 1 Meat

Paradise Pineapple Salad

Here's what I mean about the difference between old-style "diet food" and Healthy Exchanges living. Lunch used to consist of cottage cheese with some pineapple stirred into it. Well, that's a good start, but when you stir in just a few more ingredients, you'll start to smile, then break into a happy laugh. This is good eating!

Serves 8 (⅔ cup)

> 2 cups fat-free cottage cheese
> 2 cups (two 8-ounce cans) crushed pineapple, packed in fruit juice, drained
> 1 (4-serving) package JELL-O sugar-free lemon gelatin
> 1 cup Cool Whip Free
> ¼ cup (1 ounce) chopped pecans

In a large bowl, combine cottage cheese and pineapple. Stir in dry gelatin. Fold in Cool Whip Free and pecans. Cover and refrigerate for at least 15 minutes. Gently stir again just before serving.

Each serving equals:

HE: ½ Protein • ½ Fruit • ½ Fat • ¼ Slider

110 Calories • 2 gm Fat • 8 gm Protein • 15 gm Carbohydrate • 244 mg Sodium • 33 mg Calcium • 0 gm Fiber

DIABETIC: 1 Meat • ½ Fruit • ½ Fat • ½ Starch/Carbohydrate

Peaches-and-More Salad

I like layering flavors in my recipes, so that if something involves peaches, you don't just get a bite or two of fruit, you also get the luscious addition of peach-flavored yogurt. What, you still want more? You've got it, with some crunchy walnuts mixed in! ☻ Serves 4 (¾ cup)

1½ cups fat-free cottage cheese
1 (6-ounce) container Yoplait sugar- and fat-free peach yogurt
2 cups (one 16-ounce can) sliced peaches, packed in fruit juice, drained, and
    coarsely chopped
¼ cup (1 ounce) chopped walnuts
⅛ teaspoon ground cinnamon

In a medium bowl, combine cottage cheese and yogurt. Add peaches, walnuts, and cinnamon. Mix gently to combine. Cover and refrigerate for at least 15 minutes. Gently stir again just before serving.

Each serving equals:

HE: 1 Protein • 1 Fruit • ½ Fat • ¼ Skim Milk

180 Calories • 4 gm Fat • 15 gm Protein • 21 gm Carbohydrate • 354 mg Sodium • 136 mg Calcium • 2 gm Fiber

DIABETIC: 1 Meat • 1 Fruit • 1 Fat

Creamy Strawberry-Rice Salad

For people like me, who think the season for fresh strawberries is just too, too short, I had to come up with tasty ways to enjoy my favorite fruit all year long! This is so cool and creamy, it would make a yummy dessert, but I like to serve it for a contrast with a spicy main dish. ☻ Serves 8 (¾ cup)

1 (4-serving) package JELL-O sugar-free vanilla cook-and-serve pudding mix
1 (4-serving) package JELL-O sugar-free strawberry gelatin
2 cups skim milk
1 cup Cool Whip Free
1 teaspoon almond extract
3 cups frozen unsweetened strawberries, thawed, chopped and drained
3 cups cold cooked rice

In a medium saucepan, combine dry pudding mix, dry gelatin, and skim milk. Cook over medium heat until mixture thickens and starts to boil, stirring constantly. Remove from heat. Place saucepan on a wire rack and allow to cool completely. Blend in Cool Whip Free and almond extract. Add strawberries and rice. Mix gently to combine. Pour mixture into a medium bowl. Cover and refrigerate for at least 15 minutes. Gently stir again just before serving.

HINT: 2 cups uncooked rice usually cooks to about 3 cups.

Each serving equals:

HE: ¾ Bread • ⅓ Fruit • ¼ Skim Milk • ¼ Slider •
14 Optional Calories

124 Calories • 0 gm Fat • 4 gm Protein • 27 gm Carbohydrate •
124 mg Sodium • 88 mg Calcium • 1 gm Fiber

DIABETIC: 1½ Starch/Carbohydrate

Vegetable-Bean Pasta Salad

Too hot to turn on the oven, but you've got a houseful of ravenous kids to feed? Here's a delectable pasta salad that will fill up everyone's tummies—but not fill out your hips! This features one of my favorite tangy dressings, and I hope you'll agree it's a dish to be savored again and again. ❂ Serves 8 (¾ cup)

2 cups cold cooked rotini pasta, rinsed and drained

10 ounces (one 16-ounce can) red kidney beans, rinsed and drained

¼ cup chopped onion

¼ cup chopped green bell pepper

2 cups (one 16-ounce can) cut green beans, rinsed and drained

1 tablespoon + 1 teaspoon all-purpose flour

1½ teaspoons lemon pepper

½ cup white vinegar

½ cup Sugar Twin or Sprinkle Sweet

⅓ cup water

4 teaspoons reduced-calorie margarine

1 tablespoon prepared mustard

In a large bowl, combine rotini pasta, kidney beans, onion, green pepper, and green beans. In a covered jar, combine flour, lemon pepper, vinegar, Sugar Twin, and water. Shake well to blend. Pour mixture into a medium saucepan sprayed with butter-flavored cooking spray. Add margarine and mustard. Mix well to combine. Cook over medium heat until mixture thickens, stirring constantly. Place saucepan on a wire rack and let set for 5 minutes. Stir sauce mixture into pasta mixture. Cover and refrigerate for at least 30 minutes. Gently stir again just before serving.

HINT: 1½ cups uncooked rotini pasta usually cooks to about 2 cups.

Each serving equals:

HE: ⅔ Protein • ⅔ Vegetable • ½ Bread • ¼ Fat •
11 Optional Calories

105 Calories • 1 gm Fat • 4 gm Protein • 20 gm Carbohydrate •
169 mg Sodium • 24 mg Calcium • 3 gm Fiber

DIABETIC: 1 Vegetable • 1 Starch

Dijon Tuna Macaroni Salad

If you picked up a half dozen cans of tuna on sale, but you're tired of tuna casserole and tuna sandwiches, here's a fresh and fun way to stir up a little lunchtime excitement at your house! Yes, a jar of "gourmet" mustard may cost a little more, but a little of it goes such a long way toward making your meals extra-special!

☺ Serves 4 (1 full cup)

> 1½ cups cold cooked elbow macaroni, rinsed and drained
> ½ cup frozen peas, thawed
> ¾ cup finely diced celery
> ¼ cup finely chopped onion
> ½ cup Kraft fat-free mayonnaise
> 1 tablespoon white vinegar
> Sugar substitute to equal 1 tablespoon sugar
> 1 tablespoon Grey Poupon Country Dijon Mustard
> ¼ teaspoon black pepper
> 1 teaspoon dried parsley flakes
> 2 (6-ounce) cans white tuna, packed in water, drained and flaked
> 1 hard-boiled egg, finely chopped

In a large bowl, combine macaroni, peas, celery, and onion. In a small bowl, combine mayonnaise, vinegar, sugar substitute, mustard, black pepper, and parsley flakes. Add mayonnaise mixture to macaroni mixture. Mix well to combine. Stir in tuna and egg. Cover and refrigerate for at least 30 minutes. Gently stir again just before serving.

HINTS: 1. 1 cup uncooked macaroni usually cooks to about 1½ cups.
2. Thaw peas by placing in a colander and rinsing under hot water for one minute.
3. If you want the look and feel of egg without the cholesterol, toss out the yolk and dice the whites.

Each serving equals:

HE: 1¾ Protein • 1 Bread • ½ Vegetable • ¼ Slider •
2 Optional Calories

235 Calories • 3 gm Fat • 27 gm Protein • 25 gm Carbohydrate •
675 mg Sodium • 37 mg Calcium • 2 gm Fiber

DIABETIC: 3 Meat • 1½ Starch

Oriental Tuna and Green Bean Salad

There's something irresistible about a crunchy salad, and this one is about the crunchiest you'll ever meet! The dressing perks up your taste buds, and the almonds give this succulent blend a little added pizzazz. Do as the great Asian chefs do—slice your celery on a slant to make it prettier and tastier.

● Serves 6 (¾ cup)

> 3 cups frozen French-style green beans
> 1½ cups water
> ½ cup Kraft fat-free mayonnaise
> 1 tablespoon lemon juice
> 1½ tablespoons reduced-sodium soy sauce
> ¼ teaspoon dried minced garlic
> 1 (6-ounce) can white tuna, packed in water, drained and flaked
> 1 cup thinly sliced celery
> 2 tablespoons (½ ounce) slivered almonds
> 1 cup (2¼ ounces) coarsely chopped chow mein noodles

In a medium saucepan, cook beans in water just until tender. Drain well and cool. In a large bowl, combine mayonnaise, lemon juice, soy sauce, and garlic. Add green beans, tuna, and celery. Mix gently to combine. Cover and refrigerate for at least 30 minutes. Just before serving, stir in almonds and chow mein noodles.

Each serving equals:

HE: 1⅓ Vegetable • ½ Protein • ½ Bread • ¼ Slider •
5 Optional Calories

128 Calories • 4 gm Fat • 10 gm Protein • 13 gm Carbohydrate •
447 mg Sodium • 38 mg Calcium • 2 gm Fiber

DIABETIC: 1 Vegetable • 1 Meat • ½ Fat • ½ Starch/Carbohydrate

Chicken Mexicali Pasta Salad

Here's a truly festive mix of flavors and textures that's bound to elicit an "Olé" or two around your table! Go as hot as you dare with the salsa, but first be sure that everyone at the table enjoys steam coming out of their ears the way Cliff does!

☻ Serves 4 (¾ cup)

> 1 full cup (6 ounces) diced cooked chicken breast
> ⅓ cup Kraft fat-free mayonnaise
> ½ cup chunky salsa (mild, medium, or hot)
> ¼ teaspoon dried minced garlic
> 1 teaspoon dried parsley flakes
> 1½ cups cold cooked rotini pasta, rinsed and drained
> ½ cup frozen whole-kernel corn, thawed

In a medium bowl, combine chicken, mayonnaise, salsa, garlic, and parsley flakes. Add rotini pasta and corn. Mix gently to combine. Cover and refrigerate for at least 30 minutes. Gently stir again just before serving.

HINTS: 1. If you don't have leftovers, purchase a chunk of cooked chicken breast from your local deli.
2. 1 cup uncooked rotini pasta usually cooks to about 1½ cups.
3. Thaw corn by placing in a colander and rinsing under hot water for one minute.

Each serving equals:

HE: 1½ Protein • 1 Bread • ¼ Vegetable • 13 Optional Calories

201 Calories • 1 gm Fat • 16 gm Protein • 23 gm Carbohydrate • 315 mg Sodium • 52 mg Calcium • 1 gm Fiber

DIABETIC: 1½ Meat • 1½ Starch • ½ Vegetable

BBQ Chicken and Macaroni Salad

If you're struggling to make ends meet, must you go to the extra expense of buying healthy versions of popular products like barbecue sauce? Here's my philosophy: first, a little goes a long way toward making your healthy recipe extra-yummy, and second, spending a little more to ensure good health always saves you money—if not now, then later on!   ☻   Serves 6 (⅔ cup)

> 2 cups cold cooked elbow macaroni, rinsed and drained
>
> 1 cup frozen peas, thawed
>
> 1 full cup (6 ounces) diced cooked chicken breast
>
> ½ cup Kraft fat-free mayonnaise
>
> 3 tablespoons Healthy Choice BBQ sauce
>
> 1 teaspoon dried parsley flakes

In a large bowl, combine macaroni, peas, and chicken. In a small bowl, combine mayonnaise, BBQ sauce, and parsley flakes. Add mayonnaise mixture to macaroni mixture. Mix gently to combine. Cover and refrigerate for at least 30 minutes. Gently stir again just before serving.

HINTS: 1. 1⅓ cups uncooked elbow macaroni usually cooks to about 2 cups.
2. Thaw peas by placing in a colander and rinsing under hot water for one minute.
3. If you don't have leftovers, purchase a chunk of cooked chicken breast from your local deli.

Each serving equals:

HE: 1 Bread • 1 Protein • ¼ Slider • 1 Optional Calorie

142 Calories • 1 gm Fat • 12 gm Protein • 21 gm Carbohydrate • 260 mg Sodium • 15 mg Calcium • 2 gm Fiber

DIABETIC: 1½ Starch/Carbohydrate • 1 Meat

Chunky Chicken Club Salad

That wonderful all-American lunch tradition known as the club sandwich is very high in calories and fat when prepared in classic style. Why not enjoy all those scrumptious flavors in an easy-to-fix main-dish salad, and join the "club" devoted to a lifetime of good health?   ☻   Serves 4 (2 cups)

1 full cup (6 ounces) diced Dubuque 97% fat-free ham or any extra-lean ham
1 full cup (6 ounces) diced cooked chicken breast
⅓ cup Kraft Fat Free French Dressing
¼ cup chopped onion
½ cup chopped celery
2 tablespoons Hormel Bacon Bits
2¾ cups finely shredded lettuce
1 cup chopped fresh tomato
2 slices reduced-calorie bread, toasted and cubed

In a large bowl, combine ham, chicken, French dressing, onion, celery, and bacon bits. Just before serving, add lettuce, tomato, and toast cubes. Toss gently to combine.

HINT: If you don't have leftovers, purchase a chunk of cooked chicken breast from your local deli.

Each serving equals:

HE: 2½ Bread • 2¼ Vegetable • ¼ Bread • ½ Slider • 6 Optional Calories

204 Calories • 4 gm Fat • 24 gm Protein • 18 gm Carbohydrate • 793 mg Sodium • 33 mg Calcium • 3 gm Fiber

DIABETIC: 2½ Meat • 1 Vegetable • ½ Starch

Roman Carrot and Ham Pasta Salad

Budget meals don't have to look or taste as if you're scrimping, as long as you toss together such crunchy and colorful ingredients as this inviting salad does! Can't you just imagine sitting in a cafe in the Eternal City and nibbling on this delight as you gaze at its beautiful sights? (If you can't afford a plane ticket, stir this up for lunch and borrow a video of Italy from the library!) ❂ Serves 6 (1 cup)

2 cups (one 16-ounce can) sliced carrots, rinsed and drained

½ cup chopped onion

½ cup chopped green bell pepper

1 (10¾-ounce) can Healthy Request Tomato Soup

2 tablespoons Sugar Twin or Sprinkle Sweet

½ cup Kraft Fat Free Italian Dressing

2 tablespoons cider vinegar

2 teaspoons prepared mustard

2 teaspoons Worcestershire sauce

1½ cups (9 ounces) diced Dubuque 97% fat-free ham or any extra-lean ham

2 cups cold cooked rotini pasta, rinsed and drained

In a medium bowl, combine carrots, onion, and green pepper. In a small saucepan, combine tomato soup, Sugar Twin, Italian dressing, vinegar, mustard, and Worcestershire sauce. Bring mixture to a boil. Remove from heat. Pour hot mixture over carrot mixture. Mix gently to combine. Cover and refrigerate for at least 30 minutes. Stir in ham and rotini pasta. Re-cover and refrigerate for at least 30 minutes. Gently stir again just before serving.

HINT: 1 cup uncooked rotini pasta usually cooks to about 1½ cups.

Each serving equals:

HE: 1 Protein • 1 Vegetable • ⅔ Bread • ½ Slider •
3 Optional Calories

126 Calories • 2 gm Fat • 7 gm Protein • 20 gm Carbohydrate •
586 mg Sodium • 21 mg Calcium • 1 gm Fiber

DIABETIC: 1 Meat • 1 Starch/Carbohydrate • ½ Vegetable

Summertime Ham Pasta Salad

I find myself serving main-dish salads often during July and August, usually because the sunny days create an appetite for food that is inviting and light. This delicious blend is sure to become a family favorite at your house as it has at ours!

☻ Serves 4 (1 full cup)

1½ cups cold cooked rotini pasta, rinsed and drained

1 full cup (6 ounces) Dubuque 97% fat-free ham or any extra-lean ham

2 cups (one 16-ounce can) cut green beans, rinsed and drained

2 tablespoons dill pickle relish

1 teaspoon dried parsley flakes

1 teaspoon prepared mustard

¼ teaspoon black pepper

⅓ cup Kraft fat-free mayonnaise

1 hard-boiled egg, chopped

In a medium bowl, combine rotini pasta, ham, and green beans. In a small bowl, combine dill pickle relish, parsley flakes, mustard, black pepper, and mayonnaise. Add dressing mixture to pasta mixture. Mix gently to combine. Fold in egg. Cover and refrigerate for at least 30 minutes. Gently stir again just before serving.

HINTS: 1. 1 cup uncooked rotini pasta usually cooks to about 11/2 cups.

2. If you want the look and feel of egg without the cholesterol, toss out the yolk and dice the whites.

Each serving equals:

HE: 1¼ Protein (¼ limited) • 1 Vegetable • ¾ Bread •
10 Optional Calories

183 Calories • 3 gm Fat • 12 gm Protein • 27 gm Carbohydrate •
633 mg Sodium • 34 mg Calcium • 2 gm Fiber

DIABETIC: 1½ Starch • 1 Vegetable • 1 Meat

Italian Chef's Salad

Why do they always call this entree salad the "chef's" salad? you may wonder. Probably because the first chef who served it was tidying up his larder and decided to toss in a bit of this and the last little piece of that, creating the delectable tradition that blends meat and cheese with assorted veggies. *Delicioso!*

♥ Serves 2

> 3 cups finely shredded lettuce
> ⅓ cup (1½ ounces) shredded Kraft reduced-fat mozzarella cheese
> ½ cup (3 ounces) finely diced Dubuque 97% fat-free ham or any extra-lean ham
> ¼ cup diced green bell pepper
> ¼ cup diced onion
> ½ cup sliced celery
> 1 cup diced fresh tomato
> 2 tablespoons (½ ounce) sliced ripe olives
> ¼ cup Kraft Fat Free Italian Dressing
> 1 hard-boiled egg, sliced

In a medium bowl, combine lettuce, mozzarella cheese, ham, green pepper, onion, celery, tomato, olives, and Italian dressing. Evenly divide onto 2 serving plates and garnish each with half the sliced egg.

Each serving equals:

> HE: 2½ Protein (½ limited) • 5 Vegetable • ¼ Fat •
> 16 Optional Calories
> _____
> 196 Calories • 8 gm Fat • 18 gm Protein • 13 gm Carbohydrate •
> 842 mg Sodium • 192 mg Calcium • 2 gm Fiber
> _____
> DIABETIC: 3 Vegetable • 2 Meat • ½ Fat

Creamy Italian Pasta Salad

If it's been a while since your husband or kids smacked their lips over lunch, why not wake them up with this flavorful blend that's almost as irresistible as a vacation on the Isle of Capri? A little pastrami goes a long way because it's such a rich-tasting meat, and the olives give it that extra taste of the Mediterranean.

♥ Serves 6 (1 cup)

> 3 cups cold cooked rotini pasta, rinsed and drained
> 2 (2.5-ounce) packages Carl Buddig 90% lean pastrami, diced
> ¾ cup (3 ounces) shredded Kraft reduced-fat mozzarella cheese
> ⅓ cup (1½ ounces) sliced ripe olives
> ⅓ cup Kraft Fat Free Italian Dressing
> ¼ cup Kraft fat-free mayonnaise
> ⅛ teaspoon black pepper

In a large bowl combine pasta, pastrami, mozzarella cheese, and olives. In a small bowl combine Italian dressing, mayonnaise, and black pepper. Add dressing mixture to pasta mixture. Mix gent-ly to combine. Cover and refrigerate for at least 30 minutes. Gently stir again just before serving.

HINT: 2¼ cups uncooked rotini pasta usually cooks to about 3 cups.

Each serving equals:

HE: 1½ Protein • 1 Bread • ¼ Fat • 14 Optional Calories

185 Calories • 5 gm Fat • 12 gm Protein • 23 gm Carbohydrate • 628 mg Sodium • 103 mg Calcium • 1 gm Fiber

DIABETIC: 1½ Starch • 1 Meat • 1 Fat

Victory Garden Veggies

Even though I'm too young to remember the patriotic "Victory Gardens" people planted during World War II, I grew up hearing stories of how Americans everywhere did their part for the war effort by becoming as self-sufficient as possible—and growing vegetables on whatever little plots of land they could!

I've always loved working in my own gardens, and I've tried to teach my children some of the "virtues" of home-grown vegetables. Gardening teaches you patience (you have to wait and wait and wait, but the reward for waiting is something delicious), it teaches you about commitment (if you don't tackle the weeds regularly, you won't have anything to nibble on when the summer harvest arrives), and it can even teach you something about caring for others (when you've got an abundance of cucumbers or tomatoes, you don't let them sit on the vines and go bad—you pick them and share them with your neighbors and relatives).

Veggies are an important ingredient in every smart eating plan, but don't sacrifice flavor and fun for what seems easier—just eating string beans from a can, for example. These fast and festive recipes deliver so much more for not much time spent chopping and cooking. Cliff particularly enjoyed testing my **Easy Creole Green Bean Side Dish** (tangy and made with his favorite vegetable), and we both smiled as we tried out **Bavarian Kraut and Bacon**. For an especially delightful and fresh accompaniment, I hope you'll give **Aztec Tomato Sauté** a try—maybe tonight?

Skillet Scalloped Cabbage and Mushrooms

This dish is especially good for last-minute suppers, since everything in it is on the pantry shelf (the soup and mushrooms), in the fridge (skim milk, shredded cheese), or purchased on the way home (the shredded cabbage)! You'll be amazed to see how quickly these ingredients join together and satisfy your ravenous family. ☻ Serves 4 (1 cup)

1 (10¾-ounce) can Healthy Request Cream of Mushroom Soup
½ cup skim milk
¾ cup (3 ounces) shredded Kraft reduced-fat Cheddar cheese
2 teaspoons dried onion flakes
½ cup (one 2.5-ounce jar) sliced mushrooms, undrained
4 cups shredded cabbage

In a large skillet sprayed with butter-flavored cooking spray, combine mushroom soup, skim milk, Cheddar cheese, onion flakes, and undrained mushrooms. Cook over medium heat for 5 minutes or until cheese melts, stirring often. Add cabbage. Mix well to combine. Lower heat and simmer for 15 minutes, or until cabbage is tender, stirring often.

Each serving equals:

HE: 2¼ Vegetable • 1 Protein • ½ Slider • 12 Optional Calories

129 Calories • 5 gm Fat • 8 gm Protein • 13 gm Carbohydrate • 590 mg Sodium • 264 mg Calcium • 2 gm Fiber

DIABETIC: 1 Vegetable • 1 Meat • ½ Starch/Carbohydrate

Aztec Tomato Sauté

If you're not used to cooking with Brown Sugar Twin, you'll soon discover that adding it to cooked dishes gives them a tangy, almost barbecued flavor. This veggie blend quickly sizzles up and sends your tastebuds to Mexico!

❍ Serves 4 (full ¾ cup)

½ cup chopped onion
½ cup chopped green bell pepper
1 cup peeled and chopped fresh tomatoes
2 cups (one 16-ounce can) whole-kernel corn, rinsed and drained
1 tablespoon Brown Sugar Twin
1 tablespoon chopped fresh parsley or 1 teaspoon dried parsley flakes
1 teaspoon chili seasoning

In a large skillet sprayed with butter-flavored cooking spray, sauté onion and green pepper for 5 minutes or until tender. Add tomatoes and corn. Mix well to combine. Continue cooking for about 5 minutes. Stir in Brown Sugar Twin, parsley, and chili seasoning. Lower heat and simmer for 5 minutes, stirring occasionally.

Each serving equals:

HE: 1 Bread • 1 Vegetable • 1 Optional Calorie

96 Calories • 0 gm Fat • 3 gm Protein • 21 gm Carbohydrate • 270 mg Sodium • 13 mg Calcium • 3 gm Fiber

DIABETIC: 1 Starch • 1 Vegetable

Italian Vegetable Platter

A charming tradition in Italian restaurants is to serve what's called an antipasto platter as the appetizer for a festive meal. It's usually composed of colorful vegetables served raw or cooked just enough to soften them. Then they're drizzled with a delectable dressing and presented in all their colorful glory.

☻ Serves 4 (1½ cups)

> 2 cups chopped fresh broccoli
> 2 cups chopped fresh cauliflower
> 2 cups sliced unpeeled zucchini
> 2 cups peeled and chopped fresh tomatoes
> ¼ cup Kraft Fat Free Italian Dressing
> ¾ cup (3 ounces) shredded Kraft fat-free mozzarella cheese

Place broccoli, cauliflower, and zucchini in an 8-by-8-inch glass baking dish. Cover and microwave on HIGH (100% power) for 8 to 10 minutes, or until vegetables are tender. Drain off moisture, if necessary. Stir in tomatoes. Drizzle Italian dressing over vegetables. Sprinkle mozzarella cheese evenly over top. Re-cover and microwave on HIGH for 3 minutes. Let set for 1 to 2 minutes. Gently stir just before serving.

Each serving equals:

HE: 4 Vegetable • 1 Protein • 8 Optional Calories

116 Calories • 4 gm Fat • 8 gm Protein • 12 gm Carbohydrate • 331 mg Sodium • 184 mg Calcium • 4 gm Fiber

DIABETIC: 3 Vegetable • ½ Meat

Easy Creole Green Bean Side Dish

Here's a scrumptious skillet recipe for that man-pleasing vegetable, the string bean, that will bring any hungry man running to the dinner table! This is so rich with tomato flavor, I bet the man in your life will ask for it often.

⏺ Serves 6 (1 cup)

¼ cup chopped onion

1¾ cups (one 14½-ounce can) stewed tomatoes, undrained

¼ cup Heinz Light Harvest Ketchup or any reduced-sodium ketchup

¼ cup Hormel Bacon Bits

1 teaspoon dried parsley flakes

6 cups (three 16-ounce cans) cut green beans, rinsed and drained

In a large skillet sprayed with butter-flavored cooking spray, sauté onion for about 5 minutes or until tender. Stir in undrained stewed tomatoes, ketchup, bacon bits, and parsley flakes. Add green beans. Mix well to combine. Lower heat and simmer for 5 minutes, stirring often.

Each serving equals:

HE: 2⅔ Vegetable • ¼ Slider • 7 Optional Calories

77 Calories • 1 gm Fat • 4 gm Protein • 13 gm Carbohydrate • 457 mg Sodium • 74 mg Calcium • 2 gm Fiber

DIABETIC: 2 Vegetable

Celery and Carrots in Beef Gravy

Sometimes the best dishes are the simplest, when you blend the perfect ingredients together and invent a new classic! Cooking the veggies in the fat-free gravy couldn't be easier, but nothing gives plain veggies like carrots, celery, and onion more pizzazz than this. ☻ Serves 6 (⅔ cup)

3 cups chopped celery
3 cups chopped carrots
1½ cups sliced onion
2 cups hot water
1 (12-ounce) jar Heinz Fat Free Beef Gravy
½ cup (one 2.5-ounce jar) sliced mushrooms, undrained
2 teaspoons dried parsley flakes

In a large saucepan, combine celery, carrots, onion, and water. Bring mixture to a boil. Lower heat, cover, and simmer for 15 minutes, or until vegetables are tender, stirring occasionally. Drain and return vegetables to saucepan. Add beef gravy, undrained mushrooms, and parsley flakes. Mix well to combine. Continue simmering for 6 to 8 minutes, stirring often.

Each serving equals:

HE: 2½ Vegetable • ¼ Slider • 5 Optional Calories

64 Calories • 0 gm Fat • 2 gm Protein • 14 gm Carbohydrate •
459 mg Sodium • 47 mg Calcium • 3 gm Fiber

DIABETIC: 1½ Vegetable • ½ Starch

Creamed Carrots and Bacon Side Dish

What could be more cozy and comfy than an old-fashioned dish of creamed vegetables? The real comfort comes from learning that you don't have to give up such luscious treats once you decide to eat healthy. (If you can't find the celery soup, give this dish a try with cream of mushroom or broccoli!)

❍ Serves 6 (1 cup)

> ½ cup finely diced onion
> 4 cups (two 16-ounce cans) sliced carrots, rinsed and drained
> 1 (10¾-ounce can) Healthy Request Cream of Celery Soup
> 6 tablespoons Hormel Bacon Bits
> 2 tablespoons Land O Lakes no-fat sour cream
> 1 teaspoon dried parsley flakes
> ⅛ teaspoon black pepper

In a large saucepan sprayed with butter-flavored cooking spray, sauté onion for 5 minutes or until tender. Stir in carrots. Add celery soup, bacon bits, sour cream, parsley flakes, and black pepper. Mix well to combine. Lower heat, cover, and simmer for 6 to 8 minutes or until mixture is heated through, stirring often.

Each serving equals:

HE: 1½ Vegetable • ½ Slider • 18 Optional Calories

91 Calories • 3 gm Fat • 4 gm Protein • 12 gm Carbohydrate • 498 mg Sodium • 67 mg Calcium • 2 gm Fiber

DIABETIC: 1½ Vegetable • ½ Starch/Carbohydrate

Skillet Corn with Pimiento

I almost named this "Colorful Corn" because that's what it is. The veggies go from pretty tasty to lip-smacking great when they're stirred together with a tomato-y sauce that's both sweet and savory.   ☻   Serves 6 (½ cup)

¾ cup chopped onion

¼ cup chopped green bell pepper

1 cup (one 8-ounce can) Hunt's Tomato Sauce

1 tablespoon Brown Sugar Twin

1 teaspoon prepared mustard

1 teaspoon dried parsley flakes

3 cups frozen whole-kernel corn, thawed

¼ cup (one 2-ounce jar) chopped pimiento, undrained

In a large skillet sprayed with butter-flavored cooking spray, sauté onion and green pepper for 5 minutes or until tender. Stir in tomato sauce, Brown Sugar Twin, mustard, and parsley flakes. Add corn and undrained pimiento. Mix well to combine. Lower heat and simmer for 6 to 8 minutes, stirring occasionally.

HINT: Thaw corn by placing in a colander and rinsing under hot water for one
minute.

Each serving equals:

HE: 1 Bread • 1 Vegetable • 1 Optional Calorie

100 Calories • 0 gm Fat • 3 gm Protein • 22 gm Carbohydrate •
264 mg Sodium • 14 mg Calcium • 3 gm Fiber

DIABETIC: 1 Starch • 1 Vegetable

Dilled Peas with Mushrooms

It's amazing how quickly the flavors in this recipe join together and produce something that's more scrumptiously special than any of them could be all alone! This is a great dish to serve when you've had no time to shop, but you've still got a few cans and jars in your kitchen cabinet. ☻ Serves 4 (½ cup)

½ cup finely chopped onion
2 cups frozen peas, thawed
¼ cup (one 2-ounce jar) chopped pimiento, undrained
1 cup (one 4-ounce can) sliced mushrooms, undrained
½ teaspoon dried dill weed

In a large skillet sprayed with butter-flavored cooking spray, sauté onion for about 5 minutes or until tender. Add peas, undrained pimiento, undrained mushrooms, and dill weed. Mix well to combine. Lower heat, cover, and simmer for 5 minutes or until mixture is heated through, stirring often.

HINT: Thaw peas by placing in a colander and rinsing under hot water for one minute.

Each serving equals:

HE: 1 Bread • ¾ Vegetable

80 Calories • 0 gm Fat • 5 gm Protein • 15 gm Carbohydrate •
172 mg Sodium • 30 mg Calcium • 5 gm Fiber

DIABETIC: 1 Starch • 1 Vegetable

Bavarian Kraut and Bacon

Did you think that sauerkraut was only for serving with hot dogs? Not at our house, where this wonderfully satisfying dish would be perfect served with all kinds of main dishes. The applesauce may seem a bit of a surprise, but it adds a real old-timey taste.　◐　Serves 4 (¾ cup)

½ cup chopped onion
¼ cup Hormel Bacon Bits
1 teaspoon dried parsley flakes
⅛ teaspoon black pepper
1 cup unsweetened applesauce
1¾ cups (one 14½-ounce can) Frank's Bavarian-style sauerkraut, drained

In a large skillet sprayed with butter-flavored cooking spray, sauté onion for 5 minutes or until tender. Add bacon bits, parsley flakes, and black pepper. Mix well to combine. Stir in applesauce and sauerkraut. Lower heat and simmer for 6 to 8 minutes, or until mixture is heated through, stirring occasionally.

HINT:　If you can't find Bavarian sauerkraut, use regular sauerkraut, ½ teaspoon caraway seeds, and 1 teaspoon Brown Sugar Twin.

Each serving equals:

HE: 1¼ Vegetable • ½ Fruit • ¼ Slider • 5 Optional Calories

109 Calories • 1 gm Fat • 5 gm Protein • 20 gm Carbohydrate • 847 mg Sodium • 6 mg Calcium • 3 gm Fiber

DIABETIC: 1 Vegetable • ½ Fruit • ½ Starch/Carbohydrate

Campfire Simmered Beans

Beans make such a healthy, high-fiber meal, especially when they're prepared without all that added fat and sugar so many traditional recipes include. But that's not the only reason to serve this again and again. You'll keep bringing it to the table because everyone who tries it will smile "thank-you" with every bite.

☻ Serves 6 (¾ cup)

> 1½ cups chopped onion
>
> 1¾ cups (one 15-ounce can) Hunt's Tomato Sauce
>
> ¼ cup pourable Sugar Twin
>
> 1 teaspoon prepared mustard
>
> 1 tablespoon white vinegar
>
> 1 teaspoon dried parsley flakes
>
> 2 tablespoons Hormel Bacon Bits
>
> 10 ounces (one 16-ounce can) pinto beans, rinsed and drained
>
> 10 ounces (one 16-ounce can) red kidney beans, rinsed and drained
>
> 10 ounces (one 16-ounce can) butter or lima beans, rinsed and drained

In a large skillet sprayed with butter-flavored cooking spray, sauté onion for about 5 minutes or until tender. Stir in tomato sauce, Sugar Twin, mustard, vinegar, and parsley flakes. Add bacon bits, pinto beans, kidney beans, and butter beans. Mix well to combine. Lower heat, cover, and simmer for 10 minutes, stirring occasionally.

Each serving equals:

HE: 2½ Protein • 1⅔ Vegetable • 12 Optional Calories

229 Calories • 1 gm Fat • 13 gm Protein • 42 gm Carbohydrate • 646 mg Sodium • 95 mg Calcium • 12 gm Fiber

DIABETIC: 1½ Meat • 1½ Starch • 1 Vegetable

Broccoli Rice Quiche

If you've ever made a traditional quiche, you know it's not only full of pricey ingredients but also high in fat and cholesterol. But now you can enjoy the special flavors of this French import without any guilt, just pure culinary pleasure. The rice crust is unusual, but you'll find it's unusually good. It's so luscious and golden-brown as it emerges from the oven, your taste buds will go into overdrive!

❂ Serves 6

2 cups hot cooked rice

¾ cup (3 ounces) grated Kraft reduced-fat Cheddar cheese☆

4 eggs, beaten, or equivalent in egg substitute☆

1½ cups frozen chopped broccoli, thawed

½ cup (one 2.5-ounce jar) sliced mushrooms, drained

½ cup chopped onion

1 teaspoon lemon pepper

Preheat oven to 375 degrees. Spray a 9-inch pie plate with butter-flavored cooking spray. In a large bowl, combine rice, ½ cup Cheddar cheese, and 1 egg. Evenly spread mixture into prepared pie plate. In a medium bowl, combine remaining 3 eggs, broccoli, mushrooms, onion, and lemon pepper. Spread mixture in crust. Bake for 15 to 20 minutes. Sprinkle remaining ¼ cup Cheddar cheese evenly over top. Bake for additional 10 minutes. Place pie plate on a wire rack and let set for 10 minutes. Cut into 6 wedges.

HINT: 1⅓ cups uncooked rice usually cooks to about 2 cups.

Each serving equals:

HE: 1⅓ Protein (⅔ limited) • ⅔ Bread • ⅓ Vegetable

233 Calories • 9 gm Fat • 15 gm Protein • 23 gm Carbohydrate • 619 mg Sodium • 206 mg Calcium • 2 gm Fiber

DIABETIC: 2 Meat • 1 Starch • 1 Vegetable

Tomato Pot Pie

This inventive combination takes a classic family favorite—the pot pie—but stirs in entirely new ingredients for a taste sensation that's sure to please! In addition to that irresistible cheese-and-tomato flavor, you also get a healthy amount of protein and fiber. ☻ Serves 6

> 1 cup finely chopped celery
> ½ cup finely chopped onion
> 1 (10¾-ounce) can Healthy Request Tomato Soup
> 3 cups (one 28-ounce can) tomatoes, coarsely chopped, drained, and ⅓ cup juice
>   reserved
> 1 teaspoon dried parsley flakes
> 1½ cups (6 ounces) shredded Kraft reduced-fat Cheddar cheese ☆
> 1 (7.5-ounce) package Pillsbury refrigerated buttermilk biscuits

Preheat oven to 375 degrees. Spray an 8-by-8-inch baking dish with butter-flavored cooking spray. In a large skillet sprayed with butter-flavored cooking spray, sauté celery and onion for 10 minutes or just until vegetables are tender. Stir in tomato soup, reserved tomato juice, parsley flakes, and 1 cup Cheddar cheese. Continue cooking for 5 minutes or until cheese melts, stirring often. Add tomatoes. Mix well to combine. Spread mixture into prepared baking dish. Separate biscuits and cut each into 4 pieces. Evenly sprinkle biscuit pieces over tomato mixture. Lightly spray tops with butter-flavored cooking spray. Sprinkle remaining ½ cup Cheddar cheese over top. Bake 12 to 15 minutes or until biscuits are golden brown. Place baking dish on a wire rack and let set for 5 minutes. Divide into 6 servings.

HINT: If you like tomatoes on the sweeter side, stir in 1 tablespoon Sugar Twin when adding parsley flakes.

Each serving equals:

HE: 1½ Vegetable • 1⅓ Protein • 1¼ Bread • ¼ Slider •
10 Optional Calories

226 Calories • 6 gm Fat • 12 gm Protein • 31 gm Carbohydrate •
908 mg Sodium • 235 mg Calcium • 3 gm Fiber

DIABETIC: 1½ Starch • 1 Vegetable • 1 Meat

Cheesy Main Dish Strata

Three—count 'em—three cheeses in this gorgeous baked entree make it a mouth-watering choice, one your family is sure to request again and again. Even though it takes a bit more time to prepare than most of my recipes (not more work, just an extra hour or so in the fridge before baking!), it's definitely worth the wait!

○ Serves 8

> 12 slices reduced-calorie Italian bread, cut into 1-inch cubes
> 1 (10¾-ounce) can Healthy Request Cream of Mushroom Soup
> ⅔ cup Carnation Nonfat Dry Milk Powder
> 1½ cups water
> 4 eggs, beaten, or equivalent in egg substitute
> ¼ cup (¾ ounce) grated Kraft fat-free Parmesan cheese
> 1½ cups (6 ounces) shredded Kraft reduced-fat Cheddar cheese
> 7 (¾-ounce) slices Kraft reduced-fat Swiss cheese, shredded

Spray a 9-by-13-inch baking dish with butter-flavored cooking spray. Evenly arrange bread cubes in prepared baking dish. In a large bowl, combine mushroom soup, dry milk powder, water, and eggs. Stir in Parmesan cheese, Cheddar cheese, and Swiss cheese. Pour soup mixture evenly over bread. Cover and refrigerate at least 1 hour or up to 24 hours. Uncover and bake at 350 degrees for 40 to 45 minutes or until a knife inserted near the center comes out clean. Place baking dish on a wire rack and let set for 5 minutes. Cut into 8 servings.

Each serving equals:

HE: 2½ Protein • ¾ Bread • ¼ Skim Milk • ¼ Slider •
1 Optional Calorie

---

244 Calories • 8 gm Fat • 20 gm Protein • 23 gm Carbohydrate •
668 mg Sodium • 451 mg Calcium • 4 gm Fiber

DIABETIC: 2 Meat • 1½ Starch/Carbohydrate

Cabbage and Potato Patties

Here's a simple dinner that belongs in your "Smart Leftovers" recipe section! I created this one evening when I spotted a bowl of leftover mashed potatoes and a bag of shredded cabbage in the refrigerator. You know how they say that necessity is the mother of invention? Well, this mother invented a lip-smacking meal to feed her family that was not only cost-effective but QUICK, QUICK, QUICK!

♥ Serves 4

½ cup finely chopped onion
2 cups cooked shredded cabbage
2 cups cold mashed potatoes
2 teaspoons reduced-calorie margarine

In a large bowl, combine onion, cabbage, and potatoes. Mix well to combine. Pat mixture into 4 patties. In a large skillet, melt margarine. Evenly arrange patties in skillet. Brown patties for 5 minutes on each side. Serve at once.

Each serving equals:

HE: 1¼ Vegetable • 1 Bread • ¼ Fat

109 Calories • 1 gm Fat • 3 gm Protein • 22 gm Carbohydrate • 334 mg Sodium • 48 mg Calcium • 3 gm Fiber

DIABETIC: 1 Vegetable • 1 Starch • ½ Fat

Garden Macaroni and Cheese Skillet

Here's a tasty and quick way to serve this beloved American classic with the addition of some healthy veggies! Stirred up on the stove top, it's just perfect to feed the healthy appetites of your busy family. ☻ Serves 4 (1 cup)

1 (10¾-ounce) can Healthy Request Cream of Mushroom Soup

⅓ cup Carnation Nonfat Dry Milk Powder

½ cup water

¼ cup (¾ ounce) grated Kraft fat-free Parmesan cheese

¾ cup (3 ounces) shredded Kraft reduced-fat Cheddar cheese

¾ cup (3 ounces) shredded Kraft reduced-fat mozzarella cheese

2 cups hot cooked elbow macaroni, rinsed and drained

1 teaspoon dried parsley flakes

⅛ teaspoon black pepper

1 cup (one 8-ounce can) cut green beans, rinsed and drained

1 cup (one 8-ounce can) sliced carrots, rinsed and drained

In a large skillet sprayed with butter-flavored cooking spray, combine mushroom soup, dry milk powder, water, and Parmesan cheese. Stir in Cheddar and mozzarella cheeses. Cook over medium heat until cheeses melt, stirring often. Add macaroni, parsley flakes, and black pepper. Mix well to combine. Stir in green beans and carrots. Lower heat and simmer for 10 minutes, stirring occasionally.

HINT: 1⅓ cups uncooked elbow macaroni usually cooks to about 2 cups.

Each serving equals:

HE: 2¼ Protein • 1 Bread • 1 Vegetable • ¼ Skim Milk • ½ Slider
• 1 Optional Calorie

313 Calories • 9 gm Fat • 20 gm Protein • 38 gm Carbohydrate •
813 mg Sodium • 452 mg Calcium • 3 gm Fiber

DIABETIC: 2 Meat • 2 Starch/Carbohydrate • 1 Vegetable

Southwest Corn Bake

If your kids relish a succulent corn pudding as much as mine do, then this should be a big hit at your house! It puffs up so beautifully and smells so good, they will gobble it down with grins on their faces—then maybe even offer to wash the car!

◐ Serves 4

⅔ cup Carnation Nonfat Dry Milk Powder

1 cup water

3 tablespoons all-purpose flour

1½ cups frozen whole-kernel corn, thawed

¾ cup (3 ounces) shredded Kraft reduced-fat Cheddar cheese

¼ cup chopped onion

¼ cup chunky salsa (mild, medium, or hot)

2 tablespoons chopped fresh parsley or 1 teaspoon dried parsley flakes

⅛ teaspoon black pepper

4 eggs or equivalent in egg substitute

Preheat oven to 350 degrees. Spray an 8-by-8-inch baking dish with butter-flavored cooking spray. In a covered jar, combine dry milk powder, water, and flour. Shake well to blend. Pour milk mixture into a medium saucepan sprayed with butter-flavored cooking spray. Cook over medium heat until mixture starts to thicken, stirring constantly. Stir in corn, cheese, onion, salsa, parsley, and black pepper. Continue cooking 2 to 3 minutes or until cheese melts. Remove from heat. Separate eggs. Stir yolks into corn mixture. In a large bowl, beat egg whites with an electric mixer until almost stiff. Fold ⅓ of beaten egg whites into corn mixture. Gently fold corn mixture into remaining egg whites. Pour mixture into prepared baking dish. Bake 40 to 45 minutes. Place baking dish on a wire rack and let set for 5 minutes. Divide into 4 servings.

Each serving equals:

HE: 1½ Protein (½ limited) • 1 Bread • ½ Skim Milk • ¼ Vegetable

214 Calories • 6 gm Fat • 15 gm Protein • 25 gm Carbohydrate • 330 mg Sodium • 314 mg Calcium • 2 gm Fiber

DIABETIC: 2 Meat • 1 Starch • ½ Skim Milk

Vegetable Enchiladas

Through the magic of microwavery, this dish arrives at your table in minutes—and utterly mouthwatering! There's just no substitute for serving tasty, fresh vegetables in today's favorite wrap, the tortilla, especially when they're topped with cheese and sour cream. Diet food? It sure doesn't look or taste like it!

☻ Serves 4

1 cup chopped fresh tomato
¼ cup chopped onion
¼ cup chopped green bell pepper
1½ cups frozen or fresh whole-kernel corn
2 teaspoons reduced-calorie margarine
4 (6-inch) flour or corn tortillas
⅓ cup (1½ ounces) shredded Kraft reduced-fat Cheddar cheese
¼ cup Land O Lakes no-fat sour cream

In a 4-cup glass measuring cup, combine tomato, onion, green pepper, corn, and margarine. Microwave on MEDIUM (50% power) for 4 to 5 minutes. Spoon about ½ cup of the vegetable mixture on each tortilla. Evenly sprinkle about 1½ tablespoons Cheddar cheese over each. Place tortillas in a microwavable baking dish and continue to microwave on MEDIUM for 2 to 3 minutes or until cheese melts. Top each with 1 tablespoon sour cream. Roll up and serve at once.

Each serving equals:

HE: 1¾ Bread • ¾ Vegetable • ½ Protein • ¼ Fat •
15 Optional Calories

209 Calories • 5 gm Fat • 8 gm Protein • 33 gm Carbohydrate •
285 mg Sodium • 99 mg Calcium • 2 gm Fiber

DIABETIC: 2 Starch • ½ Vegetable • ½ Meat

Mexican Pizza

Here's a fast and inexpensive kid-pleasing lunch that's easy, healthy, and oh-so-good. Pizza is so beloved by all the kids we feed at the local day care centers in DeWitt, Iowa, I created this dish with their hungry tummies in mind!

☾ Serves 4

> 4 (6-inch) flour tortillas
> ¼ cup Heinz Light Harvest Ketchup or any reduced-sodium ketchup
> 1 cup chunky salsa (mild, medium, or hot)
> ¾ cup (3 ounces) shredded Kraft reduced-fat Cheddar cheese

Preheat oven to 375 degrees. Spray a baking sheet with olive oil–flavored cooking spray. Place tortillas on prepared sheet. For each pizza, spread 1 tablespoon ketchup over a tortilla, spoon ¼ cup salsa over ketchup and top with 3 tablespoons Cheddar cheese. Bake for 15 minutes.

HINT: Good topped with 1 tablespoon Land O Lakes no-fat sour cream, but don't forget to count the few additional calories.

Each serving equals:

HE: 1 Bread • 1 Protein • ½ Vegetable • 15 Optional Calories

169 Calories • 5 gm Fat • 9 gm Protein • 22 mg Carbohydrate • 573 mg Sodium • 246 mg Calcium • 0 gm Fiber

DIABETIC: 1 Starch • 1 Meat • 1 Vegetable

Baked Omelet with Mushroom Sauce

Is breakfast or brunch time somewhat chaotic at your house? Nothing is ever ready at the same time, whether it's the eggs or the toast, and everyone tends to eat and run. Well, I hope this tasty dish will bring a little more peace and culinary pleasure to your table. I suggest preparing the first part of the recipe the night before, so when you wake up, you're ready to bake it and eat! ☻ Serves 6

8 slices reduced-calorie bread, cut into 1-inch cubes
¾ cup (3 ounces) shredded Kraft reduced-fat Cheddar cheese
3 eggs or equivalent in egg substitute
3 cups skim milk ☆
¼ teaspoon lemon pepper
1 (10¾-ounce) can Healthy Request Cream of Mushroom Soup
1 teaspoon dried parsley flakes
¼ cup (¾ ounce) grated Kraft fat-free Parmesan cheese

Spray an 8-by-8-inch baking dish with butter-flavored cooking spray. Evenly arrange bread cubes in prepared baking dish. Sprinkle Cheddar cheese over top. In a large bowl, combine eggs, 2½ cups milk, and lemon pepper. Mix well using a wire whisk. Evenly pour egg mixture over bread and cheese. Cover and refrigerate for at least 1 hour or up to 24 hours. Uncover and bake at 350 degrees for 35 to 40 minutes, or until a knife inserted in center comes out clean. Just before omelet is done, in a small saucepan, combine mushroom soup, remaining ½ cup skim milk, parsley flakes, and Parmesan cheese. Cook over medium heat until mixture is heated through, stirring often. Cut omelet into 6 pieces. When serving, spoon about ¼ cup soup mixture over each piece.

Each serving equals:

HE: 1⅓ Protein (½ limited) • ⅔ Bread • ½ Skim Milk • ¼ Slider • 8 Optional Calories

222 Calories • 6 gm Fat • 16 gm Protein • 26 gm Carbohydrate • 653 mg Sodium • 322 mg Calcium • 4 gm Fiber

DIABETIC: 1 Meat • 1 Starch • ½ Skim Milk

Chili Pasta Grande

What's great about a recipe like this one is not only that it fits perfectly into your budget, but also that it's so full of crunch and flavor, no one will ever miss the meat! Pasta added to a traditional chili with beans provides additional texture and flavor, and also helps stretch the ingredients a little further.   ☻   Serves 4 (1 cup)

½ cup chopped onion
½ cup chopped green bell pepper
1¾ cups (one 15-ounce can) Hunt's Chunky Tomato Sauce
2 teaspoons chili seasoning
1 tablespoon Brown Sugar Twin
1 teaspoon dried parsley flakes
½ cup Land O Lakes no-fat sour cream
10 ounces (one 16-ounce can) red kidney beans, rinsed and drained
2 cups hot cooked rotini pasta, rinsed and drained

In a large skillet sprayed with olive oil–flavored cooking spray, sauté onion and green pepper for 5 minutes or just until tender. Stir in tomato sauce, chili seasoning, Brown Sugar Twin, parsley flakes, and sour cream. Add kidney beans and rotini pasta. Mix well to combine. Lower heat and simmer for 5 minutes or until mixture is heated through, stirring often.

HINT: 1½ cups uncooked rotini pasta usually cooks to about 2 cups.

Each serving equals:

HE: 2¼ Vegetable • 1¼ Protein • 1 Bread • ¼ Skim Milk •
11 Optional Calories

212 Calories • 0 gm Fat • 9 gm Protein • 44 gm Carbohydrate •
743 mg Sodium • 61 mg Calcium • 8 gm Fiber

DIABETIC: 2 Vegetable • 2 Starch

Budget Main Dishes

When you hear the word "budget," what's the first thing you think of? Maybe it means s-t-r-e-t-c-h-ing too little money to pay for all the things you need. Maybe it suggests you're not going to be able to have or do all the things you want to. Maybe, just maybe, it means deprivation.

But what "budget" means to me, and has, even before I began creating Healthy Exchanges recipes, is planning. I once heard someone say, "If you fail to plan, you plan to fail." That may be putting it a bit strongly, but I agree with the reasoning behind the motto. Healthy eating does take planning, especially when it comes to filling your pantry and refrigerator. Sure, you could throw half a dozen frozen entrees into your freezer each week, then slide them into the microwave when you get home late from work. But that's not my idea of a healthy, satisfying lifestyle.

Instead, plan by stocking your shelves and cabinets with the ingredients you'll need to nourish yourself and your family. If your goals include losing some weight, recovering your health, or simply eating better, you need a plan to meet those goals. Just imagine how good you'll feel when you open your cabinet to reveal cans of veggies, fruits, and healthy soups, packages of your favorite JELL-O puddings and gelatins, cans of tuna and salmon, and boxes of pasta in every shape you can buy!

You don't have to spend a lot to eat well, and this section will prove that again and again. Whether you stir up my **Dinner Bell Skillet** or **Scalloped Tuna and Potatoes**, **Western Hoedown Burgers** or **Supper Time Pizza Casserole**, you'll discover how quickly and easily you can prepare a satisfying, good-tasting, and good-for-you meal!

132

Marinara Bread Casserole

"Bread" is actually the main ingredient in this Italian-inspired baked entree, which may seem a bit strange, but once you combine it with lots of tasty veggies and two luscious cheeses, you'll be ready to hop on a plane for Rome! ☻ Serves 4

½ cup chopped onion

½ cup chopped green bell pepper

1 cup (one 8-ounce can) Hunt's Tomato Sauce

¾ cup water

1 cup (one 8-ounce can) tomatoes, chopped and undrained

½ cup (one 2.5-ounce jar) sliced mushrooms, drained

¼ cup (¾ ounce) grated Kraft fat-free Parmesan cheese

1½ teaspoons Italian seasoning

½ teaspoon dried minced garlic

1 teaspoon dried parsley flakes

1 tablespoon pourable Sugar Twin

8 slices reduced-calorie Italian bread, torn into large pieces

*½ cup + 1 tablespoon (2¼ ounces) shredded Kraft reduced-fat
    mozzarella cheese*

Preheat oven to 375 degrees. Spray an 8-by-8-inch baking dish with olive oil–flavored cooking spray. In a large skillet sprayed with olive oil–flavored cooking spray, sauté onion and green pepper for 5 minutes or until tender. Stir in tomato sauce, water, undrained tomatoes, and mushrooms. Add Parmesan cheese, Italian seasoning, garlic, parsley flakes, and Sugar Twin. Mix well to combine. Fold in bread pieces. Spoon hot mixture into prepared baking dish. Evenly sprinkle mozzarella cheese over top. Bake for 25 to 30 minutes. Place baking dish on a wire rack and let set for 5 minutes. Divide into 4 servings.

Each serving equals:

HE: 3 Vegetable • 1 Bread • 1 Protein • 1 Optional Calorie

195 Calories • 3 gm Fat • 12 gm Protein • 30 gm Carbohydrate •
945 mg Sodium • 178 mg Calcium • 9 gm Fiber

DIABETIC: 3 Vegetable • 1 Starch • 1 Meat

Italian Fresh Tomato Scramble

I haven't traveled around Italy (except in my imagination), but I suspect that every home outside the cities has a garden, and every garden has a tomato patch! How else would they produce all the wonderful fresh tomatoes they need for dishes like this one? But even if you can't keep yourself in home-grown tomatoes, enjoy them often when they're at their ripest! ☻   Serves 4 (1 cup)

2 cups peeled and chopped fresh tomatoes
¾ cup chopped onion
¾ cup chopped green bell pepper
1 (10¾-ounce) can Healthy Request Tomato Soup
1½ teaspoons Italian seasoning
¼ cup (¾ ounce) grated Kraft fat-free Parmesan cheese
¾ cup (3 ounces) shredded Kraft reduced-fat mozzarella cheese
2 cups hot cooked noodles, rinsed and drained

In a large skillet sprayed with olive oil–flavored cooking spray, sauté tomatoes, onion, and green pepper for about 10 minutes, or until vegetables are tender. Stir in tomato soup, Italian seasoning, Parmesan cheese, and mozzarella cheese. Add noodles. Mix well to combine. Lower heat and simmer for 5 minutes or until cheese melts, stirring occasionally.

HINT: 1¾ cups uncooked noodles usually cooks to about 2 cups.

Each serving equals:

HE: 1¾ Vegetable • 1¼ Protein • 1 Bread • ½ Slider •
5 Optional Calories

253 Calories • 5 gm Fat • 12 gm Protein • 40 gm Carbohydrate •
464 mg Sodium • 167 mg Calcium • 4 gm Fiber

DIABETIC: 2 Starch • 1½ Vegetable • 1 Meat

Bountiful Harvest Vegetable-Cheese Pie

Here's my idea for a healthy vegetable quiche that doesn't contain a bit of cream, and only 2 grams of fat! As you bite into a dish of such joyful abundance, you'll know you made the right decision to live as healthily as you can.

◐ Serves 6

> 1½ cups chopped unpeeled zucchini
> ½ cup chopped onion
> 1 cup chopped fresh tomato
> ¼ cup (¾ ounce) grated Kraft fat-free Parmesan cheese
> ⅓ cup (1½ ounces) shredded Kraft reduced-fat Cheddar cheese
> 1½ cups (one 12-fluid-ounce can) Carnation Evaporated Skim Milk
> ¾ cup Bisquick Reduced Fat Baking Mix
> 1 teaspoon dried parsley flakes
> ⅛ teaspoon black pepper

Preheat oven to 400 degrees. Spray a 10-inch deep-dish pie plate or quiche dish with butter-flavored cooking spray. Evenly layer zucchini, onion, and tomato into prepared pie plate. Sprinkle Parmesan cheese and Cheddar cheese evenly over vegetables. In a medium bowl, combine evaporated skim milk, baking mix, parsley flakes, and black pepper. Mix well using a wire whisk. Pour mixture evenly over top. Bake for 25 to 30 minutes or until a knife inserted near the center comes out clean. Place pie plate on a wire rack and let set for 5 minutes. Cut into 6 servings.

Each serving equals:

HE: 1 Vegetable • ⅔ Bread • ½ Skim Milk • ½ Protein

150 Calories • 2 gm Fat • 9 gm Protein • 24 gm Carbohydrate • 362 mg Sodium • 252 mg Calcium • 2 gm Fiber

DIABETIC: 1 Vegetable • ½ Starch • ½ Skim Milk • ½ Meat

Cabbage and Noodles Au Gratin Skillet ❄

What if you had a bag of coleslaw mix, a jar of salsa, and some cooked noodles—and then you stirred in some cheese and let it all bubble together? Your kitchen would fill with a wonderful fragrance, your kids would peek into the room wondering what was for dinner, and you'd feel all the stress disappear from your shoulders because dinner was just about ready! ☻ Serves 4 (1¼ cups)

1 cup finely chopped celery
½ cup finely chopped onion
2 cups purchased coleslaw mix
1½ cups chunky salsa (mild, medium, or hot)
2 cups hot cooked noodles, rinsed and drained
⅔ cup Carnation Nonfat Dry Milk Powder
1 cup water
1½ cups (6 ounces) shredded Kraft reduced-fat Cheddar cheese
⅛ teaspoon black pepper

In a large skillet sprayed with butter-flavored cooking spray, sauté celery and onion for 5 minutes or until tender. Stir in coleslaw mix. Continue cooking for 3 to 5 minutes or until cabbage is just tender. Add salsa and noodles. Mix well to combine. In a small bowl, combine dry milk powder and water. Add milk mixture, Cheddar cheese, and black pepper to vegetable mixture. Mix well to combine. Lower heat and simmer for 5 minutes, or until cheese melts and mixture is heated through, stirring often.

HINTS: 1. 1½ cups shredded cabbage and ½ cup shredded carrots may be used in place of purchased coleslaw mix.
2. 1¾ cups uncooked noodles usually cooks to about 2 cups.

Each serving equals:

HE: 2½ Vegetable • 2 Protein • 1 Bread • ½ Skim Milk

252 Calories • 8 gm Fat • 19 gm Protein • 36 gm Carbohydrate • 790 mg Sodium • 581 mg Calcium • 3 gm Fiber

DIABETIC: 2 Vegetable • 1½ Meat • 1 Starch • ½ Skim Milk

Three-Cheese Noodle Dish

It's as easy as one-two-three, and it's as unforgettably yummy as any dish layered with three cheeses can be! If you're trying to serve more meatless meals and boost your calcium intake, here's a recipe that's sure to become a regular on your table.

◐ Serves 4 (1 cup)

> 1 (10¾-ounce) can Healthy Request Cream of Mushroom Soup
> 1 teaspoon Italian seasoning
> ½ cup (one 2.5-ounce jar) sliced mushrooms, undrained
> ¼ cup (¾ ounce) grated Kraft fat-free Parmesan cheese
> ⅓ cup (1½ ounces) shredded Kraft reduced-fat mozzarella cheese
> ⅓ cup (1½ ounces) shredded Kraft reduced-fat Cheddar cheese
> 1½ cups hot cooked noodles, rinsed and drained
> ½ cup frozen whole-kernel corn, thawed

In a large skillet sprayed with butter-flavored cooking spray, combine mushroom soup, Italian seasoning, undrained mushrooms, and Parmesan cheese. Mix well to combine. Stir in mozzarella cheese and Cheddar cheese. Cook over medium heat for about 3 minutes, or until cheeses melt, stirring often. Add noodles and corn. Mix well to combine. Lower heat and simmer for about 5 minutes, or until mixture is heated through, stirring occasionally.

HINTS: 1. 1¼ cups uncooked noodles usually cooks to about 1½ cups.
2. Thaw corn by placing in a colander and rinsing under hot water for one minute.

Each serving equals:

HE: 1¼ Protein • 1 Bread • ¼ Vegetable • ½ Slider •
1 Optional Calorie

214 Calories • 6 gm Fat • 10 gm Protein • 30 gm Carbohydrate •
627 mg Sodium • 198 mg Calcium • 2 gm Fiber

DIABETIC: 1½ Starch/Carbohydrate • 1 Meat

Confetti Macaroni and Cheese

Macaroni and cheese is probably America's favorite casserole, and I've created dozens of versions of this popular and well-loved dish. I hope you'll agree that this one is definitely cause for celebration! ☻ Serves 6 (1 cup)

1 (10¾-ounce) can Healthy Request Cream of Mushroom Soup

½ cup skim milk

1 teaspoon Worcestershire sauce

2 teaspoons prepared mustard

⅛ teaspoon black pepper

¼ cup finely diced onion

1½ cups (6 ounces) shredded Kraft reduced-fat Cheddar cheese

3 cups warm cooked elbow macaroni, rinsed and drained

½ cup (one 2.5-ounce jar) sliced mushrooms, drained

¼ cup (one 2-ounce jar) chopped pimiento, drained

2 teaspoons dried parsley flakes

In a large skillet sprayed with butter-flavored cooking spray, combine mushroom soup, skim milk, Worcestershire sauce, mustard, and black pepper. Add onion and Cheddar cheese. Mix well to combine. Cook over medium heat for 5 minutes or until cheese melts, stirring often. Stir in macaroni, mushrooms, pimiento, and parsley flakes. Lower heat and simmer for 10 minutes, or until mixture is heated through, stirring occasionally.

HINT: 2 cups uncooked elbow macaroni usually cooks to about 3 cups.

Each serving equals:

HE: 1⅓ Protein • 1 Bread • ¼ Vegetable • ¼ Slider • 15 Optional Calories

214 Calories • 6 gm Fat • 12 gm Protein • 28 gm Carbohydrate • 537 mg Sodium • 256 mg Calcium • 2 gm Fiber

DIABETIC: 1½ Meat • 1½ Starch

Home Again Macaroni Bake

Are you curious why I don't use fat-free cheeses in my recipes? It's simple. I've tested many, and I've found that they don't taste like cheese, they don't melt properly, and they ruin an otherwise good-tasting dish. On the other hand, the low-fat cheeses I *do* use deliver the texture and flavor that you expect, and that you deserve! ☻ Serves 6

¾ cup sliced onion

½ cup finely chopped celery

1¾ cups (one 14½-ounce can) stewed tomatoes, chopped and undrained

1 (10¾-ounce) can Healthy Request Tomato Soup

1½ teaspoons Worcestershire sauce

1 teaspoon dried parsley flakes

⅛ teaspoon black pepper

3 cups hot cooked elbow macaroni, rinsed and drained

1 cup + 2 tablespoons (4½ ounces) shredded Kraft reduced-fat Cheddar cheese☆

Preheat oven to 375 degrees. Spray an 8-by-12-inch baking dish with butter-flavored cooking spray. In a large skillet sprayed with butter-flavored cooking spray, sauté onion and celery for 6 to 8 minutes or until tender. Stir in undrained stewed tomatoes, tomato soup, Worcestershire sauce, parsley flakes, and black pepper. Add macaroni and ¾ cup Cheddar cheese. Mix well to combine. Spread mixture into prepared baking dish. Sprinkle remaining Cheddar cheese evenly over top. Bake for 25 to 30 minutes. Place baking dish on a wire rack and let set for 5 minutes. Divide into 6 servings.

HINT: 2 cups uncooked elbow macaroni usually cooks to about 3 cups.

Each serving equals:

HE: 1 Bread • 1 Protein • 1 Vegetable • ¼ Slider •
10 Optional Calories

221 Calories • 5 gm Fat • 11 gm Protein • 33 gm Carbohydrate •
583 mg Sodium • 212 mg Calcium • 3 gm Fiber

DIABETIC: 1 Starch • 1 Meat • 1 Vegetable

Tucson Supper Skillet

I hope my recipes will introduce you to some foods you've never tried or don't eat often, like the great northern beans that provide this recipe's protein. It's too easy to get into a "food rut," where you eat the same foods all the time—and you get bored. Boredom can lead to feeling deprived, so it's important to keep surprising your mouth!   ☻   Serves 4 (1½ cups)

¾ cup chopped onion

2 cups (one 16-ounce can) cut green beans, rinsed and drained

10 ounces (one 16-ounce can) great northern beans, rinsed and drained

½ cup (one 2.5-ounce jar) sliced mushrooms, drained

1 cup hot cooked rotini pasta, rinsed and drained

1¾ cups (one 14½-ounce can) stewed tomatoes, undrained

1 (10¾-ounce) can Healthy Request Cream of Celery or Mushroom Soup

1 teaspoon Italian seasoning

⅛ teaspoon black pepper

¼ cup (¾ ounce) grated Kraft fat-free Parmesan cheese

In a large skillet sprayed with olive oil–flavored cooking spray, sauté onion for 5 minutes or until tender. Stir in green beans, great northern beans, mushrooms, and rotini pasta. Add undrained tomatoes, celery soup, Italian seasoning, and black pepper. Mix well to combine. Stir in Parmesan cheese. Lower heat and simmer for 10 minutes or until mixture is heated through, stirring occasionally.

HINT: ¾ cup uncooked rotini pasta usually cooks to about 1 cup.

Each serving equals:

HE: 2½ Vegetable • 1½ Protein • ½ Bread

246 Calories • 2 gm Fat • 12 gm Protein • 45 gm Carbohydrate • 781 mg Sodium • 180 mg Calcium • 7 gm Fiber

DIABETIC: 2 Vegetable • 2 Starch/Carbohydrate • 1 Meat

Italian Fish Skillet

White fish, like flounder and sole, has a delicate flavor on its own, so it's good to prepare it in ways that bring out its subtle pleasures. This "saucy" approach is deliciously simple, but the finished result is delectably good. ☻ Serves 4

16 ounces white fish, cut into 4 pieces
1 (10¾-ounce) can Healthy Request Tomato Soup
½ cup (one 2.5-ounce jar) sliced mushrooms, undrained
1 teaspoon Italian seasoning
1 teaspoon dried onion flakes
¼ cup (¾ ounce) grated Kraft fat-free Parmesan cheese

In a large skillet sprayed with olive oil–flavored cooking spray, brown fish pieces for 2 to 3 minutes on each side. In a medium bowl, combine tomato soup and undrained mushrooms. Add Italian seasoning, onion flakes, and Parmesan cheese. Mix well to combine. Spoon sauce mixture evenly over fish. Lower heat, cover, and simmer for 15 to 20 minutes or until fish flakes easily. When serving, evenly spoon sauce over fish pieces.

Each serving equals:

HE: 1¾ Protein • ¼ Vegetable • ½ Slider • 5 Optional Calories

162 Calories • 2 gm Fat • 23 gm Protein • 13 gm Carbohydrate •
485 mg Sodium • 54 mg Calcium • 2 gm Fiber

DIABETIC: 3 Meat • 1 Starch/Carbohydrate

Scalloped Tuna and Potatoes

When your favorite brand of canned tuna is on sale, why not pick up a few extra cans? The white tuna is a little pricier than the darker version, but it also has less fat and a lighter taste. Not only that, but this recipe feeds four on just one six-ounce can, so it's easy on the pocketbook and luscious on the lips. ☻ Serves 4

3 cups (10 ounces) shredded loose-packed frozen potatoes

½ cup frozen peas, thawed

⅓ cup (1½ ounces) shredded Kraft reduced-fat Cheddar cheese

½ cup chopped onion

½ cup (one 2.5-ounce jar) sliced mushrooms, drained

3 tablespoons all-purpose flour

2 cups skim milk

1 (6-ounce) can white tuna, packed in water, drained and flaked

¼ cup (one 2-ounce jar) diced pimiento, drained

⅛ teaspoon black pepper

Preheat oven to 375 degrees. Spray an 8-by-8-inch baking dish with butter-flavored cooking spray. In a medium bowl, combine potatoes, peas, and Cheddar cheese. Spread mixture evenly in prepared baking dish. In a large skillet sprayed with butter-flavored cooking spray, sauté onion for 5 minutes or until tender. Add mushrooms. Mix well to combine. In a covered jar, combine flour and skim milk. Shake well to blend. Pour milk mixture into skillet with onion. Cook over medium heat until mixture starts to thicken, stirring often. Add tuna, pimiento, and black pepper. Mix well to combine. Pour tuna mixture over potato mixture. Bake for 25 to 30 minutes. Place baking dish on a wire rack and let set for 5 minutes. Divide into 4 servings.

HINT: Thaw peas by placing in a colander and rinsing under hot water for one minute.

Each serving equals:

HE: 1¼ Protein • 1 Bread • ½ Skim Milk • ½ Vegetable

215 Calories • 3 gm Fat • 22 gm Protein • 25 gm Carbohydrate • 610 mg Sodium • 242 mg Calcium • 5 gm Fiber

DIABETIC: 2 Meat • 1½ Starch • ½ Skim Milk

Baked Macaroni and Cheese with Tuna

When I was naming this recipe, I had to decide whether it was a tuna casserole with cheese, or macaroni and cheese with tuna. Well, I had to, but you probably won't care very much. What's important is how tasty and thrifty it is!

☻ Serves 4

1 (10¾-ounce) can Healthy Request Cream of Mushroom Soup

⅓ cup skim milk

1 teaspoon dried parsley flakes

⅛ teaspoon black pepper

1 cup + 2 tablespoons (4½ ounces) shredded Kraft reduced-fat Cheddar cheese

2 cups hot cooked elbow macaroni, rinsed and drained

1 (6-ounce) can white tuna, packed in water, drained and flaked

¼ cup (one 2-ounce jar) chopped pimiento, drained

Preheat oven to 375 degrees. Spray an 8-by-8-inch baking dish with butter-flavored cooking spray. In a large skillet, combine mushroom soup, skim milk, parsley flakes, and black pepper. Stir in Cheddar cheese. Cook over medium heat until cheese melts, stirring often. Add macaroni, tuna, and pimiento. Mix well to combine. Spread mixture evenly into prepared baking dish. Bake for 20 to 25 minutes. Place baking dish on a wire rack and let set for 5 minutes. Divide into 4 servings.

HINT: 1⅓ cups uncooked macaroni usually cooks to about 2 cups.

Each serving equals:

HE: 2¼ Protein • 1 Bread • ½ Slider • 9 Optional Calories

280 Calories • 8 gm Fat • 24 gm Protein • 28 gm Carbohydrate • 723 mg Sodium • 296 mg Calcium • 1 gm Fiber

DIABETIC: 2½ Meat • 1½ Starch/Carbohydrate

Tuna-Cabbage Buns

Instead of serving tuna fish sandwiches with coleslaw on the side, I decided to blend the crunchy cabbage right in! This could be the start of a whole new tradition—a perfect "meal-in-a-bun"!   ☻   Serves 4

> 1 cup finely shredded cabbage
>
> 1 (6-ounce) can white tuna, packed in water, drained and flaked
>
> ⅓ cup Kraft fat-free mayonnaise
>
> 1 teaspoon dried parsley flakes
>
> 2 teaspoons dried onion flakes
>
> 4 reduced-calorie hamburger buns

In a small bowl, combine cabbage, tuna, mayonnaise, parsley flakes, and onion flakes. Mix well. For each sandwich, spoon about ½ cup tuna mixture between a bun. Serve at once or refrigerate until ready to serve.

Each serving equals:

HE: 1 Bread • ¾ Protein • ½ Vegetable • 13 Optional Calories

137 Calories • 1 gm Fat • 13 gm Protein • 19 gm Carbohydrate • 479 mg Sodium • 18 mg Calcium • 1 gm Fiber

DIABETIC: 1½ Meat • 1 Starch/Carbohydrate

Macaroni and Cheese–Tuna Salad Stuffed Tomatoes

Here's another fun combo that invites two already tasty foods to "tango" with a tomato! I like taking a dinner favorite like stuffed tomatoes and giving it that extra sparkle you don't expect. This might also be fun if you substituted shredded reduced-fat Swiss cheese for the Cheddar! ☻ Serves 4

4 medium-sized fresh tomatoes

1 (6-ounce) can white tuna, packed in water, drained and flaked

1½ cups cold cooked elbow macaroni, rinsed and drained

1 cup diced celery

2 teaspoons dried onion flakes

1 teaspoon dried parsley flakes

½ cup Kraft fat-free mayonnaise

¼ cup (one 2-ounce jar) chopped pimiento, drained

⅓ cup (1½ ounces) shredded Kraft reduced-fat Cheddar cheese

Cut tops off tomatoes. Cut tomatoes into quarters, being careful not to cut all the way through the bottom. Spread wedges slightly apart. In a medium bowl, combine tuna, macaroni, celery, onion flakes, and parsley flakes. Add mayonnaise and pimiento. Mix well to combine. Stir in Cheddar cheese. Evenly spoon about ⅔ cup tuna mixture into center of each tomato. Serve at once or refrigerate until ready to serve.

HINT: 1 cup uncooked elbow macaroni usually cooks to about 1½ cups.

Each serving equals:

HE: 1½ Vegetable • 1¼ Protein • ¾ Bread • ¼ Slider

203 Calories • 3 gm Fat • 17 gm Protein • 27 gm Carbohydrate • 532 mg Sodium • 97 mg Calcium • 3 gm Fiber

DIABETIC: 1½ Meat • 1 Vegetable • 1 Starch

Tuna Skillet Pot Pie

Cliff really loved this top-of-the-stove surprise that's just right for steamy summer evenings when you'd rather not turn on your oven. It's delightfully creamy and cheesy, the biscuits are beautifully golden brown, and the flavor—well, it's simply out of this world! ☾ Serves 6

> 2 (6-ounce) cans white tuna, packed in water, drained and flaked
> 1 cup frozen peas, thawed
> 1 (10¾-ounce) can Healthy Request Cream of Mushroom Soup
> ⅔ cup Carnation Nonfat Dry Milk Powder
> ¾ cup water
> ¾ cup Bisquick Reduced Fat Baking Mix
> 1 teaspoon dried parsley flakes
> ⅓ cup (1½ ounces) shredded Kraft reduced-fat Cheddar cheese

In a large skillet sprayed with butter-flavored cooking spray, combine tuna, peas, and mushroom soup. Cook over medium heat, stirring occasionally. Meanwhile, in a small bowl, combine dry milk powder and water. Stir ½ cup of milk mixture into tuna mixture. Lower heat and simmer while preparing biscuits. In a medium bowl, combine baking mix, parsley flakes, Cheddar cheese, and remaining ⅓ cup milk mixture. Mix just to combine. Using a full tablespoon as a guide, drop biscuit mixture onto tuna mixture to form 6 biscuits. Cover and continue simmering for 15 minutes or until biscuits are golden brown. Divide into 6 servings.

HINT: Thaw peas by placing in a colander and rinsing under hot water for one minute.

Each serving equals:

HE: 1⅓ Protein • 1 Bread • ⅓ Skim Milk • ¼ Slider •
8 Optional Calories

155 Calories • 3 gm Fat • 16 gm Protein • 16 gm Carbohydrate •
496 mg Sodium • 147 mg Calcium • 1 gm Fiber

DIABETIC: 2 Meat • 1½ Starch/Carbohydrate

Creamy Tuna and Vegetable Skillet

This is another super skillet combination that is just as mouthwatering as it is good for your bones! (Yes, it's got lots of healthy calcium, as well as so much nourishment for the dollar, you'll be amazed!) If you've vowed to add more fish meals to your menu, here's one the whole family will surely love. ☻ Serves 6 (1 cup)

1 (6-ounce) can white tuna, packed in water, drained and flaked

1 (10¾-ounce) can Healthy Request Cream of Celery Soup

⅓ cup skim milk

¾ cup (3 ounces) shredded Kraft reduced-fat Cheddar cheese

¼ cup (¾ ounce) grated Kraft fat-free Parmesan cheese

1 teaspoon dried parsley flakes

1 teaspoon dried onion flakes

¼ teaspoon black pepper

2 cups (one 16-ounce can) sliced carrots, rinsed and drained

2 cups (one 16-ounce can) cut green beans, rinsed and drained

½ cup (one 2.5-ounce jar) sliced mushrooms, drained

2 cups hot cooked noodles, rinsed and drained

In a large skillet, combine tuna, celery soup, and skim milk. Stir in Cheddar cheese, Parmesan cheese, parsley flakes, onion flakes, and black pepper. Cook over medium heat until cheese melts, stirring often. Add carrots, green beans, mushrooms, and noodles. Mix well to combine. Lower heat and simmer for 10 minutes, or until mixture is heated through, stirring often.

Each serving equals:

HE: 1½ Vegetable • 1⅓ Protein • ⅔ Bread • ¼ Slider • 8 Optional Calories

217 Calories • 5 gm Fat • 16 gm Protein • 27 gm Carbohydrate • 533 mg Sodium • 187 mg Calcium • 3 gm Fiber

DIABETIC: 2 Meat • 1½ Vegetable • 1½ Starch

Tuna Rice à la King Skillet

Even if the only royalty you're serving dinner to is the king of your castle (your hubby) or the little princess you call your daughter, here's a luscious and satisfying meal to please their palates (not to mention your own!). This cooks up so thick and rich, everyone will be dazzled. ☻ Serves 4 (1 cup)

2 cups skim milk

3 tablespoons all-purpose flour

½ cup (4 ounces) Philadelphia fat-free cream cheese

½ cup (one 2.5-ounce jar) sliced mushrooms, undrained

1 cup frozen peas, thawed

1 (6-ounce) can white tuna, packed in water, drained and flaked

1 teaspoon dried parsley flakes

¼ cup (one 2-ounce jar) chopped pimiento, drained

¼ teaspoon black pepper

1 cup (3 ounces) uncooked Minute Rice

In a covered jar, combine skim milk and flour. Shake well to blend. Pour milk mixture into a large skillet sprayed with butter-flavored cooking spray. Stir in cream cheese. Cook over medium heat until mixture starts to thicken, stirring constantly. Add undrained mushrooms, peas, tuna, parsley flakes, pimiento, and black pepper. Mix well to combine. Continue cooking just until mixture starts to boil. Stir in uncooked rice. Remove from heat. Cover and let set for 5 minutes. Fluff with a fork before serving.

HINT: Thaw peas by placing in a colander and rinsing under hot water for one minute.

Each serving equals:

HE: 1½ Bread • 1¼ Protein • ½ Skim Milk • ¼ Vegetable

233 Calories • 1 gm Fat • 27 gm Protein • 29 gm Carbohydrate • 552 mg Sodium • 172 mg Calcium • 3 gm Fiber

DIABETIC: 2 Meat • 1½ Starch • ½ Skim Milk

Heartland Tuna Bake

You heard it first in *The Music Man*—we Iowans can be quite stubborn, especially when it comes to tasty food! We just won't settle for less than the best we can get, even if we're working hard to make ends meet. But when we've got some "Iowa pride" (corn) to stir into a baked tuna entree, we're sure we couldn't do any better!

● Serves 6

1½ cups finely chopped celery
½ cup chopped onion
1½ cups hot cooked rice
1½ cups frozen whole-kernel corn, thawed
⅔ cup Carnation Nonfat Dry Milk Powder
½ cup water
2 (6-ounce) cans white tuna, packed in water, drained and flaked
¾ cup (3 ounces) shredded Kraft reduced-fat Cheddar cheese
1 teaspoon dried parsley flakes
¼ teaspoon lemon pepper

Preheat oven to 325 degrees. Spray an 8-by-8-inch baking dish with butter-flavored cooking spray. In a large skillet sprayed with butter-flavored cooking spray, sauté celery and onion for 5 minutes or just until tender. Stir in rice and corn. In a small bowl, combine dry milk powder and water. Stir milk mixture into celery mixture. Add tuna, Cheddar cheese, parsley flakes, and lemon pepper. Mix well to combine. Pour mixture into prepared baking dish. Cover and bake for 45 minutes. Uncover and continue to bake an additional 10 minutes. Place baking dish on a wire rack and let set for 5 minutes. Divide into 6 servings.

HINT: 1 cup uncooked rice usually cooks to about 1½ cups.

Each serving equals:

HE: 1⅔ Protein • 1 Bread • ⅔ Vegetable • ⅓ Skim Milk

215 Calories • 3 gm Fat • 23 gm Protein • 24 gm Carbohydrate • 382 mg Sodium • 210 mg Calcium • 2 gm Fiber

DIABETIC: 2½ Meat • 1½ Starch/Carbohydrate

New Orleans Fish and Rice

The Cajuns of New Orleans have a motto: *"Laissez le bon temps rouler!"* Translated, it means, "Let the good times roll!" It's equally true when it comes to the foods they love—they're always good and spicy! By adding a touch of Southern heat, you too can bring those good times home! ◐ Serves 4

½ cup chopped onion

1 cup chopped green bell pepper

1¾ cups (one 15-ounce can) Hunt's Chunky Tomato Sauce

½ teaspoon dried minced garlic

1 teaspoon Tabasco sauce

1 tablespoon Brown Sugar Twin

2 teaspoons dried parsley flakes

16 ounces white fish, cut into 16 pieces

2 cups hot cooked rice

In a large skillet sprayed with butter-flavored cooking spray, sauté onion and green pepper for 5 minutes or until tender. Stir in tomato sauce, garlic, Tabasco sauce, Brown Sugar Twin, and parsley flakes. Add fish pieces. Mix gently to combine. Lower heat, cover, and simmer for 20 to 25 minutes, or until fish is tender, stirring occasionally. For each serving, place ½ cup rice on a plate and spoon about 1 full cup sauce mixture over top.

HINT: 1⅓ cups uncooked rice usually cooks to about 2 cups.

Each serving equals:

HE: 2½ Vegetable • 1½ Protein • 1 Bread • 1 Optional Calorie

213 Calories • 1 gm Fat • 25 gm Protein • 26 gm Carbohydrate • 796 mg Sodium • 57 mg Calcium • 3 gm Fiber

DIABETIC: 3 Meat • 2 Vegetable • 1 Starch

Seaside Spaghetti and Fish

Pasta and fish just seem right together—like sea and sand or hot dogs with mustard! Here's a fresh way to serve this classic dish: with a seafood twist that boosts the protein sky-high and delivers a succulent meal at a surprisingly low cost. Better than that, it's scrumptious! ❂ Serves 4

3 tablespoons all-purpose flour

1 teaspoon Italian seasoning

16 ounces white fish, cut into 16 pieces

2 tablespoons skim milk

1¾ cups (one 15-ounce can) Hunt's Chunky Tomato Sauce

½ cup chunky salsa (mild, medium, or hot)

2 cups hot cooked spaghetti, rinsed and drained

¼ cup (¾ ounce) grated Kraft fat-free Parmesan cheese

In a saucer, combine flour and Italian seasoning. Dip fish pieces in skim milk, then into flour mixture. (Reserve any remaining flour mixture.) Place fish in a large skillet sprayed with olive oil–flavored cooking spray. Brown fish pieces on both sides. In a medium bowl, combine tomato sauce, salsa, and any remaining flour mixture. Pour sauce mixture over fish. Lower heat, cover, and simmer for 20 to 25 minutes, or until fish is tender, stirring occasionally. For each serving, place ½ cup spaghetti on a plate, spoon about 1 full cup sauce mixture over top, and garnish with 1 tablespoon Parmesan cheese.

HINT: 1½ cups broken spaghetti usually cooks to about 2 cups.

Each serving equals:

HE: 2 Vegetable • 1¾ Protein • 1¼ Bread • 3 Optional Calories

266 Calories • 2 gm Fat • 27 gm Protein • 35 gm Carbohydrate • 1,019 mg Sodium • 98 mg Calcium • 4 gm Fiber

DIABETIC: 3½ Meat • 3 Vegetable • 1 Starch *or* 3½ Meat • 2 Starch • 1 Vegetable

Salmon Cups with Creamed Peas

Looking for a lovely main dish to serve at a summer lunch for friends but can't afford anything with a fancy price? Here's a particularly pretty and delectable entree that looks special but isn't hard on your budget or your overbooked schedule! ☻ Serves 6

> 1 (14½-ounce drained weight) can pink salmon, packed in water,
>   drained and flaked
> 14 small fat-free saltine crackers, made into fine crumbs
> 1 egg or equivalent in egg substitute
> 1½ cups (one 12-fluid-ounce can) Carnation Evaporated Skim Milk☆
> 1 teaspoon dried onion flakes
> 2 teaspoons dried parsley flakes
> 3 tablespoons all-purpose flour
> 1½ cups frozen peas, thawed
> ¼ teaspoon lemon pepper

Preheat oven to 350 degrees. Spray a 6-hole muffin pan with butter-flavored cooking spray. In a medium bowl, combine salmon, cracker crumbs, egg, ¼ cup evaporated skim milk, onion flakes, and parsley flakes. Mix well. Evenly pat about ⅓ cup of salmon mixture into each prepared muffin cup. Press mixture up sides to form a cup. In a covered jar, combine remaining 1¼ cups evaporated skim milk and flour. Shake well to blend. Pour milk mixture into a medium saucepan sprayed with butter-flavored cooking spray. Add peas and lemon pepper. Mix well to combine. Cook over medium heat until mixture thickens, stirring often. Spoon about ⅓ cup of pea sauce into center of each salmon cup. Bake for 30 minutes. Place muffin pan on a wire rack and let set for 5 minutes.

HINTS: 1. A self-seal sandwich bag works great for crushing crackers.
2. Thaw peas by placing in a colander and rinsing under hot water for one minute.

Each serving equals:

HE: 2½ Protein • 1 Bread • ½ Skim Milk • 5 Optional Calories

195 Calories • 3 gm Fat • 21 gm Protein • 21 gm Carbohydrate • 508 mg Sodium • 295 mg Calcium • 2 gm Fiber

DIABETIC: 2½ Meat • 1 Starch • ½ Skim Milk

Shrimp and Vegetables

Ordering shrimp cocktail in restaurants means paying a high price for this beloved seafood treat. Why not enjoy the shrimp you love, but prepared at home in a tangy sauce and coupled with lots of delicious vegetables? You get the flavor you crave, but the only "belt-tightening" required will be when your healthy lifestyle means taking in the waist of your slacks!   ☻   Serves 4 (1½ cups)

1 cup coarsely chopped onion
1 cup coarsely chopped green bell pepper
3 full cups (16 ounces) diced cooked potatoes
2 cups peeled and coarsely chopped fresh tomatoes
¼ cup shrimp sauce
½ teaspoon dried minced garlic
1 teaspoon dried parsley flakes
¼ teaspoon black pepper
2 (4.5-ounce drained weight) cans small shrimp, rinsed and drained

In a large skillet sprayed with olive oil–flavored cooking spray, sauté onion and green pepper for 5 minutes. Add potatoes. Mix well to combine. Simmer for 5 minutes, stirring often. Stir in tomatoes, shrimp sauce, garlic, parsley flakes, black pepper, and shrimp. Continue simmering for 5 minutes, stirring often.

HINT: 9 ounces frozen shrimp may be substituted for canned.

Each serving equals:

HE: 2¼ Protein • 2¼ Vegetable • 1 Bread • ¼ Slider • 5 Optional Calories

234 Calories • 2 gm Fat • 19 gm Protein • 35 gm Carbohydrate • 350 mg Sodium • 61 mg Calcium • 4 gm Fiber

DIABETIC: 1½ Vegetable • 1½ Starch • 1 Meat

Mom's Salmon Noodle Casserole

My mother was a true whiz at figuring out ways to feed her family without spending a fortune. Salmon was more of a treat than tuna, so when she served us a casserole like this one, we knew there was something worth celebrating.

☻ Serves 4

2 cups hot cooked noodles, rinsed and drained
1 (14¾-ounce) can pink salmon, drained and flaked
½ cup (one 2.5-ounce jar) sliced mushrooms, undrained
2 cups (one 16-ounce can) cut green beans, rinsed and drained
1 (10¾-ounce) can Healthy Request Cream of Mushroom Soup
1 teaspoon dried onion flakes
1 teaspoon dried parsley flakes
⅛ teaspoon black pepper
1 teaspoon dried dill weed

Preheat oven to 350 degrees. Spray an 8-by-8-inch baking dish with butter-flavored cooking spray. In a large bowl, combine noodles, salmon, mushrooms, and green beans. Add mushroom soup, onion flakes, parsley flakes, black pepper, and dill weed. Mix well to combine. Spread mixture into prepared baking dish. Bake for 25 to 30 minutes. Place baking dish on a wire rack and let set for 3 minutes. Divide into 4 servings.

HINT: 1¾ cups uncooked noodles usually cooks to about 2 cups.

Each serving equals:

HE: 3 Protein • 1¼ Vegetable • 1 Bread • ½ Slider • 1 Optional Calorie

274 Calories • 6 gm Fat • 24 gm Protein • 31 gm Carbohydrate • 907 mg Sodium • 234 mg Calcium • 3 gm Fiber

DIABETIC: 3 Meat • 1½ Starch/Carbohydrate • 1 Vegetable

Turkey Hot Dish

This recipe calls for a real mélange of ingredients, all of them irresistible on their own! Stirred together and baked into a delightfully fragrant casserole, those tasty bits of this and that will please all your senses. ❂ Serves 6

1 cup finely chopped celery

2 full cups (12 ounces) diced cooked turkey breast

½ cup (one 2.5-ounce jar) sliced mushrooms, drained

½ cup Kraft fat-free mayonnaise

1 (10¾-ounce) can Healthy Request Cream of Chicken Soup

2 teaspoons dried onion flakes

2 hard-boiled eggs, chopped

¼ cup (1 ounce) slivered almonds

1 cup (1½ ounces) crushed reduced-fat potato chips

Preheat oven to 375 degrees. Spray an 8-by-12-inch baking dish with butter-flavored cooking spray. In a large skillet sprayed with butter-flavored cooking spray, sauté celery for 6 to 8 minutes or until tender. Stir in turkey, mushrooms, mayonnaise, chicken soup, and onion flakes. Fold in eggs and almonds. Spread mixture into prepared baking dish. Evenly sprinkle crushed potato chips over top. Bake for 25 to 30 minutes. Place baking dish on a wire rack and let set for 5 minutes. Divide into 6 servings.

HINTS: 1. If you don't have leftovers, purchase a chunk of cooked turkey breast from your local deli.
2. If you want the look and feel of egg without the cholesterol, toss out the yolk and dice the whites.
3. A self-seal sandwich bag works great for crushing potato chips.

Each serving equals:

HE: 2½ Protein (⅓ limited) • ½ Vegetable • ⅓ Bread • ⅓ Fat • ½ Slider • 1 Optional Calorie

229 Calories • 9 gm Fat • 22 gm Protein • 15 gm Carbohydrate • 510 mg Sodium • 42 mg Calcium • 1 gm Fiber

DIABETIC: 2½ Meat • 1 Starch/Carbohydrate • ½ Fat

Baked Turkey and Rice Casserole

When it comes to turkey breast, you can roast a turkey and cut up the white meat leftovers to use in other recipes; you can purchase a turkey breast and serve it many times; or you can buy it already cooked by the pound. Serve it often!

❂ Serves 6

½ cup finely chopped onion

1 cup diced celery

1 (10¾-ounce) can Healthy Request Cream of Chicken Soup

¼ cup (one 2-ounce jar) chopped pimiento, undrained

1 tablespoon dried parsley flakes

⅛ teaspoon black pepper

3 cups hot cooked rice

1½ cups (8 ounces) diced cooked turkey breast

Preheat oven to 375 degrees. Spray an 8-by-12-inch baking dish with butter-flavored cooking spray. In a large skillet sprayed with butter-flavored cooking spray, sauté onion and celery for 6 to 8 minutes or until tender. Stir in chicken soup, undrained pimiento, parsley flakes, and black pepper. Add rice and turkey. Mix well to combine. Pour mixture into prepared baking dish. Bake for 25 to 30 minutes. Place baking dish on a wire rack and let set for 5 minutes. Divide into 6 servings.

HINTS: 1. 2 cups uncooked rice usually cooks to about 3 cups.
2. If you don't have leftovers, purchase a chunk of cooked turkey breast from your local deli.

Each serving equals:

HE: 1⅓ Protein • 1 Bread • ½ Vegetable • ¼ Slider • 10 Optional Calories

178 Calories • 2 gm Fat • 15 gm Protein • 25 gm Carbohydrate • 250 mg Sodium • 27 mg Calcium • 1 gm Fiber

DIABETIC: 1½ Starch/Carbohydrate • 1 Meat

After the Holiday Turkey Casserole

If you're like me, you can never get enough turkey and stuffing! (And my kids agree!) Here's a smart and frugal way to use up those leftovers, but this flavorful casserole doesn't taste like the "day after"! It's amazingly creamy and rich, but still under 200 calories a serving!   ☻   Serves 6

> 2 cups (one 16-ounce can) Healthy Request Chicken Broth ☆
> 1 cup chopped celery
> ½ cup chopped onion
> 1 cup frozen peas, thawed
> 1½ cups (3 ounces) unseasoned dry bread cubes
> 1½ cups (8 ounces) diced cooked turkey breast
> 1 teaspoon dried parsley flakes
> 1 teaspoon sage seasoning
> ⅛ teaspoon black pepper
> 1 (10¾-ounce) can Healthy Request Cream of Chicken Soup

Preheat oven to 350 degrees. Spray an 8-by-8-inch baking dish with butter-flavored cooking spray. In a large saucepan, combine 1 cup chicken broth, celery, and onion. Cook over medium heat until vegetables are just tender. Add peas, bread cubes, turkey, parsley flakes, sage seasoning, and black pepper. Mix well to combine. In a small bowl, combine remaining 1 cup chicken broth and chicken soup. Stir soup mixture into dressing mixture. Spoon mixture into prepared baking dish. Bake for 45 to 50 minutes. Place baking dish on a wire rack and let set for 5 minutes. Divide into 6 servings.

HINTS: 1. Thaw peas by placing in a colander and rinsing under hot water for one minute.
2. Pepperidge Farm bread cubes work great.

Each serving equals:

HE: 1⅓ Protein • 1 Bread • ½ Vegetable • 6 Optional Calories

179 Calories • 3 gm Fat • 17 gm Protein • 21 gm Carbohydrate •
553 mg Sodium • 22 mg Calcium • 2 gm Fiber

DIABETIC: 2 Meat • 1½ Starch/Carbohydrate

Mexican Turkey Noodle Bake

Turkey is such a healthy choice, you don't have to reserve it just for the holidays. I watch for sales on a whole turkey breast, then use it to stir up lots of dishes like this one. If you like it extra-spicy, add a pinch of extra chili seasoning, but don't set the kitchen on fire! ☻ Serves 8

1⅓ cups Carnation Nonfat Dry Milk Powder

½ cup water

1 (10¾-ounce) can Healthy Request Cream of Chicken Soup

1½ cups (8 ounces) diced cooked turkey breast

1¾ cups (one 14½-ounce can) stewed tomatoes, coarsely chopped and undrained

¼ cup finely chopped onion

1 teaspoon dried parsley flakes

1 teaspoon chili seasoning

1 cup frozen whole-kernel corn, thawed

3 cups cooked noodles, rinsed and drained

¾ cup (3 ounces) shredded Kraft reduced-fat Cheddar cheese

Preheat oven to 350 degrees. Spray a 9-by-13-inch baking dish with olive oil–flavored cooking spray. In a large bowl, combine dry milk powder, water, and chicken soup. Add turkey, undrained stewed tomatoes, onion, parsley flakes, chili seasoning, and corn. Mix well to combine. Stir in noodles and Cheddar cheese. Pour mixture into prepared baking dish. Bake for 30 minutes. Place baking dish on a wire rack and let set for 5 minutes. Cut into 8 servings.

HINTS: 1. Thaw corn by placing in a colander and rinsing under hot water for one minute.
2. 2½ cups uncooked noodles usually cooks to about 3 cups.

Each serving equals:

HE: 1½ Protein • 1 Bread • ½ Skim Milk • ½ Vegetable • ¼ Slider • 3 Optional Calories

231 Calories • 3 gm Fat • 19 gm Protein • 32 gm Carbohydrate • 461 mg Sodium • 230 mg Calcium • 2 gm Fiber

DIABETIC: 2 Starch/Carbohydrate • 1½ Meat • ½ Vegetable

Baked Turkey and Rice

This cozy classic reminded me of eating at Grandma's in the days after Christmas, when she'd keep coming up with tasty new ways to finish up the holiday turkey! If this doesn't take you back to childhood memories with just one bite, I'll be very surprised! ☻ Serves 6

3 cups hot cooked rice

1½ cups (8 ounces) diced cooked turkey breast

1 (10¾-ounce) can Healthy Request Cream of Chicken Soup

½ cup (one 2.5-ounce jar) sliced mushrooms, drained

½ cup chopped onion

½ cup finely diced celery

1 tablespoon dried parsley flakes

¼ cup (one 2-ounce jar) chopped pimiento, drained

¼ cup Kraft fat-free mayonnaise

⅛ teaspoon black pepper

Preheat oven to 350 degrees. Spray an 8-by-8-inch baking dish with butter-flavored cooking spray. In a large bowl, combine rice, turkey, and chicken soup. Stir in mushrooms, onion, celery, parsley flakes, pimiento, mayonnaise, and black pepper. Mix well to combine. Pour mixture into prepared baking dish. Bake for 60 minutes. Place baking dish on a wire rack and let set for 5 minutes. Divide into 6 servings.

HINT: 2 cups uncooked rice usually cooks to about 3 cups.

Each serving equals:

HE: 1⅓ Protein · • 1 Bread • ⅔ Vegetable • ¼ Slider •
13 Optional Calories

186 Calories • 2 gm Fat • 15 gm Protein • 27 gm Carbohydrate •
296 mg Sodium • 24 mg Calcium • 1 gm Fiber

DIABETIC: 1½ Starch/Carbohydrate • 1½ Meat

Home-Style Turkey with Biscuits

Here's an old-fashioned dish served with new-style smarts no thrifty cook can afford to be without! Healthy prepared foods like the soup and ready-made biscuits let you save money and save time—and who doesn't need to do both?

○ Serves 6

> 1½ cups (8 ounces) diced cooked turkey breast
> 1 (10¾-ounce) can Healthy Request Cream of Chicken Soup
> 1 teaspoon dried onion flakes
> 1 teaspoon dried parsley flakes
> 1 cup (one 8-ounce can) sliced carrots, rinsed and drained
> 1 cup (one 8-ounce can) cut green beans, rinsed and drained
> 1 (7.5-ounce) can Pillsbury refrigerated buttermilk biscuits
> ¼ teaspoon paprika

Preheat oven to 400 degrees. Spray an 8-by-8-inch baking dish with butter-flavored cooking spray. In a large skillet, combine turkey, chicken soup, onion flakes, parsley flakes, carrots, and green beans. Cook over medium heat for 10 minutes, stirring often. Spread hot mixture into prepared baking dish. Separate biscuits and cut each into 4 pieces. Evenly sprinkle biscuit pieces over top of turkey mixture. Lightly spray tops of biscuit pieces with butter-flavored cooking spray. Sprinkle paprika evenly over top. Bake for 15 minutes or until biscuits are golden brown. Place baking dish on a wire rack and let set for 2 to 3 minutes. Divide into 6 servings.

Each serving equals:

HE: 1⅓ Protein • 1¼ Bread • ⅔ Vegetable • ¼ Slider • 10 Optional Calories

---

191 Calories • 3 gm Fat • 17 gm Protein • 24 gm Carbohydrate • 546 mg Sodium • 20 mg Calcium • 2 gm Fiber

---

DIABETIC: 1½ Meat • 1½ Starch • 1 Vegetable

Cozy Turkey Pot Pies

This is a wonderful recipe to serve on cold winter afternoons when your kids come in from playing in the snow. It tastes delectably homemade and warms the coldest child through and through.   ♥   Serves 4

1½ cups (8 ounces) diced cooked turkey breast

½ cup (one 2.5-ounce jar) sliced mushrooms, drained

½ cup chopped onion

1 cup frozen peas, thawed

¼ teaspoon black pepper

⅓ cup (1½ ounces) shredded Kraft reduced-fat Cheddar cheese

6 tablespoons all-purpose flour

2 teaspoons baking powder

2 teaspoons dried parsley flakes

1 cup skim milk

2 eggs or equivalent in egg substitute

2 tablespoons Kraft fat-free mayonnaise

Preheat oven to 400 degrees. Spray 4 individual casseroles or (10-ounce) custard cups with butter-flavored cooking spray. In a medium bowl, combine turkey, mushrooms, onion, peas, black pepper, and Cheddar cheese. Evenly divide mixture among prepared casseroles. In a small bowl, combine flour, baking powder, and parsley flakes. Add skim milk, egg, and mayonnaise. Mix well to combine. Evenly spoon batter over top of casseroles. Bake for 30 to 35 minutes. Place casseroles on a wire rack and let set for 5 minutes.

HINT: Thaw peas by placing in a colander and rinsing under hot water for one minute.

Each serving equals:

HE: 3 Protein (½ limited) • 1 Bread • ½ Vegetable • ¼ Skim Milk • 5 Optional Calories

279 Calories • 7 gm Fat • 30 gm Protein • 24 gm Carbohydrate • 681 mg Sodium • 331 mg Calcium • 4 gm Fiber

DIABETIC: 3 Meat • 1½ Starch • ½ Vegetable

Midwest Scalloped Chicken and Corn

When I was growing up, I was convinced that creamed corn actually contained cream. I was surprised (and delighted) to discover that it's the corn itself that makes this magically creamy ingredient so good.　　⚫　Serves 6

½ cup chopped onion

1 cup chopped celery

1 cup (one 8-ounce can) cream-style corn

1 (10¾-ounce can) Healthy Request Cream of Chicken Soup

1 teaspoon dried parsley flakes

⅛ teaspoon black pepper

¾ cup (3 ounces) shredded Kraft reduced-fat Cheddar cheese

1 cup (5 ounces) diced cooked chicken breast

2 cups hot cooked elbow macaroni, rinsed and drained

Preheat oven to 375 degrees. Spray an 8-by-12-inch baking dish with butter-flavored cooking spray. In a large skillet sprayed with butter-flavored cooking spray, sauté onion and celery for 6 to 8 minutes or until tender. Stir in cream-style corn, chicken soup, parsley flakes, and black pepper. Add Cheddar cheese. Mix well to combine. Stir in chicken and elbow macaroni. Spread mixture into prepared baking dish. Bake for 20 to 25 minutes. Place baking dish on a wire rack and let set for 5 minutes. Divide into 6 servings.

HINTS: 1. If you don't have leftovers, purchase a chunk of cooked chicken breast from your local deli.
2. 1⅓ cups uncooked elbow macaroni usually cooks to about 2 cups.

Each serving equals:

HE: 1½ Protein • 1 Bread • ½ Vegetable • ¼ Slider • 10 Optional Calories

208 Calories • 4 gm Fat • 15 gm Protein • 28 gm Carbohydrate • 477 mg Sodium • 113 mg Calcium • 2 gm Fiber

DIABETIC: 2 Starch • 1½ Meat

Hot Chicken Salad Sandwiches

Here's a fun new way to stir up a little lunchtime excitement at your house! By taking an American classic like chicken salad and adding a few extra touches (like the cheese), then baking the stuffed buns in the oven—you've got a great recipe for yum-yum-yum! ☻ Serves 6

> 1½ cups (8 ounces) diced cooked chicken breast
> ¾ cup (3 ounces) shredded Kraft reduced-fat Cheddar cheese
> ½ cup finely diced celery
> ¼ cup diced onion
> 2 tablespoons sweet pickle relish
> ½ cup Kraft fat-free mayonnaise
> ¼ cup (one 2-ounce jar) chopped pimiento
> ⅛ teaspoon black pepper
> 6 reduced-calorie hamburger buns

Preheat oven to 350 degrees. In a medium bowl, combine chicken, Cheddar cheese, celery, onion, and pickle relish. Add mayonnaise, pimiento, and black pepper. Mix gently to combine. Evenly spoon about ½ cup chicken mixture between each bun. Wrap each in foil. Arrange foil packages on a baking sheet and bake for 20 minutes.

Each serving equals:

HE: 2 Protein • 1 Bread • ¼ Vegetable • 13 Optional Calories

189 Calories • 5 gm Fat • 17 gm Protein • 19 gm Carbohydrate • 471 mg Sodium • 106 mg Calcium • 1 gm Fiber

DIABETIC: 2 Meat • 1 Starch

Skillet Chicken Stew

This stove-top stew has such a wonderfully old-fashioned flavor, your kids may wonder if Grandma stopped by to make dinner! By stirring in lots of veggies along with spaghetti noodles, you get tremendous chicken-y goodness out of a modest amount of meat. 🔄 Serves 4 (1 full cup)

> 2 cups (one 16-ounce can) Healthy Request Chicken Broth
>
> 1 full cup (3 ounces) uncooked broken spaghetti
>
> 1 cup shredded carrots
>
> 1 cup chopped celery
>
> 2 cups shredded cabbage
>
> ½ cup chopped onion
>
> 1 full cup (6 ounces) diced cooked chicken breast
>
> ½ cup (one 2.5-ounce jar) sliced mushrooms, drained
>
> ¼ cup (one 2-ounce jar) chopped pimiento, drained
>
> 2 tablespoons reduced-sodium soy sauce

In a medium saucepan, bring chicken broth to a boil. Stir in uncooked spaghetti. Add carrots, celery, cabbage, and onion. Mix well to combine. Bring mixture to a boil. Lower heat and simmer for 15 minutes, stirring often. Stir in chicken, mushrooms, pimiento, and soy sauce. Continue simmering for 10 minutes, stirring occasionally.

Each serving equals:

HE: 2½ Vegetable • 1½ Protein • 1 Bread

---

166 Calories • 2 gm Fat • 18 gm Protein • 19 gm Carbohydrate • 627 mg Sodium • 41 mg Calcium • 3 gm Fiber

---

DIABETIC: 1½ Vegetable • 1½ Meat • 1 Starch

Cheesy Chicken and Green Beans over Noodles

Each month, new "healthy" products appear in our local grocery stores, but many of them promise more than they deliver. One that really works great is the fat-free chicken gravy I used in this recipe, and I give it this high praise: if you didn't know it was fat-free, you'd never believe it! ☻ Serves 4

½ cup finely chopped onion

1 (12-ounce) jar Heinz Fat Free Chicken Gravy

¼ cup (one 2-ounce jar) chopped pimiento, undrained

¾ cup (3 ounces) shredded Kraft reduced-fat Cheddar cheese

¼ teaspoon black pepper

1 teaspoon dried parsley flakes

1 cup (5 ounces) diced cooked chicken breast

2 cups (one 16-ounce can) cut green beans, rinsed and drained

2 cups hot cooked noodles, rinsed and drained

In a large skillet sprayed with butter-flavored cooking spray, sauté onion for 5 minutes or until just tender. Stir in chicken gravy, undrained pimiento, Cheddar cheese, black pepper, and parsley flakes. Continue cooking until cheese melts, stirring often. Add chicken and green beans. Mix well to combine. Lower heat and simmer for 5 minutes or until mixture is heated through, stirring occasionally. For each serving, place ½ cup noodles on a plate and spoon about ¾ cup chicken mixture over top.

HINT: 1¾ cups uncooked noodles usually cooks to about 2 cups.

Each serving equals:

HE: 2¼ Protein • 1¼ Vegetable • 1 Bread • ¼ Slider •
1 Optional Calorie

262 Calories • 6 gm Fat • 23 gm Protein • 29 gm Carbohydrate •
708 mg Sodium • 176 mg Calcium • 2 gm Fiber

DIABETIC: 2 Meat • 1½ Starch • 1 Vegetable

Fiesta Chicken Skillet

All across America, when it was time for Sunday supper, you'd often find a heaping platter of chicken and noodles carried steaming to the table! It's still one of the coziest main dishes anyone can serve, and I love discovering lively new ways to prepare it. This spicy version is a special favorite of my husband, Cliff's, and my son Tommy's—it must be the salsa! ◐ Serves 4 (1 cup)

1 full cup (6 ounces) diced cooked chicken breast
½ cup chunky salsa (mild, medium, or hot)
1 (12-ounce) jar Heinz Fat Free Chicken Gravy
2 cups hot cooked noodles, rinsed and drained
1 teaspoon dried parsley flakes

In a large skillet sprayed with olive oil–flavored cooking spray, combine chicken, salsa, and chicken gravy. Bring mixture to a boil. Add noodles and parsley flakes. Mix well to combine. Lower heat and simmer for 10 minutes or until mixture is heated through, stirring occasionally.

Each serving equals:

HE: 1½ Protein • 1 Bread • ¼ Vegetable • ¼ Slider • 18 Optional Calories

199 Calories • 3 gm Fat • 18 gm Protein • 25 gm Carbohydrate • 643 mg Sodium • 56 mg Calcium • 1 gm Fiber

DIABETIC: 1½ Meat • 1½ Starch • 1 Vegetable

Skillet Chicken Cacciatore

I think cooking with fat-free dressing is one of the thrifty chef's best secrets! It makes a wonderful marinade, and when stirred together with other tasty ingredients, it produces a family favorite like chicken cacciatore that's even better than the original! ❤ Serves 4

¼ cup Kraft Fat Free Italian Dressing
½ cup sliced onion
¼ cup sliced green bell pepper
16 ounces skinned and boned uncooked chicken breasts, cut into 16 pieces
2 teaspoons Italian seasoning
2 teaspoons Sugar Twin or Sprinkle Sweet
1¾ cups (one 14 ½-ounce can) stewed tomatoes, undrained
2 cups hot cooked noodles, rinsed and drained

In a large skillet, heat Italian dressing. Add onion, green pepper, and chicken. Mix well to combine. Cook for 6 to 8 minutes, stirring occasionally. In a small bowl, combine Italian seasoning, Sugar Twin, and undrained stewed tomatoes. Spoon tomato mixture evenly over chicken. Lower heat and simmer for 12 to 15 minutes, or until chicken is tender, stirring occasionally. For each serving, place ½ cup noodles on a plate and spoon about 1 cup chicken mixture over top.

HINT: 1¾ cups uncooked noodles usually cooks to about 2 cups.

Each serving equals:

HE: 3 Protein • 1¾ Vegetable • 1 Bread • 9 Optional Calories

258 Calories • 2 gm Fat • 31 gm Protein • 29 gm Carbohydrate • 550 mg Sodium • 82 mg Calcium • 2 gm Fiber

DIABETIC: 3 Meat • 1½ Vegetable • 1 Starch

Nacho Chicken Potato Dish

Cutting corners never has to mean cutting back on flavor, and this spicy fiesta combination is a sizzling example! By drawing protein from three different sources (beans, cheese, and chicken), I never sacrifice on nutrition—but by stirring together lots of wonderful flavors, I create fireworks on a plate! ♥ Serves 6

¼ cup chopped onion
¼ cup chopped green bell pepper
1 full cup (6 ounces) diced cooked chicken breast
1 cup (one 8-ounce can) Hunt's Tomato Sauce
1 teaspoon taco seasoning
3 cups (10 ounces) shredded loose packed frozen potatoes
10 ounces (one 16-ounce can) red kidney beans, rinsed and drained
1 (10¾-ounce) can Healthy Request Tomato Soup
½ cup chunky salsa (mild, medium, or hot)
1 teaspoon dried parsley flakes
¾ cup (3 ounces) shredded Kraft reduced-fat Cheddar cheese

Preheat oven to 350 degrees. Spray an 8-by-8-inch baking dish with olive oil–flavored cooking spray. In a large skillet sprayed with olive oil–flavored cooking spray, sauté onion and green pepper for 5 minutes. Stir in chicken, tomato sauce, and taco seasoning. Continue simmering for 2 to 3 minutes or until mixture is heated through. Spread mixture in prepared baking dish. Evenly layer potatoes and kidney beans over chicken mixture. In a small bowl, combine tomato soup, salsa, and parsley flakes. Spoon soup mixture evenly over top. Bake for 30 minutes. Sprinkle Cheddar cheese evenly over top. Continue baking for 10 to 15 minutes or until cheese melts. Place baking dish on a wire rack and let set for 5 minutes. Cut into 6 servings.

HINT: Mr. Dell's frozen shredded potatoes are a good choice. Raw shredded potatoes may be used in place of frozen potatoes.

Each serving equals:

HE: 2½ Protein • 1 Vegetable • ⅓ Bread • ¼ Slider • 10 Optional Calories

213 Calories • 5 gm Fat • 17 gm Protein • 25 gm Carbohydrate • 646 mg Sodium • 152 mg Calcium • 5 gm Fiber

DIABETIC: 2 Meat • 1½ Starch • 1 Vegetable

Chicken and Macaroni Stew

My kids always loved the kind of stove-top stews that filled the house with lip-smacking aromas like this one does! The ingredients are simple, the cooking time is short, but the payoff in flavor and soul satisfaction is off the charts!

❂   Serves 4 (1¾ cup)

> 1½ cups (8 ounces) diced cooked chicken breast
>
> ¼ cup chopped onion
>
> 1 cup (two 2.5-ounce jars) sliced mushrooms, drained
>
> 2 cups shredded carrots
>
> 2 cups frozen cut green beans, thawed
>
> 1¾ cups (one 14½-ounce can) stewed tomatoes, undrained
>
> 1½ cups water
>
> 1⅓ cups (3 ounces) uncooked elbow macaroni
>
> ½ teaspoon black pepper
>
> 2 teaspoons Italian seasoning

In a large skillet sprayed with olive oil–flavored cooking spray, sauté chicken and onion for 5 minutes. Add mushrooms, carrots, green beans, undrained stewed tomatoes, and water. Mix well to combine. Bring mixture to a boil. Stir in uncooked macaroni, black pepper, and Italian seasoning. Lower heat, cover, and simmer for 20 minutes or until macaroni is tender, stirring occasionally.

HINT: Thaw green beans by placing in a colander and rinsing under hot water for one minute.

Each serving equals:

HE: 3½ Vegetable • 2 Protein • 1 Bread

279 Calories • 3 gm Fat • 26 gm Protein • 37 gm Carbohydrate • 563 mg Sodium • 115 mg Calcium • 5 gm Fiber

DIABETIC: 3 Vegetable • 2 Meat • 1½ Starch

Chicken Cola Bake

You might think I let the kids take over the kitchen when I was creating this slightly strange but savory sauced chicken dish! I promise you, it sounds odd but the blend of diet cola, cream soup, and spices is simply marvelous! In fact, most people you serve it to will never believe there's cola in the gravy. . . .

● Serves 4

> 16 ounces skinned and boned uncooked chicken breasts, cut into 4 pieces
> ½ cup Diet Pepsi or Diet Coke
> 1 (10¾-ounce) can Healthy Request Cream of Mushroom Soup
> 2 tablespoons dried onion flakes
> 1 tablespoon dried parsley flakes

Preheat oven to 350 degrees. Place chicken pieces in an 8-by-8-inch baking dish. In a medium bowl, combine diet cola, mushroom soup, onion flakes, and parsley flakes using a wire whisk. Pour soup mixture over chicken pieces. Cover and bake for 1 to 1½ hours, or until chicken is tender.

HINT: This "gravy" (the soup mixture without the chicken) is also delicious over rice or mashed potatoes.

Each serving equals:

HE: 3 Protein • ½ Slider • 10 Optional Calories

163 Calories • 3 gm Fat • 27 gm Protein • 7 gm Carbohydrate •
534 mg Sodium • 67 mg Calcium • 0 gm Fiber

DIABETIC: 3 Meat • ½ Starch/Carbohydrate

Baked Chicken in Sweet and Sour Sauce

Some like it sweet, and some like it tangy, but everyone who taste-tested this recipe gave it a perfect "10"! If you've always relished "sweet and sour" dishes but never tried one at home, give this scrumptious blend a whirl.   ♥   Serves 4

16 ounces skinned and boned uncooked chicken breasts, cut into 4 pieces

1 tablespoon dried onion flakes

⅓ cup Kraft Fat Free French Dressing

¼ cup grape spreadable fruit

1 teaspoon dried parsley flakes

Preheat oven to 325 degrees. Spray an 8-by-8-inch baking dish with butter-flavored cooking spray. Evenly arrange chicken pieces in prepared baking dish. In a small bowl, combine onion flakes, French dressing, spreadable fruit, and parsley flakes. Evenly spoon mixture over chicken. Cover and bake for 30 minutes. Uncover and continue baking for 20 minutes or until chicken is tender. When serving, evenly spoon sauce over chicken pieces.

Each serving equals:

HE: 3 Protein • 1 Fruit • ¼ Slider • 13 Optional Calories

185 Calories • 1 gm Fat • 26 gm Protein • 18 gm Carbohydrate • 234 mg Sodium • 19 mg Calcium • 0 gm Fiber

DIABETIC: 3 Meat • 1 Fruit

Southern Delight ChickenBreasts

Oh, no, JoAnna's cooking with soda again! Yes, I figured if chicken and cola went together like old friends, why not glaze a Southern-style chicken dish with this delightful combination? I bet your family will agree it's "finger-lickin'" good!

● Serves 4

2 teaspoons reduced-calorie margarine
16 ounces skinless and boned uncooked chicken breasts, cut into 4 pieces
½ cup Diet 7UP☆
¼ cup apricot spreadable fruit
2 tablespoons (½ ounce) chopped pecans

In a large skillet, melt margarine. Arrange chicken pieces in skillet and brown for 4 to 5 minutes on each side. Reserve 1 tablespoon Diet 7UP. Pour remaining Diet 7UP over chicken. Lower heat, cover, and simmer for 15 minutes or until chicken is tender. In a small bowl, combine remaining 1 tablespoon Diet 7UP, spreadable fruit, and pecans. Evenly drizzle mixture over chicken pieces. Continue to simmer for 1 to 2 minutes or until sauce is heated through. When serving, drizzle sauce evenly over chicken pieces.

Each serving equals:

HE: 3 Protein • 1 Fruit • ¾ Fat

184 Calories • 4 gm Fat • 26 gm Protein • 11 gm Carbohydrate • 83 mg Sodium • 14 mg Calcium • 0 gm Fiber

DIABETIC: 3 Meat • 1 Fruit • 1 Fat

Easy "Fried" Chicken

Here's a wonderful example of the magic of cooking sprays. I know it seems almost impossible that skinned chicken breasts could taste anything like "real" fried chicken, but give this approach a chance before you decide. The spices play an active role, of course, but it's the right amount of heat, coupled with the spray oil, that makes it work.   ☻   Serves 4

16 ounces skinned and boned chicken breast, cut into 4 pieces
1 teaspoon lemon pepper
½ teaspoon paprika

Evenly sprinkle chicken pieces with lemon pepper and paprika. Place chicken pieces in a large skillet sprayed with butter-flavored cooking spray. Cover, and "fry" over medium heat for 20 to 25 minutes or until brown and well done, turning chicken occasionally.

HINT: Add a little water, if necessary, toward the end of the "frying" time.

Each serving equals:

HE: 3 Protein

176 Calories • 4 gm Fat • 35 gm Protein • 0 gm Carbohydrate •
84 mg Sodium • 17 mg Calcium • 0 gm Fiber

DIABETIC: 3 Meat

Western Hoedown Burgers

Back in pioneer times, hardworking men and women used to get together for lively dances and dinners. These "hoedowns" were energetic and festive occasions, and the food served was plentiful but definitely "down-home." The next time you're heading out for some Texas two-stepping with friends, why not have them over for a quick dinner before the dancing? ○ Serves 8

16 ounces ground 90% lean turkey or beef
1 cup chopped onion
½ cup chopped green bell pepper
10 ounces (one 16-ounce can) pinto beans, rinsed and drained
1¾ cups (one 15-ounce can) Hunt's Tomato Sauce
2 teaspoons chili seasoning
⅛ teaspoon black pepper
2 tablespoons Hormel Bacon Bits
½ cup + 1 tablespoon (2¼ ounces) shredded Kraft reduced-fat Cheddar cheese
4 English muffins, split and toasted

In a large skillet sprayed with butter-flavored cooking spray, brown meat, onion, and green pepper. Stir in pinto beans, tomato sauce, chili seasoning, and black pepper. Add bacon bits and Cheddar cheese. Mix well to combine. Lower heat and simmer for 10 minutes or until cheese melts and mixture is heated through, stirring often. For each serving, place an English muffin half on a plate and spoon about ½ cup meat mixture over top.

Each serving equals:

HE: 2½ Protein • 1¼ Vegetable • 1 Bread • 6 Optional Calories

251 Calories • 7 gm Fat • 19 gm Protein • 28 gm Carbohydrate • 640 mg Sodium • 131 mg Calcium • 5 gm Fiber

DIABETIC: 2 Meat • 1 Vegetable • 1 Starch

Campfire Chili Burgers

Here's a clever way to stretch your meat budget a little—and to "stuff" lots of tangy flavor into an American classic! If you've never considered serving chili on a bun, keep this recipe handy for your next family camping trip.   ◐   Serves 6

16 ounces ground 90% lean turkey or beef
½ cup chopped onion
½ cup chunky salsa (mild, medium, or hot)
6 ounces (one 8-ounce can) kidney beans, rinsed and drained
¼ cup Heinz Light Harvest Ketchup or any reduced-sodium ketchup
1 teaspoon chili seasoning
6 reduced-calorie hamburger buns

In a large skillet sprayed with butter-flavored cooking spray, brown meat and onion. Add salsa, kidney beans, ketchup, and chili seasoning. Mix well to combine. Lower heat and simmer for 10 minutes, stirring occasionally. For each sandwich, spoon a full ⅓ cup mixture between a bun.

Each serving equals:

HE: 2½ Protein • 1 Bread • ⅓ Vegetable • 17 Optional Calories

223 Calories • 7 gm Fat • 17 gm Protein • 23 gm Carbohydrate • 307 mg Sodium • 40 mg Calcium • 3 gm Fiber

DIABETIC: 2 Meat • 1 Starch • ½ Vegetable

Grande Fiesta Burgers

Spicy, crunchy, tangy—and served up fast! This is a great budget meal that doesn't taste like you're watching the purse strings. The secret—abundant flavor makes a meal taste like a banquet! ☻ Serves 6

16 ounces ground 90% lean turkey or beef
½ cup chopped onion
½ cup chopped green bell pepper
1 (10¾-ounce) can Healthy Request Tomato Soup
2 teaspoons chili seasoning
1 teaspoon dried parsley flakes
¼ teaspoon black pepper
6 reduced-calorie hamburger buns

In a large skillet sprayed with olive oil–flavored cooking spray, brown meat, onion, and green pepper. Add tomato soup, chili seasoning, parsley flakes, and black pepper. Mix well to combine. Lower heat and simmer for 10 minutes, stirring occasionally. For each serving, spoon a full ⅓ cup meat mixture between a bun.

Each serving equals:

HE: 2 Protein • 1 Bread • ⅓ Vegetable • ¼ Slider • 10 Optional Calories

224 Calories • 8 gm Fat • 16 gm Protein • 22 gm Carbohydrate • 385 mg Sodium • 11 mg Calcium • 2 gm Fiber

DIABETIC: 2 Meat • 1½ Starch

Skillet Pizza Burgers

Pizza burgers were always a favorite of my boys when they were growing up, so when I asked them to taste this healthy version of their childhood treat, I held my breath for a moment. Phew! They absolutely loved it—and I bet your kids will too! ❂   Serves 6

16 ounces ground 90% lean turkey or beef

6 tablespoons (1½ ounces) dried fine bread crumbs

½ cup finely chopped onion

⅛ teaspoon black pepper

1½ teaspoons Italian seasoning

¼ cup Heinz Light Harvest Ketchup or any reduced-sodium ketchup

3 (¾-ounce) slices Kraft reduced-fat mozzarella cheese

6 lettuce leaves

1 medium-sized fresh tomato, cut into 6 slices

6 reduced-calorie hamburger buns

In a large bowl, combine meat, bread crumbs, onion, black pepper, Italian seasoning, and ketchup. Mix well to combine. Using a ⅓ cup measuring cup as a guide, form into 6 patties. Arrange patties in a large skillet sprayed with olive oil–flavored cooking spray. Brown for 4 to 5 minutes on each side or until cooked to desired doneness. Cut mozzarella cheese slices in half. Place 1 piece of cheese on each patty and continue cooking for 1 minute or until cheese melts. For each sandwich, place a lettuce leaf and a tomato slice on bun bottom, arrange meat patty over tomato, and place bun top over meat.

Each serving equals:

HE: 2½ Protein • 1⅓ Bread • ⅓ Vegetable • 10 Optional Calories

257 Calories • 9 gm Fat • 20 gm Protein • 24 gm Carbohydrate • 359 mg Sodium • 91 mg Calcium • 2 gm Fiber

DIABETIC: 2 Meat • 1½ Starch/Carbohydrate

Southwestern Meat Loaf

As Cliff and I have driven all across America to share my Healthy Exchanges recipes, we've thoroughly enjoyed tasting regional variations of traditional recipes. When I stirred cornmeal instead of bread crumbs into this meat loaf mix, it brought back tasty memories of our time in the Southwest.   ☻   Serves 6

16 ounces ground 90% lean turkey or beef
¼ cup (1½ ounces) yellow cornmeal
½ cup finely chopped onion
½ cup finely chopped green bell pepper
1¾ cups (one 15-ounce can) Hunt's Chunky Tomato Sauce☆
1½ teaspoons chili seasoning
1 tablespoon Brown Sugar Twin
1 teaspoon dried parsley flakes
¼ teaspoon dried minced garlic

Preheat oven to 350 degrees. Spray an 8-by-8-inch baking dish with olive oil–flavored cooking spray. In a large bowl, combine meat, cornmeal, onion, green pepper, ¼ cup tomato sauce, and chili seasoning. Mix well to combine. Pat mixture into prepared baking dish. In a small bowl, combine remaining 1½ cups tomato sauce, Brown Sugar Twin, parsley flakes, and garlic. Pour mixture evenly over meat loaf. Bake for 50 to 55 minutes. Place baking dish on a wire rack and let set for 5 minutes. Cut into 6 servings.

Each serving equals:

HE: 2 Protein • 1½ Vegetable • ⅓ Bread • 1 Optional Calorie

154 Calories • 6 gm Fat • 15 gm Protein • 10 gm Carbohydrate • 539 mg Sodium • 5 mg Calcium • 2 gm Fiber

DIABETIC: 2 Meat • 1 Vegetable • ½ Starch

Budgetville Meat Loaf

Most of my life I've lived in "Budgetville," stretching limited dollars to feed my family. Even now, though it's just Cliff and me, I still tend to shop the sales and plan menus with an eye to economy. But with dishes like this appetizing meat loaf, frugal can still mean flavorful!   ❤   Serves 6

⅔ cup Carnation Nonfat Dry Milk Powder

¾ cup water

2 teaspoons dried parsley flakes

1 teaspoon lemon juice

2 tablespoons dried onion flakes

1 teaspoon prepared mustard

⅛ teaspoon dried minced garlic

16 ounces ground 90% lean turkey or beef

½ cup + 1 tablespoon dried fine bread crumbs

Preheat oven to 350 degrees. Spray a 9-by-5-inch loaf pan with butter-flavored cooking spray. In a large bowl, combine dry milk powder, water, parsley flakes, lemon juice, onion flakes, mustard, and garlic. Add meat and bread crumbs. Mix well to combine. Pat mixture into prepared pan. Bake for 1 hour. Place pan on a wire rack and let set for 5 minutes. Cut into 6 servings.

Each serving equals:

HE: 2 Protein • ½ Bread • ⅓ Skim Milk

175 Calories • 7 gm Fat • 17 gm Protein • 11 gm Carbohydrate • 193 mg Sodium • 113 mg Calcium • 0 gm Fiber

DIABETIC: 2 Meat • ½ Starch/Carbohydrate *or* 2 Meat • ½ Skim Milk

Mexican Tomato Meat Loaf Bake

Yes, I'm actually telling you that nacho chips can be part of a healthy lifestyle—isn't it amazing! As long you keep moderation as your watchword, you can treat your taste buds to such formerly forbidden foods. This spicy recipe won applause from Cliff, who loves Mexican food enough to eat it every day.

○ Serves 6

> 16 ounces ground 90% lean turkey or beef
> 1¾ cups (one 14½-ounce can) stewed tomatoes, coarsely chopped and undrained
> 2 tablespoons chili seasoning
> ½ cup (1½ ounces) crushed Doritos Reduced Fat Nacho Chips
> ¾ cup chopped green bell pepper
> ½ cup chopped onion
> ⅓ cup (1½ ounces) shredded Kraft reduced-fat Cheddar cheese

Preheat oven to 375 degrees. Spray an 8-by-8-inch baking dish with butter-flavored cooking spray. In a medium bowl, combine meat, undrained stewed tomatoes, chili seasoning, nacho chips, green pepper, and onion. Spread mixture into prepared baking dish. Bake for 40 to 45 minutes. Evenly sprinkle Cheddar cheese over top and continue baking for 5 minutes or until cheese melts. Place baking dish on a wire rack and let set for 5 minutes. Divide into 6 servings.

HINTS: Good served with 1 tablespoon Land O Lakes no-fat sour cream, but don't forget to count the few additional calories.

Each serving equals:

HE: 2⅓ Protein • 1 Vegetable • ⅓ Bread

207 Calories • 9 gm Fat • 17 gm Protein • 12 gm Carbohydrate • 394 mg Sodium • 92 mg Calcium • 1 gm Fiber

DIABETIC: 2 Meat • 1 Vegetable • ½ Starch

Nacho Squares

Here's another easy make-at-home Mexican dish that's a true man-pleaser! (I tested it on my truck drivin' man, and Cliff said, "Thumbs up!") I think the topping on these is so much tastier than the kind you get in restaurants, and without all that extra fat, there's just good-for-you goodness piled high!

● Serves 8

8 ounces ground 90% lean turkey or beef
1 cup chopped green bell pepper
½ cup chopped onion
1¾ cups (one 15-ounce can) Hunt's Chunky Tomato Sauce
6 ounces (one 8-ounce can) red kidney beans, drained and slightly mashed
1 tablespoon taco seasoning
1 (8-ounce) can Pillsbury Reduced Fat Crescent Rolls
⅔ cup (2¼ ounces) shredded Kraft reduced-fat Cheddar cheese

Preheat oven to 415 degrees. In a large skillet sprayed with olive oil–flavored cooking spray, brown meat, green pepper, and onion. Add tomato sauce, kidney beans, and taco seasoning. Mix well to combine. Lower heat and simmer, stirring occasionally. Meanwhile, pat rolls into an ungreased 10-by-15-inch baking sheet. Gently press dough to cover bottom of pan, being sure to seal perforations. Bake for 5 to 7 minutes or until lightly browned. Spread hot meat mixture over crust and continue baking for 10 minutes. Evenly sprinkle Cheddar cheese over top and continue baking 5 minutes or until cheese melts. Place baking sheet on a wire rack and let set for 5 minutes. Cut into 8 servings.

HINT: Do not use inexpensive rolls as they don't cover the pan properly.

Each serving equals:

HE: 1½ Protein • 1¼ Vegetable • 1 Bread

200 Calories • 8 gm Fat • 12 gm Protein • 20 gm Carbohydrate • 674 mg Sodium • 61 mg Calcium • 2 gm Fiber

DIABETIC: 1 Meat • 1 Vegetable • 1 Starch

Skillet Hash

It's not a bit fancy, but it sure is good—that's what everyone who sampled this hurry-up hash told me, and I agree! This is a great Sunday supper dish, and would even be a welcome treat at a weekend brunch, so give it a try soon!

○ Serves 4 (1 full cup)

1½ cups (8 ounces) diced cooked lean roast beef

3 full cups (16 ounces) finely chopped cooked potatoes

1 cup chopped onion

2 teaspoons dried parsley flakes

⅛ teaspoon black pepper

1 cup skim milk

In a medium bowl, combine beef, potatoes, onion, parsley flakes, and black pepper. In a medium skillet sprayed with butter-flavored cooking spray, spread mixture evenly over bottom. Cook over medium heat for 15 minutes, or until bottom browns, without stirring. Add skim milk. Mix well to combine. Lower heat, and simmer for 15 minutes or until most of the liquid is absorbed and potatoes are crisp.

Each serving equals:

HE: 2 Protein • 1 Bread • ½ Vegetable • ¼ Skim Milk

236 Calories • 4 gm Fat • 21 gm Protein • 29 gm Carbohydrate • 74 mg Sodium • 92 mg Calcium • 3 gm Fiber

DIABETIC: 2 Meat • 1½ Starch/Carbohydrate

Sweet-and-Sour Loose Meat Sandwiches

Loose meat sandwiches are distinctly an Iowa tradition, but I've been doing my part to spread the word around the country as I've traveled to spread the word about Healthy Exchanges. This sweet-and-sour version is especially flavorful and makes a great choice for a children's birthday party lunch. ☻ Serves 6

16 ounces ground 90% lean turkey or beef
1 cup chopped onion
1 cup chopped green bell pepper
1 cup (one 8-ounce can) Hunt's Tomato Sauce
1 tablespoon white vinegar
1/4 cup grape spreadable fruit
6 reduced-calorie hamburger buns

In a large skillet sprayed with butter-flavored cooking spray, brown meat, onion, and green pepper. Stir in tomato sauce, vinegar, and spreadable fruit. Mix well to combine. Lower heat, cover, and simmer for 10 minutes, stirring occasionally. For each serving, spoon about 1/3 cup meat mixture into a hamburger bun.

Each serving equals:

HE: 2 Protein • 1 1/3 Vegetable • 1 Bread • 2/3 Fruit

227 Calories • 7 gm Fat • 16 gm Protein • 25 gm Carbohydrate • 478 mg Sodium • 10 mg Calcium • 2 gm Fiber

DIABETIC: 2 Meat • 1 Vegetable • 1 Starch • 1 Fruit

Santa Fe Trail Meat Patties

Imagine what it must have been like to travel west via one of the great "trails" like the Santa Fe. . . . You're exhausted, you're dusty, and you're wondering if you'll ever get where you're going. Then you smell something utterly delicious, and you know it'll give you the strength to go on! (Well, it's fun to fantasize, but why not enjoy eating the real thing?)   ☻   Serves 6

16 ounces ground 90% lean turkey or beef
1 cup (1½ ounces) crushed cornflakes
1 cup frozen whole-kernel corn, thawed
1 cup chunky salsa, (mild, medium, or hot) ☆
2 tablespoons Heinz Light Harvest Ketchup or any reduced-sodium ketchup
⅛ teaspoon black pepper

In a large bowl, combine meat, cornflakes, corn, ¼ cup salsa, ketchup, and black pepper. Mix well to combine. Using a ½-cup measure as a guide, form mixture into 6 patties. Place patties in a large skillet sprayed with butter-flavored cooking spray. Brown patties for 6 to 8 minutes on each side or until cooked to desired doneness. When serving, top each patty with 2 tablespoons salsa.

HINT: Thaw corn by placing in a colander and rinsing under hot water for one minute.

Each serving equals:

HE: 2 Protein • ⅔ Bread • ⅓ Vegetable • 5 Optional Calories

154 Calories • 6 gm Fat • 14 gm Protein • 11 gm Carbohydrate • 263 mg Sodium • 41 mg Calcium • 1 gm Fiber

DIABETIC: 2 Meat • ½ Starch

Cabbage Meatloaf Patties

Are you one of those clever moms who manage to sneak vegetables into nearly every food on your kids' plates? I'd be happy to help! These tangy patties are delightfully appetizing, and great for a change from the same old burgers.

☻ Serves 6

16 ounces ground 90% lean turkey or beef
½ cup chopped onion
1½ cups shredded cabbage
1 cup cold cooked rice
1 (10¾-ounce) can Healthy Request Tomato Soup ☆
½ cup water
1 teaspoon dried parsley flakes

In a large bowl, combine meat, onion, cabbage, rice, and ¼ cup tomato soup. Mix well to combine. Using a ½-cup measure as a guide, form mixture into 6 patties. Place patties in a large skillet sprayed with butter-flavored cooking spray. Brown patties for 6 to 8 minutes on each side. Stir water and parsley flakes into remaining soup. Evenly spoon soup mixture over patties. Continue cooking for 6 minutes or until meat is cooked through. When serving, evenly spoon sauce over top of patties.

HINT: ⅔ cup uncooked rice usually cooks to about 1 cup.

Each serving equals:

HE: 2 Protein • ⅔ Vegetable • ⅓ Bread • ¼ Slider • 10 Optional Calories

167 Calories • 7 gm Fat • 14 gm Protein • 12 gm Carbohydrate • 229 mg Sodium • 19 mg Calcium • 1 gm Fiber

DIABETIC: 2 Meat • 1 Starch/Carbohydrate

Easy Pizza Meatloaf

Here's a delicious way to combine two of your family favorites in one savory dish! By flavoring a classic meatloaf with those ingredients that usually top your chosen pizza, you give your tastebuds an easy surprise. ☻ Serves 6

16 ounces ground 90% lean turkey or beef
6 tablespoons (1½ ounces) dried fine bread crumbs
½ cup finely chopped onion
½ cup finely chopped green bell pepper
½ cup (one 2.5-ounce jar) sliced mushrooms, drained
⅓ cup (1½ ounces) sliced ripe olives
1¾ cups (one 15-ounce can) Hunt's Tomato Sauce ☆
2 teaspoons Italian seasoning ☆
½ teaspoon pourable Sugar Twin
¾ cup (3 ounces) shredded Kraft reduced-fat mozzarella cheese

Place a small custard cup in center of a deep-dish 9-inch glass pie plate or use microwave ring mold. Spray pie plate with olive oil–flavored cooking spray. In a large bowl, combine meat, bread crumbs, onion, green pepper, mushrooms, olives, ½ cup tomato sauce, and 1 teaspoon Italian seasoning. Mix well to combine. Evenly spread meat mixture into pie plate. Stir remaining 1 teaspoon Italian seasoning and Sugar Twin into remaining tomato sauce. Spread sauce mixture evenly over meat mixture. Microwave on HIGH (100% power) for 10 minutes. Sprinkle mozzarella cheese evenly over top. Turn dish and continue microwaving on HIGH an additional 8 minutes. Place pie plate on a wire rack and let set for 5 minutes. Cut into 6 servings.

Each serving equals:

HE: 2⅔ Protein • 1⅔ Vegetable • ⅓ Bread • ¼ Fat

215 Calories • 9 gm Fat • 19 gm Protein • 12 gm Carbohydrate • 771 mg Sodium • 127 mg Calcium • 2 gm Fiber

DIABETIC: 2½ Meat • 2 Vegetable

Micro-Sausage Meatloaf

This recipe could lead you to sample a couple of firsts: your first meatloaf in the microwave (it works great!) and your first sausage-flavored meatloaf (unusual but oh-so-good!). And don't you just love a dish that is served in its baking dish?

◑ Serves 6

16 ounces ground 90% lean turkey or beef

½ cup + 1 tablespoon (2¼ ounces) dried fine bread crumbs

1 teaspoon poultry seasoning

¼ teaspoon ground sage

¼ teaspoon garlic powder

2 teaspoons dried onion flakes

⅛ teaspoon black pepper

1 cup (one 8-ounce can) Hunt's Tomato Sauce ☆

1 tablespoon Brown Sugar Twin

1 teaspoon dried parsley flakes

Place a 1-cup glass custard cup upside down in center of a 9-inch-deep glass pie plate or use a microwave ring mold. Spray pie plate with butter-flavored cooking spray. In a large bowl, combine meat, bread crumbs, poultry seasoning, sage, garlic powder, onion flakes, black pepper, and ¾ cup tomato sauce. Mix well to combine. Pat meat mixture evenly into prepared pie plate. In a small bowl, combine remaining ¼ cup tomato sauce, Brown Sugar Twin, and parsley flakes. Spread sauce mixture evenly over top of meatloaf mixture. Cover with waxed paper and microwave on ROAST (70% power) for 15 minutes, turning dish after 8 minutes. Place covered glass pie plate on a wire rack and let set for 5 minutes. Cut into 6 servings.

Each serving equals:

HE: 2 Protein • ⅔ Vegetable • ½ Bread • 1 Optional Calorie

163 Calories • 7 gm Fat • 15 gm Protein • 10 gm Carbohydrate • 399 mg Sodium • 29 mg Calcium • 1 gm Fiber

DIABETIC: 2 Meat • ½ Starch

Scalloped Grande Skillet Potatoes

I'm a big fan of skillet suppers, and not only because they leave you with just one pan to wash! This lip-smacking combo is perfect for a last-minute supper, and it's also a great choice for a holiday buffet. ☻ Serves 4 (1 cup)

> 8 ounces ground 97% lean turkey or beef
> ½ cup chopped onion
> 3 cups (10 ounces) shredded loose-packed frozen potatoes
> 1 cup (one 8-ounce can) whole-kernel corn, rinsed and drained
> ½ cup chunky salsa (mild, medium, or hot)
> 1 (10¾-ounce) can Healthy Request Tomato Soup
> 2 teaspoons dried parsley flakes
> ⅓ cup (1½ ounces) shredded Kraft reduced-fat Cheddar cheese

In a large skillet sprayed with olive oil–flavored cooking spray, brown meat and onion. Stir in potatoes, corn, salsa, tomato soup, and parsley flakes. Add Cheddar cheese. Mix well to combine. Lower heat and simmer for 15 minutes, stirring occasionally.

HINT: Mr. Dell's frozen shredded potatoes are a good choice or raw shredded potatoes may be used instead. If using raw, just be sure to bake for at least 15 minutes longer.

Each serving equals:

HE: 2 Protein • 1 Bread • ½ Vegetable • ½ Slider •
5 Optional Calories

264 Calories • 8 gm Fat • 16 gm Protein • 32 gm Carbohydrate •
486 mg Sodium • 126 mg Calcium • 3 gm Fiber

DIABETIC: 2 Meat • 1½ Starch • ½ Vegetable

Supper Time Pizza Casserole

If you've only been using your microwave to heat frozen dinners (or, admit it, to reheat cups of coffee), it's time to learn a few new lessons about what this handy appliance can do for you! This dish is so simple to prepare, your older kids could actually make it some night when you're late getting home.

🙂 Serves 4 (1 full cup)

> 8 ounces ground 90% lean turkey or beef
> ½ cup chopped onion
> ½ cup chopped green bell pepper
> ½ cup (one 2.5-ounce jar) sliced mushrooms, drained
> 1¾ cups (one 15-ounce can) Hunt's Tomato Sauce
> 1 teaspoon pizza or Italian seasoning
> 1 teaspoon pourable Sugar Twin
> 2 cups cooked noodles, rinsed and drained
> ¾ cup (3 ounces) shredded Kraft reduced-fat mozzarella cheese

Place meat in a plastic colander and place colander in a glass pie plate. Microwave on HIGH (100% power) for 4 to 5 minutes or until meat is browned, stirring after 2 minutes. In an 8-cup glass measuring bowl, combine browned meat, onion, green pepper, and mushrooms. Add tomato sauce, pizza seasoning, Sugar Twin, and noodles. Mix well to combine. Cover with waxed paper and microwave on HIGH for 10 minutes, stirring after 5 minutes. Stir in mozzarella cheese. Place bowl on a wire rack and let set for 5 minutes. Mix well again before serving.

HINT: 1¾ cups uncooked noodles usually cooks to about 2 cups.

Each serving equals:

HE: 2½ Protein • 2½ Vegetable • 1 Bread • 1 Optional Calorie

281 Calories • 9 gm Fat • 21 gm Protein • 29 gm Carbohydrate • 930 mg Sodium • 168 mg Calcium • 4 gm Fiber

DIABETIC: 2½ Vegetable • 2 Meat • 1 Starch

Layered Shepherd's Pie

Instead of a traditional shepherd's pie that sort of jumbles all the filling ingredients together before topping them with mashed potatoes, this recipe asks you to take a couple of minutes more to spread them out separately and let them bake together! The sour cream gives the potatoes a truly luscious taste.   ◐   Serves 6

> 8 ounces ground 90% lean turkey or beef
> ½ cup finely chopped onion
> ½ cup (one 2.5-ounce jar) sliced mushrooms, drained
> 2 cups (one 16-ounce can) cut green beans, rinsed and drained
> 1 (10¾-ounce) can Healthy Request Cream of Mushroom Soup
> ½ cup Land O Lakes no-fat sour cream ☆
> 2⅓ cups boiling water
> 2 cups (4½ ounces) instant potato flakes
> 1 teaspoon dried parsley flakes
> ¾ cup (3 ounces) shredded Kraft reduced-fat Cheddar cheese

Preheat oven to 375 degrees. Spray an 8-by-12-inch baking dish with butter-flavored cooking spray. In a large skillet sprayed with butter-flavored cooking spray, brown meat and onion. Spread meat mixture into prepared baking dish. Layer mushrooms and green beans over top. In a small bowl, combine mushroom soup and ¼ cup sour cream. Spoon soup mixture over green beans. In a medium saucepan, combine boiling water and potato flakes. Fold in remaining ¼ cup sour cream and parsley flakes. Spread potato mixture evenly over soup mixture. Evenly sprinkle Cheddar cheese over top. Bake for 20 to 25 minutes or until cheese melts and mixture is bubbly. Place baking dish on a wire rack and let set for 5 minutes. Divide into 6 servings.

Each serving equals:

HE: 1⅔ Protein • 1 Bread • 1 Vegetable • ½ Slider •
8 Optional Calories

211 Calories • 7 gm Fat • 13 gm Protein • 24 gm Carbohydrate •
454 mg Sodium • 169 mg Calcium • 2 gm Fiber

DIABETIC: 2 Meat • 1½ Starch/Carbohydrate • 1 Vegetable

Dinner Bell Skillet

Don't you wish that sometimes you could call the kids to dinner with a big old noisy dinner gong—anything to get their attention, right? Well, I'm happy to report that you won't need any sound effects to get them quickly to the table. The aromas this dish sends out while simmering on the stove should bring them there on the run!   ☻   Serves 4

8 ounces ground 90% lean turkey or beef
1½ cups (5 ounces) shredded loose-packed frozen potatoes
½ cup chopped onion
1 (10¾-ounce) can Healthy Request Cream of Mushroom Soup
⅓ cup (1½ ounces) shredded Kraft reduced-fat Cheddar cheese
½ cup skim milk
2 cups (one 16-ounce can) French-style green beans, rinsed and drained
½ cup (one 2.5-ounce jar) sliced mushrooms, drained

In a large skillet sprayed with butter-flavored cooking spray, brown meat, potatoes, and onion. Stir in mushroom soup, Cheddar cheese, and skim milk. Add green beans and mushrooms. Mix well to combine. Lower heat and simmer for 10 to 12 minutes or until mixture is heated through and cheese melts. Divide into 4 servings.

Each serving equals:

HE: 2 Protein • 1½ Vegetable • ¼ Bread • ½ Slider •
12 Optional Calories

216 Calories • 8 gm Fat • 16 gm Protein • 20 gm Carbohydrate •
543 mg Sodium • 181 mg Calcium • 3 gm Fiber

DIABETIC: 2 Meat • 1 Vegetable • 1 Starch

Man-Pleasin' Nacho Platter

It's not a mistake—you do get to enjoy *some* tortilla chips as part of this lip-smacking recipe! Here's a great way to work some Mexican microwave magic in minutes, and the finished product is meaty, cheesy, and oh-so-tasty!

◔ Serves 6

> 8 ounces ground 90% lean turkey or beef
>
> ½ cup chopped onion
>
> 10 ounces (one 16-ounce can) red kidney beans, rinsed and drained
>
> 1 cup chunky salsa (mild, medium, or hot)
>
> ¾ cup (3 ounces) shredded Kraft reduced-fat Cheddar cheese
>
> ⅓ cup (1½ ounces) sliced ripe olives
>
> ½ cup (1½ ounces) crushed Doritos Reduced Fat Tortilla Chips

Place meat and onion in a plastic colander and place colander in a glass pie plate. Cover and microwave on HIGH (100% power) for 4 to 5 minutes, stirring after 3 minutes. Break meat into small pieces and spoon into a 9-inch microwavable pie plate. Add kidney beans and salsa. Mix well to combine. Cover and continue microwaving on HIGH for 4 to 5 minutes, stirring once. Let set for 2 to 3 minutes. Top with Cheddar cheese, olives, and Dorito chips. Divide into 6 servings.

Each serving equals:

HE: 2½ Protein • ½ Vegetable • ⅓ Bread • ¼ Fat

---

184 Calories • 8 gm Fat • 13 gm Protein • 15 gm Carbohydrate • 420 mg Sodium • 168 mg Calcium • 4 gm Fiber

---

DIABETIC: 2 Meat • 1 Starch

Tex-Mex Fiesta Casserole

One bite of this spicy blend, and you'll be ready to don your sombrero and serape and head for the border! When dinner has this much sunny flavor and lively color, you'll feel terrific no matter what kind of day you've had!

☻ Serves 6

16 ounces ground 90% lean turkey or beef

½ teaspoon dried minced garlic

½ cup diced onion

½ cup diced green bell pepper

½ cup chunky salsa (mild, medium, or hot)

2 teaspoons chili seasoning

1¾ cups (one 15-ounce can) Hunt's Tomato Sauce

¼ cup Heinz Light Harvest Ketchup or any reduced-sodium ketchup

1 cup frozen whole-kernel corn, thawed

2 cups hot cooked rice

¾ cup (3 ounces) shredded Kraft reduced-fat Cheddar cheese ☆

Preheat oven to 375 degrees. Spray an 8-by-8-inch baking dish with olive oil–flavored cooking spray. In a large skillet sprayed with olive oil–flavored cooking spray, brown meat, garlic, onion, and green pepper. Add salsa, chili seasoning, tomato sauce, and ketchup. Mix well to combine. Stir in corn, rice, and ¼ cup Cheddar cheese. Pour mixture into prepared baking dish. Sprinkle remaining ½ cup Cheddar cheese evenly over top. Bake for 20 minutes or until cheese melts. Place baking dish on a wire rack and let set for 5 minutes. Divide into 6 servings.

HINTS: 1. Thaw corn by placing in a colander and rinsing under hot water for one minute.

2. 1⅓ cups uncooked rice usually cooks to about 2 cups.

Each serving equals:

HE: 2⅔ Protein • 1⅔ Vegetable • 1 Bread • 10 Optional Calories

260 Calories • 8 gm Fat • 20 gm Protein • 27 gm Carbohydrate • 776 mg Sodium • 139 mg Calcium • 2 gm Fiber

DIABETIC: 2½ Meat • 2 Vegetable • 1 Starch

Southern BBQ Pork Tenders

Try these tangy-sweet pork sandwiches at your next family picnic, and I think you'll be thrilled at how popular they are! We liked apricot spreadable fruit best with this, but peach also works really well.   ☻   Serves 4

½ cup Healthy Choice barbecue sauce
2 tablespoons apricot spreadable fruit
4 (4-ounce) lean tenderized pork tenderloins or cutlets
4 reduced-calorie hamburger buns

In a small bowl, combine barbecue sauce and spreadable fruit. Set aside. In a large skillet sprayed with butter-flavored cooking spray, brown tenderloins for 5 minutes on each side. Drizzle sauce mixture evenly over browned tenderloins. Lower heat, cover, and simmer for 6 to 8 minutes. For each sandwich, place a tenderloin in a hamburger bun.

Each serving equals:

HE: 3 Protein • 1 Bread • ½ Fruit • ½ Slider • 10 Optional Calories

267 Calories • 7 gm Fat • 28 gm Protein • 23 gm Carbohydrate •
489 mg Sodium • 32 mg Calcium • 1 gm Fiber

DIABETIC: 3 Meat • 1½ Starch

Gypsy Pork Noodle Skillet

Here's an inventive skillet supper that is both spirited and satisfying! It's lusciously creamy, prepared in the style of those Bohemian noodle dishes, but I've whisked out the fat and kept all that flavor. ☻ Serves 4 (1¼ cups)

1 full cup (6 ounces) diced cooked lean roast pork
¼ cup chopped onion
1 (10¾-ounce) can Healthy Request Cream of Mushroom Soup
2 tablespoons skim milk
½ cup (one 2.5-ounce jar) sliced mushrooms, drained
1¾ cups (one 14½-ounce can) Frank's Bavarian-style sauerkraut, well drained
2 cups cooked noodles, rinsed and drained
¼ cup (one 2-ounce jar) chopped pimiento, drained

In a large skillet sprayed with butter-flavored cooking spray, brown meat and onion. Stir in mushroom soup, skim milk, and mushrooms. Add sauerkraut, noodles, and pimiento. Mix well to combine. Lower heat and simmer for 6 to 8 minutes or until mixture is heated through, stirring occasionally.

HINTS: 1. If you don't have leftovers, purchase a chunk of cooked lean roast pork from your local deli.
2. If you can't find Bavarian sauerkraut, use regular sauerkraut, ½ teaspoon caraway seeds, and 1 teaspoon Brown Sugar Twin.
3. 1¾ cups uncooked noodles usually cooks to about 2 cups.

Each serving equals:

HE: 1½ Protein • 1¼ Vegetable • 1 Bread • ½ Slider •
4 Optional Calories

261 Calories • 5 gm Fat • 17 gm Protein • 37 gm Carbohydrate •
920 mg Sodium • 92 mg Calcium • 4 gm Fiber

DIABETIC: 2 Starch • 1½ Meat • 1 Vegetable

Simmered Grande Pork Tenders

Cliff loves pork, and now that we can purchase lean cuts everywhere, I am serving it more often. This is a perfect example of simple preparation that makes for a spectacular meal. Served with a baked potato and some fresh green beans, this makes a terrific company dish.   ☻   Serves 4

4 (4-ounce) lean tenderized pork tenderloins or cutlets

1¾ cups (one 15-ounce can) Hunt's Chunky Tomato Sauce

½ cup (one 2.5-ounce jar) sliced mushrooms, undrained

1 teaspoon chili seasoning

¼ teaspoon dried minced garlic

1 tablespoon Brown Sugar Twin

In a large skillet sprayed with olive oil–flavored cooking spray, lightly brown meat on both sides. In a medium bowl, combine tomato sauce, undrained mushrooms, chili seasoning, garlic, and Brown Sugar Twin. Evenly pour mixture over browned meat. Lower heat, cover, and simmer for 20 minutes. Uncover and continue simmering for 10 minutes, or until meat is tender. When serving, evenly spoon sauce over meat.

Each serving equals:

HE: 3 Protein • 2 Vegetable • 1 Optional Calorie

182 Calories • 6 gm Fat • 26 gm Protein • 6 gm Carbohydrate • 858 mg Sodium • 26 mg Calcium • 2 gm Fiber

DIABETIC: 3 Meat • 2 Vegetable

Pork and Green Beans Supreme

This wonderfully creamy dish is a kind of pork stroganoff and tastes as if you really splurged—when you didn't have to! Some people recommend pounding the pork tenderloins to make them even more tender, but I don't find it necessary as long as you don't try to cook this dish too quickly.   ☻   Serves 6 (1 cup)

> 16 ounces lean pork tenderloin or steak, cut into 36 pieces
> 2 cups (one 16-ounce can) cut green beans, rinsed and drained
> 3 cups hot cooked noodles, rinsed and drained
> 1 (10¾-ounce) can Healthy Request Cream of Mushroom Soup
> ¼ cup skim milk
> ¼ cup Land O Lakes no-fat sour cream
> 1 teaspoon chili seasoning
> ¼ teaspoon black pepper

In a large skillet sprayed with butter-flavored cooking spray, brown meat. Stir in green beans and noodles. Add mushroom soup, skim milk, sour cream, chili seasoning, and black pepper. Mix well to combine. Lower heat, cover, and simmer for 10 minutes, or until mixture is heated through, stirring occasionally.

HINT: 2½ cups uncooked noodles usually cooks to about 3 cups.

Each serving equals:

> HE: 2 Protein • 1 Bread • ⅔ Vegetable • ½ Slider •
> 2 Optional Calories
> _____
> 254 Calories • 6 gm Fat • 22 gm Protein • 28 gm Carbohydrate •
> 275 mg Sodium • 94 mg Calcium • 2 gm Fiber
> _____
> DIABETIC: 2 Meat • 1½ Starch • ½ Vegetable

Roast Pork with Potato Dumplings and Kraut

I've become a real fan of making fast potato dumplings with instant potatoes—you save so much time and money, and they taste absolutely delicious! Spiced with my favorite sauerkraut, this pork dish is truly "budget gourmet"!

☻   Serves 4

2 cups (10 ounces) diced lean cooked roast pork

3½ cups (two 14½-ounce cans) Frank's Bavarian-style sauerkraut, drained

⅔ cup (2 ounces) instant potato flakes

¾ cup all-purpose flour

1½ teaspoons baking powder

2 teaspoons dried parsley flakes

⅓ cup Carnation Nonfat Dry Milk Powder

⅓ cup water

1 egg or equivalent in egg substitute

In a large saucepan, combine pork and sauerkraut. Cover and cook over medium heat for 10 minutes, stirring occasionally. Meanwhile, in a large bowl, combine potato flakes, flour, baking powder, parsley flakes, dry milk powder, water, and egg. Mix well to combine. Let set for 3 minutes. Using a ¼ cup measuring cup as a guide, drop batter into hot sauerkraut mixture to form 4 dumplings. Re-cover and continue cooking for 10 minutes, or until dumplings are firm. For each serving, place 1 dumpling on a plate and spoon about 1 full cup sauerkraut mixture over top.

HINT: If you can't find Bavarian sauerkraut, use regular sauerkraut, ½ teaspoon caraway seeds, and 1 teaspoon Brown Sugar Twin.

Each serving equals:

HE: 2¾ Protein (¼ limited) • 1¾ Vegetable • 1½ Bread •
¼ Skim Milk

285 Calories • 5 gm Fat • 24 gm Protein • 36 gm Carbohydrate •
1,650 mg Sodium • 263 mg Calcium • 7 gm Fiber

DIABETIC: 3 Meat • 2 Vegetable • 1½ Starch

Pork with Kidney Beans and Macaroni

If you've been looking to increase the amount of fiber in your diet, here's a dish you'll want to serve often! It's a tummy-warming treat the whole family will love, and you didn't have to go into debt to bring it to the table.

☻ Serves 4 (1½ cups)

10 ounces (one 16-ounce can) kidney beans, rinsed and drained
1 cup (5 ounces) diced lean cooked roast pork
½ cup chopped onion
1 cup shredded carrots
1¾ cups (one 15-ounce can) Hunt's Chunky Tomato Sauce
2 cups hot cooked shell macaroni, rinsed and drained
1 teaspoon dried parsley flakes

In a large skillet sprayed with butter-flavored cooking spray, combine kidney beans, pork, onion, carrots, and tomato sauce. Bring mixture to a boil. Lower heat, cover and simmer for 15 minutes or until carrots and onion are tender. Add macaroni and parsley flakes. Mix gently to combine. Continue simmering for 5 minutes, or until mixture is heated through, stirring occasionally.

HINT: 1⅓ cups uncooked macaroni usually cooks to about 2 cups.

Each serving equals:

HE: 2½ Protein • 2½ Vegetable • 1 Bread

242 Calories • 2 gm Fat • 15 gm Protein • 41 gm Carbohydrate • 1,079 mg Sodium • 37 mg Calcium • 8 gm Fiber

DIABETIC: 2 Meat • 2 Vegetable • 2 Starch

Harvest Time Pork Casserole

Here's a dish so gorgeously golden, you'll be tempted to dig right in instead of waiting a few minutes for it to set! As the creamy, cheesy sauce bubbles away in your oven, don't be surprised to find everyone already at the table before dinner is announced.   ❤   Serves 4

> 2 cups hot cooked elbow macaroni, rinsed and drained
> 2 cups (one 16-ounce can) cut green beans, rinsed and drained
> 1/4 cup finely chopped onion
> 1 3/4 cups (one 14 1/2-ounce can) Frank's Bavarian-style sauerkraut, drained
> 1 1/2 cups (8 ounces) diced lean cooked roast pork
> 1 (10 3/4-ounce) can Healthy Request Cream of Mushroom Soup
> 1/4 cup skim milk
> 4 (3/4-ounce) slices Kraft reduced-fat Swiss cheese

Preheat oven to 350 degrees. Spray an 8-by-8-inch baking dish with butter-flavored cooking spray. In a large bowl, combine macaroni, green beans, onion, sauerkraut, and roast pork. Add mushroom soup and skim milk. Mix well to combine. Spread mixture into prepared baking dish. Bake for 30 minutes. Evenly arrange Swiss cheese slices over top. Continue baking for 10 minutes or until cheese melts. Place baking dish on a wire rack and let set for 5 minutes. Divide into 4 servings.

HINT: If you can't find Bavarian sauerkraut, use regular sauerkraut, 1/2 teaspoon caraway seeds, and 1 teaspoon Brown Sugar Twin.

Each serving equals:

HE: 3 Protein • 2 Vegetable • 1 Bread • 1/2 Slider •
7 Optional Calories

298 Calories • 6 gm Fat • 25 gm Protein • 36 gm Carbohydrate •
1,085 mg Sodium • 340 mg Calcium • 4 gm Fiber

DIABETIC: 3 Meat • 2 Vegetable • 1 1/2 Starch

Celery and Pork Bake

This is another man-pleasing dish that the whole family will gobble up with enthusiasm! It's hearty in flavor but light on the calories and fat. Best of all, it will fill your tummy and win your heart. ❤ Serves 4

1½ cups (8 ounces) diced cooked lean roast pork
1½ cups sliced celery
½ cup chopped onion
1 cup (one 8-ounce can) Hunt's Tomato Sauce
½ cup water
1 teaspoon ground chili seasoning
1½ cups hot cooked rice
1 (10¾-ounce can) Healthy Request Cream of Celery or Mushroom Soup
1 teaspoon dried parsley flakes
⅓ cup (1½ ounces) shredded Kraft reduced-fat Cheddar cheese

Preheat oven to 375 degrees. Spray an 8-by-8-inch baking dish with butter-flavored cooking spray. In a large skillet sprayed with butter-flavored cooking spray, sauté pork, celery, and onion for 5 minutes. Stir in tomato sauce, water, and chili seasoning. Add rice. Mix well to combine. Spread mixture into prepared baking dish. In a small bowl, combine celery soup, parsley flakes, and Cheddar cheese. Evenly spread soup mixture over top of rice mixture. Bake for 20 to 25 minutes. Place baking dish on a wire rack and let set for 5 minutes. Divide into 4 servings.

HINTS: 1. If you don't have leftovers, purchase a chunk of cooked lean roast pork from your local deli.
2. 1 cup uncooked rice usually cooks to about 1½ cups.

Each serving equals:

HE: 2¾ Vegetable • 2 Protein • ¾ Bread • ½ Slider •
1 Optional Calorie

234 Calories • 6 gm Fat • 19 gm Protein • 26 gm Carbohydrate •
916 mg Sodium • 174 mg Calcium • 3 gm Fiber

DIABETIC: 2 Vegetable • 2 Meat • 1 Starch

Hungarian Noodles and Peas with Ham

What a great choice for one of those odds-and-ends evenings, when you just can't decide what to serve! The ingredients are handy, there's almost no preparation, and it tastes as if you slaved over a hot stove all afternoon.

⚬ Serves 6 (1 cup)

¾ cup chopped onion

1 cup frozen peas, thawed

½ cup Land O Lakes no-fat sour cream

1 cup fat-free cottage cheese

¼ cup (¾ ounce) grated Kraft fat-free Parmesan cheese

1 teaspoon dried parsley flakes

⅛ teaspoon black pepper

1½ cups (9 ounces) diced Dubuque 97% fat-free ham or any extra-lean ham

2 cups warm cooked noodles, rinsed and drained

¼ teaspoon paprika

In a large skillet sprayed with butter-flavored cooking spray, sauté onion for about 5 minutes or until tender. Stir in peas. Add sour cream, cottage cheese, Parmesan cheese, parsley flakes, and black pepper. Mix well to combine. Stir in ham, noodles, and paprika. Lower heat and simmer for 5 minutes, stirring occasionally.

HINTS: 1. Thaw peas by placing in a colander and rinsing under hot water for one minute.
2. 1¾ cups uncooked noodles usually cooks to about 2 cups.

Each serving equals:

HE: 1½ Protein • 1 Bread • ¼ Vegetable • ¼ Slider

190 Calories • 2 gm Fat • 17 gm Protein • 26 gm Carbohydrate • 586 mg Sodium • 54 mg Calcium • 3 gm Fiber

DIABETIC: 1½ Meat • 1½ Starch

Apple-Raisin Ham Rolls

Are you one of those people who just love baked ham but tend to enjoy it only on special occasions? Here's a fresh idea for bringing that unique flavor to your table more often.　●　Serves 8

1 (8-ounce) can Pillsbury Reduced Fat Crescent Rolls
1 (6-ounce) package Oscar Mayer deli sliced 97% fat-free ham or any extra-lean thinly sliced ham
1 (4-serving) package JELL-O sugar-free vanilla cook-and-serve pudding mix
1¼ cups water
1 teaspoon apple pie spice
1 cup (2 small) cored, peeled, and finely chopped cooking apples
½ cup raisins

Preheat oven to 375 degrees. Unroll crescent rolls and separate dough into 8 triangles. Separate ham slices into 8 piles. Fold each pile of ham in half and place on large end of roll triangles. Roll each triangle up and place on an ungreased baking sheet. Bake for 10 to 15 minutes or until golden brown. Meanwhile, in a medium saucepan, combine dry pudding mix, water, and apple pie spice. Stir in apples and raisins. Cook over medium heat until mixture thickens and starts to boil, stirring often. Remove from heat. For each serving, place 1 ham crescent on a plate and spoon about 3 tablespoons warm sauce over top.

Each serving equals:

HE: 1 Bread • ¾ Fruit • ½ Protein • 10 Optional Calories
___
165 Calories • 5 gm Fat • 6 gm Protein • 24 gm Carbohydrate • 471 mg Sodium • 5 mg Calcium • 1 gm Fiber
___
DIABETIC: 1 Starch • 1 Fruit • ½ Meat • ½ Fat

Aloha Supper Skillet

Trust me when you read through the ingredients in this recipe, okay? I know that mixing up tomato soup with pineapple sounds a bit unusual, but you'll be delighted to discover how scrumptious a sauce it creates! Serve it with some tropical drinks topped with tiny umbrellas, and you'd almost believe you were wading at Waikiki. ☻ Serves 4 (1 cup)

> 1 full cup (6 ounces) diced Dubuque 97% fat-free ham, or any extra-lean ham
> ½ cup chopped onion
> ½ cup chopped green bell pepper
> 1 cup (one 8-ounce can) crushed pineapple, packed in fruit juice, undrained
> 1 (10¾-ounce) can Healthy Request Tomato Soup
> 2 cups hot cooked noodles, rinsed and drained

In a large skillet sprayed with butter-flavored cooking spray, sauté ham, onion, and green pepper for 5 minutes or until vegetables are tender. Add undrained pineapple and tomato soup. Mix well to combine. Stir in noodles. Lower heat and simmer for 10 minutes, stirring occasionally.

HINT: 1¾ cups uncooked noodles usually cooks to about 2 cups.

Each serving equals:

HE: 1 Bread • 1 Protein • ½ Fruit • ½ Vegetable • ½ Slider • 5 Optional Calories

203 Calories • 3 gm Fat • 11 gm Protein • 33 gm Carbohydrate • 367 mg Sodium • 32 mg Calcium • 2 gm Fiber

DIABETIC: 1½ Starch • 1 Meat • ½ Fruit • ½ Vegetable

Ham and Potato Skillet Hash

This savory ham hash is another terrific choice for brunch or Sunday supper. It's a favorite at our house because of the green beans (Cliff's best-loved veggie), but it's high on my list, too, because it's so creamy and rich!

○ Serves 4 (1 full cup)

1½ cups (9 ounces) diced Dubuque 97% fat-free ham or any extra-lean ham
2 full cups (12 ounces) diced cooked potatoes
½ cup chopped onion
2 cups (one 16-ounce can) cut green beans, rinsed and drained
1 (10¾-ounce) can Healthy Request Cream of Mushroom Soup
1 teaspoon dried parsley flakes
⅛ teaspoon black pepper

In a large skillet sprayed with butter-flavored cooking spray, sauté ham, potatoes, and onion for 5 minutes. Add green beans, mushroom soup, parsley flakes, and black pepper. Mix well to combine. Lower heat and simmer for 10 minutes, or until mixture is heated through, stirring occasionally.

Each serving equals:

HE: 1½ Protein • 1¼ Vegetable • ¾ Bread • ½ Slider • 1 Optional Calorie

176 Calories • 4 gm Fat • 13 gm Protein • 22 gm Carbohydrate • 846 mg Sodium • 76 mg Calcium • 2 gm Fiber

DIABETIC: 2 Meat • 1 Vegetable • 1 Starch

Creamy Potatoes and Ham

Scalloped potatoes are a classic Midwestern delight, and recipes like this one are often handed down from mother to daughter over the years. This one doesn't have a long history the way some do, but it tastes like it does! ☻ Serves 6

> 4 cups (20 ounces) diced raw potatoes
>
> 1½ cups (9 ounces) diced Dubuque 97% fat-free ham or any extra-lean ham
>
> ¾ cup finely chopped onion
>
> ⅔ cup Carnation Nonfat Dry Milk Powder
>
> ½ cup water
>
> 1 (10¾-ounce) can Healthy Request Cream of Mushroom Soup
>
> 1 teaspoon prepared mustard
>
> 1 teaspoon dried parsley flakes
>
> ¼ teaspoon black pepper
>
> ¼ teaspoon paprika

Preheat oven to 375 degrees. Spray an 8-by-8-inch baking dish with butter-flavored cooking spray. Layer half of potatoes, ham, and onion in prepared baking dish. Repeat layers. In a small bowl, combine dry milk powder, water, mushroom soup, mustard, parsley flakes, and black pepper. Pour mixture evenly over potatoes. Evenly sprinkle paprika over top. Cover and bake for 45 minutes. Remove cover and continue baking for 30 minutes, or until potatoes are tender. Place baking dish on a wire rack and let set for 5 minutes. Cut into 6 servings.

Each serving equals:

HE: 1 Protein • ⅔ Bread • ⅓ Skim Milk • ¼ Vegetable • ¼ Slider • 8 Optional Calories

167 Calories • 3 gm Fat • 12 gm Protein • 23 gm Carbohydrate • 617 mg Sodium • 138 mg Calcium • 1 gm Fiber

DIABETIC: 1½ Starch/Carbohydrate • 1 Meat

Ham with Polynesian Peach Sauce

Ham is just the perfect meat for serving with a sweet sauce like this tropical pleaser! You don't have to hop a plane to feel the sultry warmth of the islands, just take a bite of this succulent delight—and you're there in spirit!

⏺ Serves 4

4 (3-ounce) slices Dubuque 97% fat-free ham or any extra-lean ham

¾ cup chopped green bell pepper

¼ cup chopped green onions

2 cups (one 16-ounce can) sliced peaches, packed in fruit juice, drained, and ⅓ cup liquid reserved

2 tablespoons Brown Sugar Twin

1 teaspoon cornstarch

1 tablespoon Heinz Light Harvest Ketchup or any reduced-sodium ketchup

1 teaspoon lemon juice

In a large skillet sprayed with butter-flavored cooking spray, lightly brown ham on both sides. Lower heat. Meanwhile, in a medium skillet sprayed with butter-flavored cooking spray, sauté green pepper and onion for 5 minutes or just until tender. In a small bowl, combine reserved peach liquid, Brown Sugar Twin, and cornstarch. Stir mixture into vegetables. Continue cooking until mixture thickens, stirring often. Add ketchup, lemon juice, and peaches. Mix gently to combine. Continue cooking for 5 minutes or until peaches are heated through, stirring occasionally. For each serving, place a slice of ham on a plate and spoon about 1/2 cup peach sauce over top.

HINT: A 3-ounce slice is usually about 1/3-inch thick.

Each serving equals:

HE: 2 Protein • 1 Fruit • ½ Vegetable • 10 Optional Calories

191 Calories • 3 gm Fat • 15 gm Protein • 26 gm Carbohydrate • 729 mg Sodium • 25 mg Calcium • 3 gm Fiber

DIABETIC: 2 Meat • 1 Fruit • ½ Starch/Carbohydrate

Holiday Ham with Cranberry Raisin Sauce

I think this would be just delightful as the centerpiece at a Christmas morning brunch! It's fantastically festive, it'll fill the house with a luscious fragrance while it's cooking, and even the color suggests it's time for your mouth to make merry!

○ Serves 4

4 (3-ounce) slices Dubuque 97% fat-free ham or any extra-lean ham

1 (4-serving) package JELL-O sugar-free vanilla cook-and-serve pudding mix

1 cup Ocean Spray reduced-calorie cranberry juice cocktail

¼ teaspoon ground cinnamon

6 tablespoons raisins

In a large skillet sprayed with butter-flavored cooking spray, lightly brown ham on both sides. Lower heat. Meanwhile, in a medium saucepan, combine dry pudding mix and Cranapple beverage drink. Stir in cinnamon and raisins. Cook over medium heat until mixture thickens and starts to boil, stirring constantly. Remove from heat. For each serving, place 1 slice of ham on a plate and spoon a full ¼ cup sauce over top.

HINT: A 3-ounce slice of ham is usually ⅓ inch thick.

Each serving equals:

HE: 2 Protein • ¾ Fruit • ¼ Slider

167 Calories • 3 gm Fat • 14 gm Protein • 21 gm Carbohydrate •
845 mg Sodium • 8 mg Calcium • 0 gm Fiber

DIABETIC: 2 Meat • 1 Fruit

Ham and Broccoli Garden Skillet

Lean ham has transformed our expectations about what meats we can enjoy as part of a healthy lifestyle. We used to think of ham as an occasional treat, but now it can be stirred into tasty everyday dishes like this smooth skillet supper that makes it a star!   ☻   Serves 4 (1 cup)

1 full cup (6 ounces) diced Dubuque 97% fat-free or any extra-lean ham
½ cup chopped onion
1 cup finely shredded carrots
1 cup (one 8-ounce can) cream-style corn
1 (10¾-ounce) can Healthy Request Cream of Broccoli Soup
1½ cups hot cooked noodles, rinsed and drained
¼ teaspoon black pepper
1 teaspoon dried parsley flakes

In a large skillet sprayed with butter-flavored cooking spray, sauté ham, onion, and carrots for about 5 minutes. Stir in corn and broccoli soup. Add noodles, black pepper, and parsley flakes. Mix well to combine. Lower heat and simmer for 10 minutes, or until mixture is heated through, stirring occasionally.

HINT: 1¼ cups uncooked noodles usually cooks to about 1½ cups.

Each serving equals:

HE: 1¼ Bread • 1 Protein • ¾ Vegetable • ½ Slider •
1 Optional Calorie

259 Calories • 7 gm Fat • 14 gm Protein • 35 gm Carbohydrate •
796 mg Sodium • 103 mg Calcium • 3 gm Fiber

DIABETIC: 2 Starch/Carbohydrate • 1 Meat • 1 Fat • ½ Vegetable

Mexicali Ham Bake

You'll never believe just how delicious this spicy-tangy blend of flavors will be until you cut into its crust after baking—and the aroma fills your kitchen! This freezes beautifully, so even if you live alone or cook just for two, the extra servings will heat up whenever you want to serve them. ☻ Serves 4

¾ cup Bisquick Reduced Fat Baking Mix
¾ cup chunky salsa (mild, medium, or hot)
¼ cup chopped onion
1 full cup (6 ounces) diced Dubuque 97% fat-free ham or any extra-lean ham
2 cups (one 16-ounce can) cut green beans, rinsed and drained
1 teaspoon dried parsley flakes
¾ cup (3 ounces) shredded Kraft reduced-fat Cheddar cheese

Preheat oven to 350 degrees. Spray an 8-by-8-inch baking dish with butter-flavored cooking spray. In a medium bowl, combine baking mix and salsa. Add onion, ham, green beans, and parsley flakes. Mix well to combine. Spread mixture into prepared baking dish. Evenly sprinkle Cheddar cheese over top. Bake for 45 to 50 minutes. Place baking dish on a wire rack and let set for 5 minutes. Cut into 4 servings.

Each serving equals:

HE: 2½ Vegetable • 2 Protein • 1 Bread

211 Calories • 7 gm Fat • 15 gm Protein • 22 gm Carbohydrate • 968 mg Sodium • 270 mg Calcium • 1 gm Fiber

DIABETIC: 2 Vegetable • 2 Meat • 1 Starch

Brunch Cornbread-Ham Casserole

What could be more cozy than sitting down to brunch with friends and serving up this scrumptious baked dish? The ingredients are somewhat unusual, it's true, but combining them is the key to a mouthwatering meal not soon forgotten!

♥ Serves 4

½ cup (3 ounces) yellow cornmeal

1 teaspoon baking powder

½ cup Yoplait plain fat-free yogurt

⅓ cup Kraft fat-free mayonnaise

¼ cup Cary's Sugar Free Maple Syrup

¾ cup (3 ounces) grated Kraft reduced-fat Cheddar cheese

1 full cup (6 ounces) diced Dubuque 97% fat-free ham or any extra-lean ham

2 cups (one 16-ounce can) cut green beans, rinsed and drained

Preheat oven to 400 degrees. Spray an 8-by-8-inch baking dish with butter-flavored cooking spray. In a medium bowl, combine cornmeal and baking powder. Stir in yogurt, mayonnaise, and maple syrup. Add Cheddar cheese, ham, and green beans. Mix well to combine. Pour mixture into prepared baking dish. Bake for 30 to 40 minutes or until lightly browned. Place baking dish on a wire rack and let set for 5 minutes. Cut into 4 pieces.

HINT: Good served with additional Cary's Sugar Free Maple Syrup drizzled on top, but don't forget to count the few additional calories.

Each serving equals:

HE: 2 Protein • 1 Bread • 1 Vegetable • ½ Slider •
12 Optional Calories

244 Calories • 8 gm Fat • 17 gm Protein • 26 gm Carbohydrate •
870 mg Sodium • 308 mg Calcium • 2 gm Fiber

DIABETIC: 2 Meats • 1½ Starch • 1 Vegetable

Swiss Ham and Biscuit Bake

Here's another truly delightful entree that makes lunch something luscious and brunch better than you dreamed! It's crusty and creamy, and surprisingly easy to prepare, so instead of serving up the same old ham and Swiss on rye, mix up something special that really feeds the soul! ☻ Serves 4

> 1 full cup (6 ounces) diced Dubuque 97% fat-free ham or any extra-lean ham
>
> ½ cup frozen peas, thawed
>
> ½ cup (one 2.5-ounce jar) sliced mushrooms, undrained
>
> 1 (10¾-ounce) can Healthy Request Cream of Celery Soup
>
> ⅔ cup Carnation Nonfat Dry Milk Powder
>
> 1¼ cups water
>
> ¾ cup Bisquick Reduced Fat Baking Mix
>
> 1 teaspoon dried parsley flakes
>
> 2 (¾-ounce) slices Kraft reduced-fat Swiss cheese, shredded
>
> 1 teaspoon prepared mustard

Preheat oven to 400 degrees. Spray an 8-by-8-inch baking dish with butter-flavored cooking spray. In a large skillet, sprayed with butter-flavored cooking spray, combine ham, peas, undrained mushrooms, and celery soup. Cook over medium heat for 5 minutes, stirring occasionally. Meanwhile in a small bowl, combine dry milk powder and water. Pour ¾ cup of milk mixture into skillet with ham. Mix well to combine. Lower heat and simmer while preparing biscuits. In a medium bowl, combine baking mix, parsley flakes, and Swiss cheese. Stir in remaining ½ cup milk mixture and mustard. Mix just to combine. Pour ham mixture into prepared baking dish. Using a large tablespoon as a guide, evenly drop batter onto ham mixture to form 4 biscuits. Bake for 15 to 18 minutes. Place baking dish on a wire rack and let set for 5 minutes. Divide into 4 servings.

HINT: Thaw peas by placing in a colander and rinsing under hot water for one minute.

Each serving equals:

HE: 1½ Protein • 1¼ Bread • ½ Skim Milk • ¼ Vegetable • ½ Slider • 1 Optional Calorie

254 Calories • 6 gm Fat • 17 gm Protein • 33 gm Carbohydrate • 1,169 mg Sodium • 283 mg Calcium • 2 gm Fiber

DIABETIC: 2 Starch/Carbohydrate • 1 Meat

Ham 'n' Tortilla Roll-Ups

Perfect for lunch on the run, these handy "wrapped" sandwiches will surprise you! Mixing cream cheese and salsa may seem an unusual choice, but when that tangy blends "hugs" the sliced ham, you'll think it's gotta be love!   ☻   Serves 4

¼ cup (2 ounces) Philadelphia fat-free cream cheese

½ cup chunky salsa (mild, medium, or hot)

4 (6-inch) flour tortillas

1 cup (6 ounces) Healthy Choice deli sliced 97% fat-free ham or any extra-lean ham

½ cup finely shredded lettuce

In a small bowl, stir cream cheese with a spoon until soft. Add salsa. Mix well to combine. Spread about 3 tablespoons cream cheese mixture over each tortilla. Evenly divide ham slices and arrange over tortillas. Sprinkle 2 tablespoons lettuce over top of each. Roll up and wrap each tightly in aluminum foil. Refrigerate for at least 30 minutes.

Each serving equals:

HE: 1¼ Protein • 1 Bread • ½ Vegetable

170 Calories • 6 gm Fat • 12 gm Protein • 17 gm Carbohydrate • 938 mg Sodium • 51 mg Calcium • 0 gm Fiber

DIABETIC: 1 Meat • 1 Starch • 1 Vegetable

South Seas Ham Patties

Here's another quick trip to the tropics that may just shock you out of your shoes! These delectably appetizing patties are sweet and tangy—a splendid change from the same old burgers, don't you think? ☻ Serves 2

> 1 cup (one 8-ounce can) crushed pineapple, packed in fruit juice, drained, and 2 tablespoons liquid reserved
>
> 1 full cup (6 ounces) finely diced Dubuque 97% fat-free ham or any extra-lean ham
>
> 3 tablespoons purchased graham cracker crumbs or 3 (2½-inch) graham cracker squares, made into crumbs
>
> 2 tablespoons sliced green onion
>
> 2 tablespoons finely chopped green bell pepper
>
> 1 teaspoon Dijon mustard
>
> 1 teaspoon Brown Sugar Twin

Preheat oven to 375 degrees. Spray an 8-by-8-inch baking dish with butter-flavored cooking spray. In a medium bowl, combine pineapple, ham, cracker crumbs, onion, and green pepper. Add reserved pineapple liquid, mustard, and Brown Sugar Twin. Mix gently to combine. Form mixture into 2 patties. Place patties in prepared baking dish. Bake for 20 to 25 minutes.

HINT: A self-seal sandwich bag works great for crushing graham crackers.

Each serving equals:

HE: 2 Protein • 1 Fruit • ½ Bread • ¼ Vegetable • 1 Optional Calorie

191 Calories • 3 gm Fat • 14 gm Protein • 27 gm Carbohydrate • 815 mg Sodium • 20 mg Calcium • 1 gm Fiber

DIABETIC: 2 Meat • 1 Fruit • ½ Starch

Bavarian Ham and Swiss Pizza

Doesn't it seem like very long ago when the only ways you topped your pizza were with mozzarella, pepperoni, and veggies? These days, of course, the sky's the limit when it comes to pizza-topping creativity! In DeWitt, our favorite pizza spot features a special with sauerkraut on top, so it's only natural I'd come up with something special in a super sauerkraut pizza for you. ☻ Serves 8

1 (8-ounce) can Pillsbury Reduced Fat Crescent Rolls

1 cup (one 8-ounce can) Hunt's Tomato Sauce

1¾ cups (one 14½-ounce can) Frank's Bavarian-style sauerkraut, well drained

1¼ cups peeled and chopped fresh tomatoes

1 full cup (6 ounces) finely diced Dubuque 97% fat-free ham or any extra-lean ham

4 (¾-ounce) slices Kraft reduced-fat Swiss cheese, shredded

Preheat oven to 415 degrees. Spray a 10-by-15-inch rimmed baking sheet with butter-flavored cooking spray. Pat rolls in pan, being sure to seal perforations. Bake for 10 minutes. Spread tomato sauce evenly over partially baked crust. Sprinkle well-drained sauerkraut over sauce. Evenly sprinkle tomatoes over sauerkraut. Layer ham and Swiss cheese evenly over top. Continue baking for 8 to 10 minutes or until crust is golden brown and cheese melts. Place baking sheet on a wire rack and let set for 5 minutes. Cut into 8 servings.

HINT: If you can't find Bavarian sauerkraut, use regular sauerkraut, ½ teaspoon caraway seeds, and 1 teaspoon Brown Sugar Twin.

Each serving equals:

HE: 1¼ Vegetable • 1 Bread • 1 Protein

187 Calories • 7 gm Fat • 10 gm Protein • 21 gm Carbohydrate • 960 mg Sodium • 47 mg Calcium • 2 gm Fiber

DIABETIC: 1 Vegetable • 1 Starch • 1 Meat

Hot Dogs and Noodles Skillet

If you're used to serving hot dogs only on buns, I hope you'll take a fresh look at what you might do with these tasty, healthy frankfurters. They've been seasoned so beautifully, they add something remarkable to any dish you prepare—and here make a tangy partner to noodles and veggies in a festive stovetop supper.

☻ Serves 4 (1 cup)

½ cup chopped onion
8 ounces Healthy Choice 97% fat-free frankfurters, diced
1 cup (one 8-ounce can) Hunt's Tomato Sauce
¾ cup water
1 teaspoon dried parsley flakes
1 teaspoon chili seasoning
2 to 3 drops Worcestershire sauce
½ cup frozen peas
¼ cup (1 ounce) sliced ripe olives
1½ cups hot cooked noodles, rinsed and drained

In a large skillet sprayed with olive oil–flavored cooking spray, sauté onion and frankfurters for about 5 minutes or until lightly browned. Stir in tomato sauce, water, parsley flakes, chili seasoning, and Worcestershire sauce. Add peas, olives, and noodles. Mix gently to combine. Lower heat and simmer for 10 minutes, stirring occasionally.

HINT: 1¼ cups uncooked noodles usually cooks to about 1½ cups.

Each serving equals:

HE: 1¼ Vegetable • 1⅓ Protein • 1 Bread • ¼ Fat

187 Calories • 3 gm Fat • 13 gm Protein • 27 gm Carbohydrate • 903 mg Sodium • 40 mg Calcium • 4 gm Fiber

DIABETIC: 1 Vegetable • 1 Meat • 1 Starch

Mexicalli Hot Dog Dish

The more flavor I can "cram" into my recipes, the more my readers seem to like them! After years of eating bland diet dishes, I know exactly how they feel. Here, the salsa and chili give this skillet dish enough sizzle to wake up the groggiest tastebuds! ☻ Serves 4 (1 cup)

½ cup chopped onion
8 ounces Healthy Choice 97% fat-free frankfurters, diced
6 ounces (one 8-ounce can) red kidney beans, rinsed and drained
½ cup chunky salsa (mild, medium, or hot)
1 (10¾-ounce) can Healthy Request Tomato Soup
1 teaspoon chili seasoning
1½ cups hot cooked rotini pasta, rinsed and drained
½ cup frozen whole-kernel corn, thawed

In a large skillet sprayed with olive oil–flavored cooking spray, sauté onion and frankfurters for about 6 minutes or until browned. Stir in kidney beans, salsa, and tomato soup. Add chili seasoning, rotini pasta, and corn. Mix well to combine. Lower heat and simmer for 10 minutes, stirring occasionally.

HINTS: 1. 1 cup uncooked rotini pasta usually cooks to about 1½ cups.
2. Thaw corn by placing in a colander and rinsing under hot water for one minute.

Each serving equals:

HE: 2 Protein • 1 Bread • ½ Vegetable • ½ Slider • 10 Optional Calories

235 Calories • 3 gm Fat • 13 gm Protein • 39 mg Carbohydrate • 808 mg Sodium • 65 mg Calcium • 5 gm Fiber

DIABETIC: 2 Meat • 1½ Starch • ½ Vegetable

Scalloped Vegetables and Hot Dogs

You'll be pleased to see that this is almost like the filling for a franks and veggie pot pie. The skim milk and flour combine for a delectably thick sauce that hugs this man-pleasing, meat-and-potatoes combo! ☻ Serves 4

> 1½ cups (one 12-fluid-ounce can) Carnation Evaporated Skim Milk
> 3 tablespoons all-purpose flour
> ½ cup (one 2.5-ounce jar) sliced mushrooms, drained
> ⅛ teaspoon black pepper
> 2½ cups (12 ounces) diced cooked potatoes
> 2 cups (one 16-ounce can) cut green beans, rinsed and drained
> 8 ounces Healthy Choice 97% fat-free frankfurters, diced

Preheat oven to 375 degrees. Spray an 8-by-8-inch baking dish with butter-flavored cooking spray. In a covered jar, combine evaporated skim milk and flour. Shake well to blend. Pour milk mixture into a large saucepan sprayed with butter-flavored cooking spray. Add mushrooms and black pepper. Cook over medium heat, until mixture thickens, stirring constantly. Remove from heat. Stir in potatoes, green beans, and frankfurters. Spread mixture into prepared baking dish. Bake for 20 to 25 minutes. Place baking dish on a wire rack and let set for 5 minutes. Divide into 4 servings.

Each serving equals:

HE: 1⅓ Protein • 1¼ Vegetable • 1 Bread • ¾ Skim Milk

230 Calories • 2 gm Fat • 17 gm Protein • 36 gm Carbohydrate • 773 mg Sodium • 304 mg Calcium • 3 gm Fiber

DIABETIC: 1 Meat • 1 Vegetable • 1 Starch • 1 Skim Milk

Frankfurter Tortilla Bake

Here's a fresh and feisty version of a classic Mexican recipe, and I hope it'll make your mouth yell "Olé!" So many traditional South of the Border dishes are high in fat, but when you make this recipe at home, you can keep all that great flavor—but still make the fat disappear.   ☻   Serves 6

10 ounces (one 16-ounce can) pinto beans, rinsed and drained

½ cup chunky salsa, (mild, medium, or hot)

½ cup finely chopped onion

8 ounces Healthy Choice 97% fat-free frankfurters, diced

6 (6-inch) flour tortillas

1 cup (one 8-ounce can) Hunt's Tomato Sauce

½ cup water

1 teaspoon chili seasoning

½ cup + 1 tablespoon (2¼ ounces) shredded Kraft reduced-fat Cheddar cheese

2 teaspoons dried parsley flakes

Preheat oven to 375 degrees. Spray an 8-by-12-inch baking dish with olive oil–flavored cooking spray. In a large bowl, mash pinto beans with a fork. Stir in salsa and onion. Spoon ¾ cup of bean mixture into a small bowl. Stir frankfurters into remaining bean mixture. Place about ½ cup bean-frankfurter mixture on each tortilla and roll up. Place rolled tortillas in prepared baking dish, seam side down. Stir tomato sauce, water, and chili seasoning into reserved bean mixture. Spoon mixture evenly over tortillas. Sprinkle Cheddar cheese and parsley flakes evenly over top. Bake for 20 to 25 minutes. Place baking dish on a wire rack and let set for 5 minutes. Divide into 6 servings.

Each serving equals:

HE: 2¼ Protein • 1 Bread • 1 Vegetable

233 Calories • 5 gm Fat • 15 gm Protein • 32 gm Carbohydrate • 935 mg Sodium • 141 mg Calcium • 5 gm Fiber

DIABETIC: 2 Starch • 1½ Meat • 1½ Vegetable

Grande Spaghetti Skillet

Here's another stove-top sensation that combines ordinary ingredients from your pantry shelves into a dish with so much flavor I called it "grande"! Sure, you could serve spaghetti a couple times a week as a cost-cutter, but why settle for the same old thing when you can "live a little"!　　☻　Serves 6 (1 full cup)

> 8 ounces ground 90% lean turkey or beef
> ½ cup chopped onion
> ¼ cup chopped green bell pepper
> 2 cups hot cooked spaghetti, rinsed and drained
> 6 ounces (one 8-ounce can) kidney beans, rinsed and drained
> 1 cup frozen whole kernel corn, thawed
> 1¾ cups (one 14½-ounce can) stewed tomatoes, undrained
> 1 cup (one 8-ounce can) Hunt's Tomato Sauce
> ⅔ cup (2¼ ounces) shredded Kraft reduced-fat Cheddar cheese
> 2 teaspoons chili seasoning
> ⅛ teaspoon black pepper
> 6 tablespoons Land O Lakes no-fat sour cream

In a large skillet sprayed with olive oil–flavored cooking spray, brown meat, onion and green pepper. Add spaghetti, kidney beans, corn, undrained stewed tomatoes, and tomato sauce. Mix well to combine. Stir in Cheddar cheese, chili seasoning, and black pepper. Lower heat and simmer for 10 to 15 minutes, stirring occasionally. When serving, top each with 1 tablespoon sour cream.

HINT:　1½ cups broken uncooked spaghetti usually cooks to about 2 cups.

Each serving equals:

HE: 2⅓ Protein • 1½ Vegetable • 1 Bread • 15 Optional Calories

---

225 Calories • 5 gm Fat • 15 gm Protein • 30 gm Carbohydrate •
395 mg Sodium • 105 mg Calcium • 4 gm Fiber

DIABETIC: 2 Meat • 1½ Vegetable • 1½ Starch

Italian Hamburger Milk Gravy with Green Beans

Because my son Tommy loves hamburger milk gravy so much, I'm giving his wife-to-be a complete collection of my cookbooks, each of which features at least one variation on this theme! Lucky for him, Angie enjoys this old-timey dish as much as he does! ☻ Serves 4 (1 cup)

> 8 ounces ground 90% lean turkey or beef
> 1½ cups (one 12-fluid-ounce can) Carnation Evaporated Skim Milk
> 3 tablespoons all-purpose flour
> 2 cups (one 16-ounce can) French-style green beans, rinsed and drained
> ½ cup (one 2.5-ounce jar) sliced mushrooms, drained
> 1 teaspoon Italian seasoning
> 1 teaspoon dried onion flakes
> ⅛ teaspoon black pepper

In a large skillet sprayed with butter-flavored cooking spray, brown meat. In a covered jar, combine evaporated skim milk and flour. Shake well to blend. Pour milk mixture into meat mixture. Mix well to combine. Stir in green beans, mushrooms, Italian seasoning, onion flakes, and black pepper. Lower heat and simmer for 10 minutes, or until mixture is heated through, stirring occasionally.

Each serving equals:

HE: 1½ Protein • 1¼ Vegetable • ¾ Skim Milk • ¼ Bread

209 Calories • 5 gm Fat • 20 gm Protein • 21 gm Carbohydrate • 249 mg Sodium • 311 mg Calcium • 2 gm Fiber

DIABETIC: 1½ Meat • 1 Vegetable • 1 Skim Milk

Supper-Time Rice Skillet

If you're looking for inexpensive dishes that supply the people you love with plenty of calcium, seek no further than this stove-top special! It's simple, it's tasty, and it will make your family feel wonderfully satisfied. Only you need to know how good it is for them!   ☻   Serves 4 (1 cup)

8 ounces ground 90% lean turkey or beef

½ cup chopped onion

1½ cups finely chopped celery

½ cup (one 2.5-ounce jar) sliced mushrooms, drained

1⅓ cups (4 ounces) uncooked Minute Rice

1 (10¾-ounce) can Healthy Request Cream of Mushroom Soup

¼ cup (one 2-ounce jar) chopped pimiento, undrained

1⅓ cups skim milk

In a large skillet sprayed with butter-flavored cooking spray, brown meat, onion, and celery for 10 minutes or until celery is tender. Add mushrooms, uncooked rice, mushroom soup, undrained pimiento, and skim milk. Mix well to combine. Lower heat, cover, and simmer for 10 minutes, or until rice is tender, stirring occasionally.

Each serving equals:

HE: 1½ Protein • 1¼ Vegetable • 1 Bread • ¼ Skim Milk •
½ Slider • 1 Optional Calorie

---

223 Calories • 7 gm Fat • 15 gm Protein • 25 gm Carbohydrate •
513 mg Sodium • 174 mg Calcium • 2 gm Fiber

DIABETIC: 1½ Meat • 1½ Starch/Carbohydrate • ½ Vegetable

Baked Adobe Vegetable Stew

This casserole brings together lots of Southwestern flavor in a dish that's so savory, no one will notice they're getting just a touch of meat amidst all those healthy veggies and noodles! Maybe the Food Pyramid was built from this kind of "adobe"?

❂ Serves 6

8 ounces ground 90% lean turkey or beef

½ cup chopped onion

1 cup (one 8-ounce can) Hunt's Tomato Sauce

½ cup chunky salsa (mild, medium, or hot)

2 tablespoons Brown Sugar Twin

2 cups hot cooked noodles, rinsed and drained

2 cups (one 16-ounce can) cut green beans, rinsed and drained

2 cups (one 16-ounce can) sliced carrots, rinsed and drained

½ cup frozen peas, thawed

½ cup frozen corn, thawed

¾ cup (3 ounces) shredded Kraft reduced-fat Cheddar cheese

Preheat oven to 350 degrees. Spray an 8-by-8-inch baking dish with olive oil–flavored cooking spray. In a large skillet sprayed with olive oil–flavored cooking spray, brown meat and onion. Add tomato sauce, salsa, and Brown Sugar Twin. Mix well to combine. Lower heat and simmer for 10 minutes, stirring occasionally. Stir in noodles, green beans, carrots, peas, and corn. Pour mixture into prepared baking dish. Sprinkle Cheddar cheese evenly over top. Bake for 25 to 30 minutes. Place baking dish on a wire rack and let set for 5 minutes. Divide into 6 servings.

HINTS: 1. 1¾ cups uncooked noodles usually cooks to about 2 cups.

2. Thaw peas and corn by placing in a colander and rinsing under hot water for one minute.

Each serving equals:

HE: 2⅓ Vegetable • 1 Protein • 1 Bread • 1 Optional Calorie

222 Calories • 6 gm Fat • 15 gm Protein • 27 gm Carbohydrate • 532 mg Sodium • 165 mg Calcium • 4 gm Fiber

DIABETIC: 2 Vegetable • 1½ Meat • 1 Starch

Goulash Jumble

Part of my heritage is Eastern European, where hearty main dishes are always on the menu! Here's an easy combo your family is sure to relish, especially if they love the taste of cabbage cooked in a succulent broth until it's full of flavor!

● Serves 6 (1 cup)

16 ounces ground 90% lean turkey or beef

1¾ cups (one 15-ounce can) Hunt's Chunky Tomato Sauce

2 cups shredded cabbage

1 cup (one 8-ounce can) sliced carrots, rinsed and drained

1 cup hot cooked elbow macaroni, rinsed and drained

1¾ cups (one 14½-ounce can) Swanson Beef Broth

3 tablespoons all-purpose flour

⅔ cup Carnation Nonfat Dry Milk Powder

1 teaspoon dried onion flakes

1 teaspoon dried parsley flakes

In a large skillet sprayed with butter-flavored cooking spray, brown meat. Stir in tomato sauce, cabbage, carrots, and macaroni. In a covered jar, combine beef broth, flour, dry milk powder, onion flakes, and parsley flakes. Shake well to blend. Pour broth mixture into meat mixture. Mix well to combine. Lower heat and simmer for 15 minutes, stirring occasionally.

HINT: ⅔ cup uncooked elbow macaroni usually cooks to about 1 cup.

Each serving equals:

HE: 2 Protein • 2 Vegetable • ½ Bread • ⅓ Skim Milk • 6 Optional Calories

201 Calories • 7 gm Fat • 19 gm Protein • 20 gm Carbohydrate • 832 mg Sodium • 109 mg Calcium • 2 gm Fiber

DIABETIC: 2 Meat • 2 Vegetable • ½ Starch *or* 2 Meat • ½ Starch/Carbohydrate

Easy Skillet Stew

Okay, it's not a special occasion, it's just the family around the table, so what's for dinner? Why not stir up this simple but satisfying meat-and-potatoes combination that answers the question perfectly? ☻ Serves 4 (full 1 cup)

8 ounces ground 90% lean turkey or beef
½ cup chopped onion
1½ cups chopped celery
2 cups frozen cut carrots, thawed
1¾ cups (one 14½-ounce can) Swanson Beef Broth
10 ounces (one 16-ounce can) sliced cooked potatoes, rinsed and drained
1 (10¾-ounce) can Healthy Request Tomato Soup
1 teaspoon dried parsley flakes
¼ teaspoon black pepper

In a large skillet sprayed with butter-flavored cooking spray, brown meat. Stir in onion, celery, carrots, and beef broth. Cook over medium heat for about 20 minutes or until liquid is almost absorbed, stirring occasionally. Add potatoes, tomato soup, parsley flakes, and black pepper. Mix well to combine. Lower heat and simmer for 5 minutes or until mixture is heated through, stirring often.

Each serving equals:

HE: 2 Vegetable • 1½ Protein • ⅔ Bread • ½ Slider •
13 Optional Calories

229 Calories • 5 gm Fat • 14 gm Protein • 32 gm Carbohydrate •
612 mg Sodium • 43 mg Calcium • 4 gm Fiber

DIABETIC: 1½ Meat • 1½ Starch • 1 Vegetable

Heritage Corn Casserole

This is just the kind of wonderful and economical casserole my mother used to fix when she had to make one egg and a half pound of meat serve the whole family. Homemade bread crumbs give this classic baked corn dish a real old-time taste.

○ Serves 4

8 ounces ground 90% lean turkey or beef

2 cups (one 16-ounce can) whole-kernel corn, rinsed and drained

1 egg, beaten, or equivalent in egg substitute

⅓ cup water

⅓ cup Carnation Nonfat Dry Milk Powder

½ cup chopped onion

1½ teaspoons taco seasoning

¼ teaspoon black pepper

1 teaspoon dried parsley flakes

2 slices reduced-calorie white bread, made into crumbs

Preheat oven to 350 degrees. Spray an 8-by-8-inch baking dish with butter-flavored cooking spray. In a large skillet sprayed with butter-flavored cooking spray, brown meat. Remove from heat. In a large bowl, combine corn, egg, water and dry milk powder. Stir in onion, taco seasoning, black pepper, and parsley flakes. Add browned meat and bread crumbs. Mix gently to combine. Spread mixture into prepared baking dish. Bake for 40 to 45 minutes. Place baking dish on a wire rack and let set for 5 minutes. Divide into 4 servings.

Each serving equals:

HE: 1¾ Protein (¼ limited) • 1¼ Bread • ¼ Skim Milk • ¼ Vegetable

226 Calories • 6 gm Fat • 17 gm Protein • 26 gm Carbohydrate • 163 mg Sodium • 92 mg Calcium • 4 gm Fiber

DIABETIC: 2 Meat • 1½ Starch

Pizza Lover's Pizza

If making your own pizza just seemed like too much trouble, I'm here to tell you that it isn't any longer! You'll never taste fresher ingredients piled on a fresh-baked golden crust than when you try this recipe for homemade happiness. Invite your kids to help by sprinkling the veggies and cheese on top! ◐ Serves 8

16 ounces ground 90% lean turkey or beef

1 (11-ounce) can Pillsbury Crusty French Loaf

1¾ cups (one 15-ounce can) Hunt's Chunky Tomato Sauce

1 teaspoon Italian seasoning

½ cup chopped onion

½ cup chopped green bell pepper

½ cup (2 ounces) sliced ripe olives

½ cup (one 2.5-ounce jar) sliced mushrooms, drained

¾ cup (3 ounces) shredded Kraft reduced-fat Cheddar cheese

¾ cup (3 ounces) shredded Kraft reduced-fat mozzarella cheese

Preheat oven to 425 degrees. In a large skillet sprayed with olive oil–flavored cooking spray, brown meat. Meanwhile, spray a 10-by-15-inch baking sheet with olive oil–flavored cooking spray. Unroll French loaf and pat into and up sides of pan to form a rim. Bake for 5 to 6 minutes. Evenly spread tomato sauce over partially baked crust. Sprinkle Italian seasoning over sauce. Layer browned meat, onion, green pepper, olives, and mushrooms over sauce. Evenly sprinkle Cheddar and mozzarella cheese over top. Bake for 20 to 25 minutes or until crust is browned. Place baking sheet on a wire rack and let set for 5 minutes. Cut into 8 servings.

Each serving equals:

HE: 2½ Protein • 1¼ Vegetable • 1 Bread • ¼ Fat

259 Calories • 9 gm Fat • 20 gm Protein • 22 gm Carbohydrate • 840 mg Sodium • 150 mg Calcium • 2 gm Fiber

DIABETIC: 2 Meat • 1 Vegetable • 1 Starch • ½ Fat

"Sausage" Strata Casserole

If your desire for a healthier lifestyle or maybe doctor's orders have driven sausage from your table, here's a great way to enjoy the traditional flavor you love without sacrificing your health! You'll discover it's all in the spices blended into this old-fashioned dish that arrives at the table beautifully golden-brown and absolutely irresistible! ☯ Serves 6

6 slices reduced-calorie white or Italian bread, cut into 1-inch cubes

8 ounces ground 90% lean turkey or beef

½ teaspoon poultry seasoning

¼ teaspoon ground sage

¼ teaspoon garlic powder

¾ cup Yoplait plain fat-free yogurt

⅓ cup Carnation Nonfat Dry Milk Powder

1 teaspoon cornstarch

3 eggs or equivalent in egg substitute

½ cup (one 2.5-ounce jar) sliced mushrooms, drained

¼ cup sliced green onion

1 teaspoon prepared mustard

⅛ teaspoon black pepper

⅓ cup (1½ ounces) shredded Kraft reduced-fat Cheddar cheese

Preheat oven to 350 degrees. Spray an 8-by-8-inch baking dish with butter-flavored cooking spray. Evenly arrange bread cubes in prepared baking dish. In a large skillet sprayed with butter-flavored cooking spray, brown meat. Stir in poultry seasoning, sage, and garlic powder. In a large bowl, combine yogurt, dry milk powder, cornstarch, and eggs. Add mushrooms, green onion, mustard, and black pepper. Mix gently to combine. Stir in browned meat mixture. Pour over bread cubes. Bake for 30 to 35 minutes. Sprinkle Cheddar cheese evenly over top. Continue baking for 10 to 15 minutes or until center is firm and cheese melts. Place baking dish on a wire rack and let set for 5 minutes. Cut into 6 servings.

Each serving equals:

HE: 1½ Protein (½ limited) • ½ Bread • ⅓ Skim Milk • ¼ Vegetable

191 Calories • 7 gm Fat • 17 gm Protein • 15 gm Carbohydrate • 339 mg Sodium • 152 mg Calcium • 3 gm Fiber

DIABETIC: 1½ Meat • 1 Starch/Carbohydrate

Creamy Baked Tacos

Mexican food is always a terrific choice when you're cutting a few culinary corners, because it's so high in flavor, you feel satisfied! These "soft" tacos are simple to fix, and while they're baking, you can watch the news and just relax before dinner.   ☻   Serves 6

8 ounces ground 90% lean turkey or beef

½ cup water

1 tablespoon taco seasoning

6 (6-inch) flour tortillas

¾ cup (3 ounces) shredded Kraft reduced-fat Cheddar cheese

1 (10¾-ounce) can Healthy Request Cream of Mushroom Soup

⅓ cup skim milk

2 cups finely shredded lettuce

1 cup finely chopped fresh tomato

6 tablespoons Land O Lakes no-fat sour cream

Preheat oven to 325 degrees. Spray an 8-by-8-inch baking dish with olive oil–flavored cooking spray. In a large skillet sprayed with olive oil–flavored cooking spray, brown meat. Stir in water and taco seasoning. Bring mixture to a boil. Lower heat and simmer for 10 minutes, stirring occasionally. Evenly spoon about ¼ cup meat mixture onto each tortilla. Roll tortillas and place in prepared baking dish, seam side down. Evenly sprinkle Cheddar cheese over top. In a small bowl, combine mushroom soup and milk. Pour mixture evenly over top of tortillas. Bake for 30 to 35 minutes. For each serving, place 1 tortilla on plate, sprinkle ⅓ cup lettuce and full 2 tablespoons tomato over top, and garnish with 1 tablespoon sour cream.

Each serving equals:

HE: 1⅔ Protein • 1 Bread • 1 Vegetable • ½ Slider •
8 Optional Calories

232 Calories • 8 gm Fat • 15 gm Protein • 25 gm Carbohydrate •
552 mg Sodium • 183 mg Calcium • 1 gm Fiber

DIABETIC: 1½ Meat • 1½ Starch/Carbohydrate • ½ Vegetable

Faux Steak with Green Pepper Sauce

Some fancy restaurants serve steak with a tangy pepper sauce, but I'm just not willing to blow the month's food budget on a big chunk of beef. Here's a version that will tantalize your taste buds and appeal to your eyes as well. Only your pocketbook will know for sure!   ☺   Serves 6

16 ounces ground 90% lean turkey or beef
⅛ teaspoon black pepper
6 tablespoons (1½ ounces) dried fine bread crumbs
1¾ cups (one 15-ounce can) Hunt's Chunky Tomato Sauce☆
½ cup sliced onion
2 cups coarsely chopped green bell peppers
1 teaspoon prepared mustard
2 teaspoons Worcestershire sauce
1 tablespoon Brown Sugar Twin

In a large bowl, combine meat, black pepper, bread crumbs, and ¼ cup tomato sauce. Mix well to combine. Using a ⅓ cup measure as a guide, form into 6 patties. Place patties in a large skillet sprayed with butter-flavored cooking spray. Brown patties for 3 minutes on both sides. Sprinkle onion and green pepper over browned patties. Continue cooking for 4 to 5 minutes. In a small bowl, combine mustard, Worcestershire sauce, Brown Sugar Twin, and remaining 1½ cups tomato sauce. Pour sauce mixture evenly over top. Lower heat, cover, and simmer for 15 minutes. When serving, evenly spoon sauce over patties.

Each serving equals:

HE: 2 Protein • 2 Vegetable • ⅓ Bread • 1 Optional Calorie

167 Calories • 7 gm Fat • 15 gm Protein • 11 gm Carbohydrate • 622 mg Sodium • 21 mg Calcium • 2 gm Fiber

DIABETIC: 2 Meat • 2 Vegetable *or* 2 Meat • ½ Starch/Carbohydrate

Chunky Stew Pot Pie

Sometimes the best kind of thrift is not having to throw out leftovers that sat in the fridge too long! This tasty, biscuit-topped meat and veggies delight makes great use of just a little roast beef—and is delicious enough to serve to your friends.   ❤   Serves 6

1 cup chopped celery

1½ cups sliced carrots

½ cup chopped onion

¼ cup water

1½ cups (8 ounces) diced lean cooked roast beef

½ cup frozen peas, thawed

1 (12-ounce) jar Heinz Fat Free Beef Gravy

1½ tablespoons dried fine bread crumbs

1 teaspoon dried parsley flakes

½ teaspoon paprika

1 (7.5-ounce) can Pillsbury refrigerated buttermilk biscuits

Place celery, carrots, onion, and water in an 8-by-8-inch glass baking dish. Cover and microwave on HIGH (100% power) for 6 to 8 minutes or until vegetables are tender. Stir in roast beef, peas, and gravy. Re-cover and microwave on HIGH for 3 to 4 minutes. Mix well. In a small bowl, combine bread crumbs, parsley flakes, and paprika. Separate biscuits and cut each into 3 pieces. Evenly drop biscuit pieces over top of stew mixture. Lightly spray biscuit pieces with butter-flavored cooking spray. Sprinkle bread crumb mixture evenly over top. Microwave on HIGH, uncovered, 3 to 4 minutes or until biscuits spring back when lightly touched. Place baking dish on a wire rack and let set for 5 minutes. Cut into 6 servings.

HINTS: 1. If you don't have leftovers, purchase a chunk of lean cooked roast beef from your local deli.
2. Thaw peas by placing in a colander and rinsing under hot water for one minute.

Each serving equals:

HE: 1½ Bread • 1⅓ Protein • 1 Vegetable • ¼ Slider • 5 Optional Calories

204 Calories • 4 gm Fat • 16 gm Protein • 26 gm Carbohydrate • 707 mg Sodium • 30 mg Calcium • 3 gm Fiber

DIABETIC: 1½ Starch • 1 Meat • ½ Vegetable

Macaroni and Cheese Extraordinaire

This all-American family favorite is a standard budget entree, but why settle for "standard" when you can have superb? Creamier and cheesier, tangier and tastier—here's a macaroni and cheese that gives you more, more, and more of what you love! ☻ Serves 6 (1 cup)

¼ cup chopped onion

3 cups hot cooked elbow macaroni, rinsed and drained

1 full cup (6 ounces) diced Dubuque 97% fat-free ham or any extra-lean ham

1¾ cups (one 14 ½-ounce can) stewed tomatoes, undrained

1½ cups (6 ounces) shredded Kraft reduced-fat Cheddar cheese

1 (10¾-ounce) can Healthy Request Cream of Mushroom Soup

In a large skillet sprayed with butter-flavored cooking spray, sauté onion for 5 minutes or just until tender. Stir in macaroni, ham, undrained stewed tomatoes, and Cheddar cheese. Add mushroom soup. Mix well to combine. Lower heat, cover, and simmer for 15 minutes, or until mixture is heated through, stirring occasionally.

HINT: 2 cups uncooked elbow macaroni usually cooks to about 3 cups.

Each serving equals:

HE: 2 Protein • 1 Bread • ⅔ Vegetable • ¼ Slider •
8 Optional Calories

260 Calories • 8 gm Fat • 17 gm Protein • 30 gm Carbohydrate •
911 mg Sodium • 280 mg Calcium • 2 gm Fiber

DIABETIC: 1½ Meat • 1 Starch • 1 Vegetable

Desserts
in a Dash

Y̲ou've got unexpected company. Or, you're working late and you still have to make dinner for your family when you get home. Or, with the schedule you and your kids keep, you never seem to have enough time to cook. So, you race through the market, grab this and that, and then you remember you forgot dessert.

The easiest and fastest thing (ice cream, donuts, pastry) is usually not the healthiest, but quick doesn't have to mean store-bought or crammed with fat and calories! There are lots of ways to prepare a tasty homemade treat in very little time, and here are just a few of my favorite tips: Keep a pie crust or two in the freezer, so when you pour a pudding-based filling into it, it sets up super-fast! Always keep one container of whipped topping in the freezer, and another in the fridge, already thawed. When you find a few minutes to slice fruit for a salad, slice a couple of cups more for a pie, spritz with lemon juice or Fruit Fresh, and put it in a Ziploc bag for the next day. When you're making one of my pies, make two, and keep one in the freezer. It'll thaw quickly, and be ready to serve by the time you've finished dinner.

This section is brimming with scrumptious delights, from dazzling pies (**Lemon Chocolate Ambrosia Cheesecake**) to creamy puddings (**Banana Toffee Pudding**) to delicious tarts and other treats (**Pineapple Bliss Cream Tarts**, **Strawberry-Rhubarb Sundaes**). Your guests will be sure you've got some kind of magic going on in that kitchen, because they've never seen such speedy and appealing desserts before!

Applescotch Pudding Treats

When you read the name of this recipe, did it make you smile a little? I love making up my own words, joining two great flavors in one scrumptiously sweet dessert. Sure, you could gobble down a dish of plain old pudding, but you deserve a treat! ☻ Serves 4

1 (4-serving) package JELL-O sugar-free instant butterscotch pudding mix
⅓ cup Carnation Nonfat Dry Milk Powder
½ teaspoon apple pie spice
1½ cups water
½ cup unsweetened applesauce
¼ cup raisins
¼ cup Cool Whip Lite

In a large bowl, combine dry pudding mix, dry milk powder, and apple pie spice. Add water and applesauce. Mix well using a wire whisk. Stir in raisins. Evenly pour pudding mixture into 4 dessert dishes. Garnish each with 1 tablespoon Cool Whip Lite. Refrigerate for at least 30 minutes.

HINT: To plump up raisins without "cooking," place in a glass measuring cup and microwave on HIGH for 20 seconds.

Each serving equals:

HE: ¾ Fruit • ¼ Skim Milk • ¼ Slider • 13 Optional Calories

96 Calories • 0 gm Fat • 2 gm Protein • 22 gm Carbohydrate • 373 mg Sodium • 75 mg Calcium • 1 gm Fiber

DIABETIC: 1 Fruit

Apple Butter Pudding

Here's an ingredient whose name might persuade you that it's a high-fat product. But apple butter, a favorite ingredient of the Amish people, is a wonderfully intense apple product, without ANY butter in it. In this recipe, it adds a spectacular fruity flavor to a sweet and creamy blend. ☻ Serves 4

> 1 (4-serving) package JELL-O sugar-free instant vanilla pudding mix
> 2/3 cup Carnation Nonfat Dry Milk Powder
> 1 1/2 cups water
> 1/4 cup apple butter
> 6 (2 1/2-inch) graham crackers, made into coarse crumbs
> 1/4 cup Cool Whip Lite
> 1/4 teaspoon ground cinnamon

In a medium bowl, combine dry pudding mix, dry milk powder, and water. Mix well using a wire whisk. Blend in apple butter. Add graham cracker crumbs. Mix gently to combine. Evenly spoon mixture into 4 dessert dishes. Top each with 1 tablespoon Cool Whip Lite and lightly sprinkle with cinnamon.

Each serving equals:

HE: 1/2 Skim Milk • 1/2 Bread • 1/4 Slider • 15 Optional Calories

125 Calories • 1 gm Fat • 4 gm Protein • 25 gm Carbohydrate • 425 mg Sodium • 139 mg Calcium • 0 gm Fiber

DIABETIC: 1 Starch/Carbohydrate • 1/2 Skim Milk

Banana Toffee Pudding

I admire the ingenuity of candy manufacturers, who've created special products (like Heath Toffee Bits and mini chocolate chips) for healthy home cooks! You may have looked longingly at a toffee bar and thought, "Nope, not me. Not anymore." I'm so happy to tell you that one of your favorite treats is off the "no-no" list for keeps!   ☻   Serves 4

> 1 (4-serving) package JELL-O sugar-free instant banana cream pudding mix
> ⅔ cup Carnation Nonfat Dry Milk Powder
> 1⅔ cups water
> ½ cup Cool Whip Free
> 1 teaspoon vanilla extract
> 2 cups (2 medium) diced bananas
> ¼ cup (1 ounce) Heath Toffee Bits

In a large bowl, combine dry pudding mix, dry milk powder, and water. Mix well using a wire whisk. Blend in Cool Whip Free and vanilla extract. Add bananas and toffee bits. Mix gently to combine. Evenly spoon mixture into 4 dessert dishes. Refrigerate for at least 15 minutes.

HINT: To prevent bananas from turning brown, mix with 1 teaspoon lemon juice or sprinkle with Fruit Fresh.

Each serving equals:

HE: 1 Fruit • ½ Skim Milk • ¾ Slider • 18 Optional Calories

153 Calories • 1 gm Fat • 5 gm Protein • 31 gm Carbohydrate •
407 mg Sodium • 142 mg Calcium • 1 gm Fiber

DIABETIC: 1 Fruit • ½ Skim Milk • ½ Starch/Carbohydrate

Mandarin Mountain Pudding Treats

Ever since I was a child, I've loved those tiny oranges called mandarins, and now I share that pleasure with my grandchildren. I definitely had "my boys" in mind when I stirred up these creamy, fruity delights!   ♥   Serves 6 (⅔ cup)

  1 (4-serving) package JELL-O sugar-free instant vanilla pudding mix
  1 (4-serving) package JELL-O sugar-free orange gelatin
  ⅔ cup Carnation Nonfat Dry Milk Powder
  1 cup (one 8-ounce can) crushed pineapple, packed in fruit juice, undrained
  ⅔ cup Diet Mountain Dew
  ¾ cup Yoplait plain fat-free yogurt
  ¾ cup Cool Whip Free
  1 teaspoon coconut extract
  1 cup (one 11-ounce can) mandarin oranges, rinsed and drained
  1 tablespoon flaked coconut

In a large bowl, combine dry pudding mix, dry gelatin, and dry milk powder. Add undrained pineapple and Diet Mountain Dew. Mix well using a wire whisk. Blend in yogurt, Cool Whip Free, and coconut extract. Add mandarin oranges. Mix gently to combine. Evenly spoon mixture into 6 dessert dishes. Sprinkle ½ teaspoon coconut over top of each. Refrigerate for at least 10 minutes.

Each serving equals:

HE: ⅔ Fruit • ½ Skim Milk • ½ Slider • 1 Optional Calorie

120 Calories • 0 gm Fat • 5 gm Protein • 25 gm Carbohydrate • 331 mg Sodium • 159 mg Calcium • 1 gm Fiber

DIABETIC: ½ Fruit • ½ Skim Milk • ½ Starch/Carbohydrate

Chocolate Crunch Pudding

If your idea of the perfect marriage is chocolate and peanuts, then this is the dessert of your secret dreams! It's a great last-minute surprise when the kids believe that there's nothing for dessert in the house—and it's a favorite with kids of all ages. ❂ Serves 4

> 1 (4-serving) package JELL-O sugar-free instant chocolate pudding mix
> 2/3 cup Carnation Nonfat Dry Milk Powder
> 1 1/2 cups water
> 1/4 cup Cool Whip Free
> 1 teaspoon vanilla extract
> 1/4 cup (1 ounce) chopped dry-roasted peanuts
> 6 (2 1/2-inch) chocolate graham crackers, broken into bite-size pieces

In a large bowl, combine dry pudding mix, dry milk powder, and water. Mix well using a wire whisk. Blend in Cool Whip Free and vanilla extract. Add peanuts and graham cracker pieces. Mix gently to combine. Evenly spoon mixture into 4 dessert dishes. Refrigerate for at least 15 minutes.

Each serving equals:

HE: 1/2 Skim Milk • 1/2 Bread • 1/2 Fat • 1/4 Protein • 1/4 Slider • 18 Optional Calories

148 Calories • 4 gm Fat • 7 gm Protein • 21 gm Carbohydrate • 428 mg Sodium • 142 mg Calcium • 1 gm Fiber

DIABETIC: 1 Starch/Carbohydrate • 1/2 Skim Milk • 1/2 Meat • 1/2 Fat

Tropical Breeze Fruit Pudding

Here's a luscious way to take an island-hopping vacation without getting up from your comfy chair! There are just so many goodies mixed into this recipe, you'll feel as if you'd actually had a rest—amazing!   ☻   Serves 6

   1 (4-serving) package JELL-O sugar-free instant banana cream pudding mix
   ⅔ cup Carnation Nonfat Dry Milk Powder
   1½ cups Yoplait plain fat-free yogurt
   1 cup (one 8-ounce can) crushed pineapple, packed in fruit juice, undrained
   ½ cup Cool Whip Free
   1 teaspoon coconut extract
   1 teaspoon rum extract
   1 cup (1 medium) diced banana
   2 tablespoons flaked coconut

In a large bowl, combine dry pudding mix and dry milk powder. Add yogurt and undrained pineapple. Mix well using a wire whisk. Blend in Cool Whip Free, coconut extract, and rum extract. Fold in banana. Evenly spoon mixture into 6 dessert dishes. Top each with 1 teaspoon flaked coconut. Refrigerate for at least 30 minutes.

HINT: To prevent banana from turning brown, mix with 1 teaspoon lemon
   juice or sprinkle with Fruit Fresh.

Each serving equals:

HE: ⅔ Skim Milk • ⅔ Fruit • ¼ Slider • 12 Optional Calories

136 Calories • 0 gm Fat • 6 gm Protein • 28 gm Carbohydrate •
318 mg Sodium • 213 mg Calcium • 1 gm Fiber

DIABETIC: 1 Skim Milk • 1 Fruit

Jamaican Apricot-Rice Custards

The intensity of the apricot flavor in this Caribbean-inspired cool and creamy dish will win you over in just one bite! If you've always loved rice pudding, give this recipe a chance to capture your heart ☻ Serves 6

2 cups (one 16-ounce can) apricots, packed in fruit juice, undrained

1 cup water

⅔ cup (3 ounces) chopped dried apricots

1⅓ cups (4 ounces) uncooked Minute Rice

1 (4-serving) package JELL-O sugar-free vanilla cook-and-serve pudding mix

⅔ cup Carnation Nonfat Dry Milk Powder

¼ teaspoon ground nutmeg

½ teaspoon rum extract

Place undrained apricots and water in a blender container. Cover and process on HIGH for 15 seconds. In a large saucepan, combine 1½ cups blended apricot mixture and chopped dried apricots. Bring mixture to a boil. Stir in uncooked rice. Cover, remove from heat, and let set. Meanwhile, in a medium saucepan, combine dry pudding mix, dry milk powder, and remaining 1½ cups apricot mixture. Cook over medium heat until mixture thickens and starts to boil, stirring constantly. Remove from heat. Stir in nutmeg and rum extract. Add rice mixture. Mix well to combine. Evenly spoon mixture into 6 dessert dishes. Lightly sprinkle additional nutmeg over tops, if desired.

HINTS: 1. Serve warm or cold.
2. Also good with 2 tablespoons chopped pecans stirred in with nutmeg and rum extract.

Each serving equals:

HE: 1 Fruit • ⅔ Bread • ⅓ Skim Milk • 13 Optional Calories

152 Calories • 0 gm Fat • 4 gm Protein • 34 gm Carbohydrate • 124 mg Sodium • 112 mg Calcium • 3 gm Fiber

DIABETIC: 1½ Starch • 1 Fruit

Strawberry-Rhubarb Sundaes

I should have a bumper sticker on my car that says "Rhubarb Lover—and Proud of It!" (Maybe I need two bumper stickers, since everyone who knows me also knows I'm passionate about strawberries, too!) If you invite me to supper, this would be a great choice for dessert, since it features what I truly love (including pecans!).   ♥   Serves 6

> 2 cups chopped fresh or frozen rhubarb
> ⅓ cup water
> 1 (4-serving) package JELL-O sugar-free strawberry gelatin
> 2 cups sliced fresh strawberries
> 3 cups Wells' Blue Bunny sugar- and fat-free vanilla ice cream or any sugar- and
>   fat-free ice cream
> 6 tablespoons Cool Whip Lite
> 2 tablespoons (½ ounce) chopped pecans

In a medium saucepan, combine rhubarb and water. Cover and cook over medium heat for about 5 minutes, or until rhubarb is tender. Remove from heat. Stir in dry gelatin and strawberries. Refrigerate for at least 10 minutes. For each serving, place ½ cup ice cream in a dessert dish, spoon about ⅓ cup slightly cooled rhubarb sauce over ice cream, and top with 1 tablespoon Cool Whip Lite and 1 teaspoon pecans.

Each serving equals:

HE: ⅔ Vegetable • ⅓ Fruit • ⅓ Fat • ¾ Slider •
17 Optional Calories

138 Calories • 2 gm Fat • 5 gm Protein • 25 gm Carbohydrate •
88 mg Sodium • 163 mg Calcium • 2 gm Fiber

DIABETIC: 1 Fruit • ½ Starch • ½ Fat

Glorified Pineapple-Rice Pudding

I grew up loving the old-fashioned comfort of traditional rice pudding, and I've been coming up with fresh ways to serve it ever since I left home and began cooking for friends and family. I'd serve this light and pretty concoction in my favorite glass dessert dishes. If you're a fan of collecting colorful Depression glass, bring it out when you serve this special dish.   ☻   Serves 4

> 1 (4-serving) package JELL-O sugar-free instant vanilla pudding mix
> ⅔ cup Carnation Nonfat Dry Milk Powder
> ½ cup unsweetened orange juice
> 1 cup (one 8-ounce can) crushed pineapple, packed in fruit juice, undrained
> ¼ cup cold water
> ½ cup Cool Whip Free
> 1½ cups cold cooked rice

In a large bowl, combine dry pudding mix, dry milk powder, orange juice, undrained pineapple, and water. Mix well using a wire whisk. Blend in Cool Whip Free. Add rice. Mix gently to combine. Evenly spoon mixture into 4 dessert dishes. Refrigerate for at least 15 minutes.

HINT: 1 cup uncooked rice usually cooks to about 1½ cups.

Each serving equals:

HE: ¾ Bread • ¾ Fruit • ½ Skim Milk • ½ Slider

184 Calories • 0 gm Fat • 5 gm Protein • 41 gm Carbohydrate •
400 mg Sodium • 154 mg Calcium • 1 gm Fiber

DIABETIC: 1 Starch • 1 Fruit • ½ Skim Milk

Hasty Rice Pudding

It's fast! It's fabulous! It's fun to eat! And you make it in the microwave, which speeds up the process and produces a moist and sweetly fragrant delight.

○ Serves 6

> 1 (4-serving) package JELL-O sugar-free vanilla cook-and-serve pudding mix
> 1½ cups (one 12-fluid-ounce can) Carnation Evaporated Skim Milk
> 1¼ cups water
> 1 cup (3 ounces) uncooked Minute Rice
> ½ cup raisins
> ¼ teaspoon ground cinnamon

In an 8-cup glass measuring bowl, combine dry pudding mix, evaporated skim milk, and water. Mix well using a wire whisk. Stir in uncooked rice. Microwave on HIGH (100% power) for 4 minutes, stirring after 2 minutes. Stir in raisins and cinnamon. Continue microwaving on HIGH for 2 minutes. Mix gently to combine. Let set for 5 minutes. Stir well. Evenly spoon mixture into 6 dessert dishes.

HINTS: 1. Good warm or cold.
   2. Also good topped with 1 tablespoon Cool Whip Lite, but don't forget to count the few additional calories.

Each serving equals:

HE: ⅔ Fruit • ½ Skim Milk • ½ Bread • 13 Optional Calories

128 Calories • 0 gm Fat • 6 gm Protein • 26 gm Carbohydrate • 152 mg Sodium • 194 mg Calcium • 1 gm Fiber

DIABETIC: 1 Fruit • ½ Skim Milk • ½ Starch

Potpourri Apple-Rice Pudding

Here's another outrageously good pudding dessert that calls on some microwave magic to blend its ingredients into something spectacular! It's just so apple-y, with the juice and apples and pie spice, that you'll feel satisfied *and* healthy all at once. (Remember, an apple a day . . .)   ☻   Serves 4

> 1 cup unsweetened apple juice
> 1/3 cup water
> 1 cup (2 small) cored, unpeeled, and diced Red Delicious apples
> 1 teaspoon apple pie spice
> 2/3 cup (2 ounces) uncooked Minute Rice
> 3/4 cup Yoplait plain fat-free yogurt
> 1/3 cup Carnation Nonfat Dry Milk Powder
> 1/2 cup Cool Whip Free
> 1 (4-serving) package JELL-O sugar-free instant vanilla pudding mix

In an 8-cup glass measuring bowl, combine apple juice, water, apples, and apple pie spice. Cover and microwave on HIGH (100% power) for 3 minutes or until mixture starts to boil. Stir in uncooked rice. Cover and let set for 5 minutes. Fluff gently with a fork. Refrigerate for at least 10 minutes. Meanwhile, in a medium bowl, combine yogurt and dry milk powder. Stir in Cool Whip Free. Add dry pudding mix. Mix well using a wire whisk. Gently fold pudding mixture into chilled rice mixture. Spoon into 4 dessert dishes. Refrigerate for at least 15 minutes.

Each serving equals:

HE: 1 Fruit • 1/2 Skim Milk • 1/2 Bread • 1/2 Slider

144 Calories • 0 gm Fat • 5 gm Protein • 31 gm Carbohydrate • 398 mg Sodium • 162 mg Calcium • 1 gm Fiber

DIABETIC: 1 Fruit • 1/2 Skim Milk • 1/2 Starch

Prizewinning Peanut Butter Bread Pudding

The name of this recipe alone should win some kind of award! I'm the queen of bread pudding fans, and I also am a proud member of the Peanut Butter Lovers' Club, so this dish is my idea of heaven in a small place! ☻   Serves 4

¼ cup Peter Pan reduced-fat peanut butter

8 slices day old reduced-calorie bread

1 (4-serving) package JELL-O sugar-free vanilla cook-and-serve pudding mix

2 cups skim milk

1 teaspoon vanilla extract

Preheat oven to 375 degrees. Spray an 8-by-8-inch baking dish with butter-flavored cooking spray. Evenly spread peanut butter on bread. Fold each piece of bread in half and break into pieces. In a large bowl, combine dry pudding mix, skim milk, and vanilla extract. Mix well using a wire whisk. Add bread pieces. Stir gently to combine. Let set for about 5 minutes. Pour mixture into prepared baking dish. Bake for 25 to 30 minutes. Divide into 6 servings. Good warm or cold.

HINT: Could be topped with fruit of your choice. If using, count accordingly.

Each serving equals:

HE: 1 Bread • 1 Protein • 1 Fat • ½ Skim Milk • ¼ Slider

234 Calories • 6 gm Fat • 13 gm Protein • 32 gm Carbohydrate • 483 mg Sodium • 186 mg Calcium • 6 gm Fiber

DIABETIC: 1½ Starch/Carbohydrate • ½ Meat • ½ Fat • ½ Skim Milk

Pumpkin Maple Dessert

This is what I call a "Becky" dish, a recipe that my daughter, Becky, would find utterly irresistible! She's always looked forward to any dessert that featured butterscotch, and she loves the taste of pumpkin all year long, not just on holidays!

● Serves 8

> 12 (2½-inch) graham cracker squares ☆
>
> 2 (4-serving) packages JELL-O sugar-free instant butterscotch pudding mix
>
> 1⅓ cups Carnation Nonfat Dry Milk Powder
>
> 2 cups (one 15-ounce can) pumpkin
>
> ½ cup water
>
> ½ cup Cary's Sugar Free Maple Syrup
>
> 2 teaspoons pumpkin pie spice
>
> 1½ cups Cool Whip Free
>
> ¼ cup (1 ounce) chopped pecans

Place 9 graham cracker squares in bottom of a 9-by-9-inch cake pan. In a large bowl, combine dry pudding mixes and dry milk powder. Add pumpkin, water, maple syrup, and pumpkin pie spice. Mix well using a wire whisk. Spread mixture evenly over crackers. Refrigerate for 5 minutes. Evenly spread Cool Whip Free over filling. Crush remaining 3 graham cracker squares. Evenly sprinkle cracker crumbs and pecans over top. Cover and refrigerate for at least 20 minutes. Cut into 8 servings.

HINT: A self-seal sandwich bag works great for crushing graham crackers.

Each serving equals:

> HE: ½ Skim Milk • ½ Bread • ½ Fat • ½ Vegetable • ½ Slider • 8 Optional Calories
>
> ---
>
> 163 Calories • 3 gm Fat • 4 gm Protein • 30 gm Carbohydrate • 450 mg Sodium • 156 mg Calcium • 1 gm Fiber
>
> ---
>
> DIABETIC: 1½ Starch/Carbohydrate • ½ Skim Milk • ½ Fat

All-American Fruit Shortcakes

Maybe you're planning a Fourth of July picnic, or you want to have friends over for Flag Day, or you're just feeling patriotic and no holiday's in sight. Whatever the occasion, this is a dazzling dessert that's much easier to prepare than it looks!

☻ Serves 6

⅓ cup Diet Mountain Dew

2 cups sliced fresh strawberries☆

6 tablespoons pourable Sugar Twin☆

1½ cups fresh blueberries

1 cup (1 medium) diced banana

1 cup + 2 tablespoons Bisquick Reduced Fat Baking Mix

½ cup Carnation Nonfat Dry Milk Powder

3 tablespoons Kraft fat-free mayonnaise

½ cup water

2 teaspoons vanilla extract

2 cups Wells' Blue Bunny sugar- and fat-free vanilla ice cream or any sugar- and fat-free ice cream

6 tablespoons Cool Whip Lite

In a blender container, combine Diet Mountain Dew and 1 cup strawberries. Cover and process on BLEND for 15 to 20 seconds. Pour mixture into a large bowl. Stir in ¼ cup Sugar Twin, remaining 1 cup strawberries, blueberries, and banana. Cover and refrigerate until ready to serve. Preheat oven to 415 degrees. Spray a 6-hole muffin tin with butter-flavored cooking spray. In a medium bowl, combine baking mix, remaining 2 tablespoons Sugar Twin, and dry milk powder. Add mayonnaise, water, and vanilla extract. Mix well to combine. Evenly divide batter among muffin wells. Bake for 8 to 10 minutes or until lightly browned. Place muffin tin on a wire rack and let cool. Split shortcakes in half crosswise. For each serving, place bottom half of shortcake in a dessert dish, top with ⅓ cup ice cream, place top half of shortcake over ice cream, spoon about ½ cup fruit mixture over top, and garnish with 1 tablespoon Cool Whip Lite.

Each serving equals:

HE: 1 Bread • 1 Fruit • ¼ Skim Milk • ¾ Slider • 1 Optional Calorie

242 Calories • 2 gm Fat • 8 gm Protein • 48 gm Carbohydrate • 372 mg Sodium • 221 mg Calcium • 3 gm Fiber

DIABETIC: 2 Starch • 1 Fruit

Easy Fruit Cocktail Cobbler

If you've loved fruit cocktail since you were a child, here's a tasty way to feel like a kid again! What makes this special is the spices, and the two little boosts of coconut, which give something plain and simple a little culinary sparkle.

❂ Serves 6

> 2 cups (one 16-ounce can) fruit cocktail, packed in fruit juice, undrained
> 1 teaspoon coconut extract
> 1 (7.5-ounce) can Pillsbury refrigerated biscuits
> 2 tablespoons pourable Sugar Twin
> ½ teaspoon ground cinnamon
> 2 tablespoons (½ ounce) chopped pecans
> 2 tablespoons flaked coconut

Preheat oven to 400 degrees. Spray an 8-by-12-inch baking dish with butter-flavored cooking spray. In a large bowl, combine undrained fruit cocktail and coconut extract. Separate biscuits and cut each into 4 pieces. Add biscuit pieces to fruit cocktail mixture. Mix gently to combine. Spread mixture into prepared baking dish. In a small bowl, combine Sugar Twin and cinnamon. Add pecans and coconut. Mix gently to combine. Sprinkle mixture evenly over top. Bake for 15 to 20 minutes or until a toothpick inserted into biscuits comes out clean. Place baking dish on a wire rack and let set for 5 minutes. Divide into 6 servings.

HINT: Good topped with sugar- and fat-free vanilla ice cream or Cool Whip Lite, but don't forget to count the few additional calories.

Each serving equals:

HE: 1¼ Bread • ⅔ Fruit • ⅓ Fat • 7 Optional Calories

151 Calories • 3 gm Fat • 3 gm Protein • 28 gm Carbohydrate • 311 mg Sodium • 10 mg Calcium • 3 gm Fiber

DIABETIC: 1 Starch • 1 Fruit • ½ Fat

New England Walnut-Apple Tarts

Talk about great relationships—you've just got to mention apples and maple syrup! The sweetness of the maple flavor and the crunchy tartness of your favorite apples "cuddle up," and the finished product will warm your heart.

☻ Serves 6

> 1 (4-serving) package JELL-O sugar-free vanilla cook-and-serve pudding mix
> ⅔ cup Carnation Nonfat Milk Powder
> ½ cup water
> ½ cup Cary's Sugar Free Maple Syrup
> 1½ cups (3 small) cored, peeled, and diced cooking apples
> ⅓ cup (1½ ounces) chopped walnuts
> 1 (6 single-serve) package Keebler graham cracker crusts
> 6 tablespoons Cool Whip Lite

In a medium saucepan, combine dry pudding mix, dry milk powder, water, and maple syrup. Stir in apples. Cook over medium heat until mixture thickens and starts to boil, stirring constantly. Remove from heat. Add walnuts. Mix gently to combine. Evenly spoon mixture into graham cracker crusts. Refrigerate for at least 30 minutes. When serving, top each with 1 tablespoon Cool Whip Lite.

Each serving equals:

HE: ½ Bread • ½ Fruit • ½ Fat • ⅓ Skim Milk • ¼ Protein • 1 Slider • 6 Optional Calories

208 Calories • 8 gm Fat • 5 gm Protein • 29 gm Carbohydrate • 292 mg Sodium • 101 mg Calcium • 2 gm Fiber

DIABETIC: 1 Starch • 1 Fruit • ½ Fat

Pineapple Bliss Cream Tarts

Here's something fun to make and pretty enough to serve at a party. You might even want to invite your kids to help spoon the mixture into the tart shells. I never yet met children who didn't eat all their dinner when they'd helped prepare dessert.　●　Serves 6

> 1 (4-serving) package JELL-O sugar-free instant vanilla pudding mix
> ⅔ cup Carnation Nonfat Dry Milk Powder
> ½ teaspoon apple pie spice
> 1 cup (one 8-ounce can) crushed pineapple, packed in fruit juice, undrained
> ½ cup water
> ½ cup + 2 tablespoons Cool Whip Free ☆
> 1 cup (1 medium) diced banana
> 1 (6 single-serve) package Keebler graham cracker crusts
> 1 maraschino cherry

In a large bowl, combine dry pudding mix, dry milk powder, and apple pie spice. Add undrained pineapple and water. Mix well using a wire whisk. Blend in ¼ cup Cool Whip Free. Add banana. Mix gently to combine. Evenly spoon mixture into graham cracker crusts. Top each with 1 tablespoon Cool Whip Free. Cut cherry in half. Cut each half into 3 pieces. Garnish each tart with a cherry piece. Refrigerate for at least 15 minutes.

HINT: To prevent banana from turning brown, mix with 1 teaspoon lemon juice or sprinkle with Fruit Fresh.

Each serving equals:

> HE: ⅔ Fruit • ½ Bread • ⅓ Skim Milk • 1 Slider •
> 2 Optional Calories
> _____
> 223 Calories • 7 gm Fat • 4 gm Protein • 36 gm Carbohydrate •
> 402 mg Sodium • 99 mg Calcium • 1 gm Fiber
> _____
> DIABETIC: 1½ Starch/Carbohydrate • 1 Fruit • 1 Fat

Almond Surprise Apricot Pie

I love surprises, and if you do, too, this recipe might just tickle your fancy! Your tastebuds start getting excited over what they can see—in this case, the creamy filling and the nutty, fruity topping. But there's more to this pie than meets the eye!

◑ Serves 8

> ½ cup apricot spreadable fruit ☆
>
> 1 (6-ounce) Keebler graham cracker piecrust
>
> 1 (8-ounce) package Philadelphia fat-free cream cheese
>
> 1 (4-serving) package JELL-O sugar-free instant vanilla pudding mix
>
> ⅔ cup Carnation Nonfat Dry Milk Powder
>
> 1 cup water
>
> ¼ cup Cool Whip Free
>
> ½ teaspoon almond extract
>
> 2 tablespoons (½ ounce) slivered almonds

Reserve 2 tablespoons apricot spreadable fruit. Spread remaining spreadable fruit in bottom of piecrust. In a large bowl, stir cream cheese with a spoon until soft. Add dry pudding mix, dry milk powder, and water. Mix well using a wire whisk. Blend in Cool Whip Free and almond extract. Pour pudding mixture into piecrust. Place reserved spreadable fruit in a small microwavable bowl. Microwave on HIGH (100% power) for 10 seconds. Drizzle melted fruit spread over set filling. Sprinkle almonds over top. Refrigerate for at least 30 minutes. Cut into 8 servings.

HINT: Spreadable fruit spreads best at room temperature.

Each serving equals:

HE: 1 Fruit • ½ Bread • ½ Protein • ¼ Skim Milk • ¾ Slider • 15 Optional Calories

210 Calories • 6 gm Fat • 7 gm Protein • 32 gm Carbohydrate • 502 mg Sodium • 74 mg Calcium • 1 gm Fiber

DIABETIC: 1 Fruit • 1 Starch/Carbohydrate • ½ Meat • ½ Skim Milk • ½ Fat

Luscious Lime Chiffon Pie

Even if you've enjoyed a hearty meal, here's a perfect dessert to serve that's as frothy and light as it is lusciously fruity! I know it seems odd to toss the skin and seeds of a lime into your blender, but they add so much intense citrusy goodness, you'll be delighted at the result.   ◐   Serves 8

1 cup Diet Mountain Dew or water

¼ of a lime, with skin and seeds, cut into chunks

1 (4-serving) package JELL-O sugar-free instant vanilla pudding mix

1 (4-serving) package JELL-O sugar-free lime gelatin

⅔ cup Carnation Nonfat Dry Milk Powder

1½ cups Yoplait plain fat-free yogurt

1 cup Cool Whip Lite ☆

1 (6-ounce) Keebler shortbread piecrust

In a blender container, combine Diet Mountain Dew and lime chunks. Cover and process on BLEND for 60 seconds or until lime pieces almost disappear. Set aside. In a large bowl, combine dry pudding mix, dry gelatin, and dry milk powder. Add blended lime mixture and yogurt. Mix well using a wire whisk. Blend in ¼ cup Cool Whip Lite. Spread pudding mixture into piecrust. Refrigerate for 5 minutes. Drop remaining Cool Whip Lite by tablespoon to form 8 mounds. Refrigerate for at least 30 minutes. Cut into 8 servings.

Each serving equals:

HE: ½ Skim Milk • ½ Bread • 1 Slider • 7 Optional Calories

177 Calories • 5 gm Fat • 6 gm Protein • 27 gm Carbohydrate • 353 mg Sodium • 154 mg Calcium • 1 gm Fiber

DIABETIC: 1½ Starch • 1 Fat • ½ Skim Milk

Creamy Pistachio-Pineapple Pie

It's creamy, it's fruity, it's—GREEN! There's just something playful about a pie this color, something that says you're going to have a good time eating it. This is a lovely dessert to bring to a potluck supper or to welcome a new neighbor to your block. ❍ Serves 8

> 1 (4-serving) package JELL-O sugar-free instant pistachio pudding mix
> ⅔ cup Carnation Nonfat Dry Milk Powder
> 1 cup (one 8-ounce can) crushed pineapple, packed in fruit juice, undrained
> ½ cup water
> ½ cup Cool Whip Free
> 1 (6-ounce) Keebler graham cracker piecrust
> 2 tablespoons purchased graham cracker crumbs or 2 (2½-inch) graham cracker
>   squares, made into crumbs

In a large bowl, combine dry pudding mix, dry milk powder, undrained pineapple, and water. Mix well using a wire whisk. Blend in Cool Whip Free. Pour pudding mixture into piecrust. Evenly spread graham cracker crumbs over top. Refrigerate for at least 30 minutes. Cut into 8 servings.

HINT: A self-seal sandwich bag works great for crushing graham crackers.

Each serving equals:

HE: ½ Bread • ¼ Skim Milk • ¼ Fruit • ¾ Slider •
17 Optional Calories

178 Calories • 6 gm Fat • 3 gm Protein • 28 gm Carbohydrate •
340 mg Sodium • 74 mg Calcium • 1 gm Fiber

DIABETIC: 2 Starch/Carbohydrate • ½ Fat

Paradise Junction Cream Pie

What could be more heavenly than this combination of flavors stirred up all together into one delectable dessert! If you love coconut as much as I do, and you also are partial to chocolate, then this is the dish for you.　●　Serves 8

1 (8-ounce) package Philadelphia fat-free cream cheese

1 (4-serving) package JELL-O sugar-free instant chocolate pudding mix

⅔ cup Carnation Nonfat Dry Milk Powder

1 cup (one 8-ounce can) crushed pineapple, packed in fruit juice, undrained

¾ cup water

1 cup Cool Whip Free ☆

1½ teaspoons coconut extract ☆

1 (6-ounce) Keebler chocolate piecrust

2 tablespoons flaked coconut

4 maraschino cherries, halved

In a large bowl, stir cream cheese with a spoon until soft. Add dry pudding mix, dry milk powder, undrained pineapple, and water. Mix well using a wire whisk. Blend in ¼ cup Cool Whip Free and 1 teaspoon coconut extract. Spread mixture evenly into piecrust. Refrigerate for at least 15 minutes. Meanwhile, in a small bowl, combine remaining ¾ cup Cool Whip Free and remaining ½ teaspoon coconut extract. Spread topping mixture evenly over set filling. Evenly sprinkle coconut over top and garnish with cherry halves. Refrigerate for at least 15 minutes. Cut into 8 servings.

Each serving equals:

HE: ½ Bread • ½ Protein • ¼ Skim Milk • ¼ Fruit • 1 Slider • 9 Optional Calories

205 Calories • 5 gm Fat • 8 gm Protein • 32 gm Carbohydrate • 474 mg Sodium • 74 mg Calcium • 1 gm Fiber

DIABETIC: 2 Starch • 1 Fat • ½ Meat

Heavenly Strawberry-Pistachio Pie

Ever pick up a pint of ripe strawberries at the market, and then reach for another, and another? They're just so gorgeously red and sweet, you know you've got to bring them home, and you'll figure out later what you're going to do with them. Here's one scrumptious suggestion that's beautiful to look at—and oh-so-good!

♥ Serves 8

> 2 cups chopped fresh strawberries ☆
> Sugar substitute to equal 2 tablespoons sugar
> 1 (4-serving) package JELL-O sugar-free instant pistachio pudding mix
> ⅔ cup Carnation Nonfat Dry Milk Powder
> 1 cup water
> 1 (6-ounce) Keebler shortbread piecrust
> ½ cup Cool Whip Free
> 2 to 3 drops red food coloring

Reserve ¼ cup strawberries. In a medium bowl, combine remaining strawberries and sugar substitute. In a large bowl, combine dry pudding mix and dry milk powder. Add water. Mix well using a wire whisk. Stir 1¼ cups of the strawberry mixture into pudding mixture. Spread mixture evenly into piecrust. Mash remaining ½ cup strawberry mixture with a fork. Blend in Cool Whip Free and red food coloring. Spread topping mixture evenly over pudding layer. Sprinkle reserved ¼ cup strawberries over top. Refrigerate for at least 30 minutes. Cut into 8 servings.

Each serving equals:

HE: ½ Bread • ¼ Skim Milk • ¼ Fruit • ¾ Slider • 12 Optional Calories

162 Calories • 6 gm Fat • 3 gm Protein • 24 gm Carbohydrate • 329 mg Sodium • 74 mg Calcium • 1 gm Fiber

DIABETIC: 1½ Starch/Carbohydrate • 1 Fat

Hawaiian Banana-Pistachio Pie

Maybe there aren't any cheap fares at the moment, or any direct flights to Maui from where you live. (There sure aren't any from Iowa!) But I can be in Hawaii in just the few minutes it takes for this pie to set. Why not join me for a dessert luau and stir up this festive dessert right now? ☻ Serves 8

1 cup (1 medium) diced banana

1 (6-ounce) Keebler graham cracker piecrust

1 (4-serving) package JELL-O sugar-free instant pistachio pudding mix

⅔ cup Carnation Nonfat Dry Milk Powder

1 cup (one 8-ounce can) crushed pineapple, packed in fruit juice, drained, and ⅓
  cup liquid reserved

¾ cup water

1 cup Cool Whip Free ☆

1½ teaspoons coconut extract ☆

2 tablespoons flaked coconut

Layer banana in bottom of piecrust. In a large bowl, combine dry pudding mix and dry milk powder. Add reserved pineapple juice and water. Mix well using a wire whisk. Blend in ¼ cup Cool Whip Free and ½ teaspoon coconut extract. Spread pudding mixture evenly over banana. Refrigerate while preparing topping. In a medium bowl, combine remaining ¾ cup Cool Whip Free, remaining 1 teaspoon coconut extract, and pineapple. Mix gently to combine. Evenly spread topping mixture over pudding mixture. Sprinkle coconut evenly over top. Refrigerate for at least 30 minutes. Cut into 8 servings.

HINT: To prevent banana from turning brown, mix with 1 teaspoon lemon juice or sprinkle with Fruit Fresh.

Each serving equals:

HE: ½ Bread • ½ Fruit • ¼ Skim Milk • 1 Slider •
1 Optional Calorie

202 Calories • 6 gm Fat • 3 gm Protein • 34 gm Carbohydrate •
334 mg Sodium • 75 mg Calcium • 1 gm Fiber

DIABETIC: 1½ Starch/Carbohydrate • 1 Fat •
½ Fruit or 2 Starch/Carbohydrate • 1 Fat

Banana-Strawberry Cream Pie

I have to give thanks to the folks at JELL-O for creating a sugar-free banana cream pudding—thanks, guys—or how else would we be able to enjoy luscious and creamy desserts like this one? I think the combo of bananas and strawberries is an especially winning one, don't you?   ☻   Serves 8

1 cup (1 medium) sliced banana

2 cups sliced fresh strawberries

1 (6-ounce) Keebler shortbread piecrust

1 (4-serving) package JELL-O sugar-free instant banana cream pudding mix

⅔ cup Carnation Nonfat Dry Milk Powder

1⅓ cups water

¾ cup Cool Whip Lite ☆

Layer banana and strawberries in bottom of piecrust. In a medium bowl, combine dry pudding mix, dry milk powder, and water. Mix well using a wire whisk. Blend in ¼ cup Cool Whip Lite. Spread mixture evenly over fruit. Refrigerate for at least 30 minutes. Cut into 8 servings. When serving, top each piece with 1 tablespoon Cool Whip Lite.

HINT: To prevent banana from turning brown, mix with 1 teaspoon lemon juice or sprinkle with Fruit Fresh.

Each serving equals:

HE: ½ Bread • ½ Fruit • ¼ Skim Milk • ¾ Slider • 18 Optional Calories

186 Calories • 6 gm Fat • 3 gm Protein • 30 gm Carbohydrate • 340 mg Sodium • 75 mg Calcium • 1 gm Fiber

DIABETIC: 1½ Starch/Carbohydrate • ½ Fruit • ½ Fat or 2 Starch/Carbohydrate • ½ Fat

Seventh Heaven Banana Cream Pie

It just isn't enough to say this dessert deserves to be eaten by angels (though my testers and I believe it is!). It's so full of good-tasting treats, it's better than that. In fact, it's better than "better than good"—and that's pretty fantastic!

⚫ Serves 8

2 cups (2 medium) sliced bananas

1 (6-ounce) Keebler shortbread piecrust

1 (4-serving) package JELL-O sugar-free instant banana cream pudding mix

⅔ cup Carnation Nonfat Dry Milk Powder

1¼ cups Diet 7Up

1 cup Cool Whip Free ☆

¼ cup raspberry spreadable fruit

3 to 4 drops red food coloring

½ teaspoon almond extract

1 tablespoon (¼ ounce) sliced almonds

Layer bananas in piecrust. In a medium bowl, combine dry pudding mix, dry milk powder, and Diet 7Up. Mix well using a wire whisk. Blend in ¼ cup Cool Whip Free. Spread mixture evenly over bananas. In a small bowl, gently combine remaining ¾ cup Cool Whip Free and spreadable fruit. Stir in red food coloring and almond extract. Evenly spread topping mixture over set filling. Sprinkle almonds evenly over top. Cover and refrigerate for at least 30 minutes. Cut into 8 servings.

HINT: To prevent bananas from turning brown, mix with 1 teaspoon lemon juice or sprinkle with Fruit Fresh.

Each serving equals:

HE: 1 Fruit • ½ Bread • ¼ Skim Milk • 1 Slider • 2 Optional Calories

214 Calories • 6 gm Fat • 3 gm Protein • 37 gm Carbohydrate • 345 mg Sodium • 74 mg Calcium • 1 gm Fiber

DIABETIC: 1½ Starch/Carbohydrate • 1 Fruit • 1 Fat

Chocolate Fancier's Cream Pie

Here's a chocolate lover's fantasy that layers chocolate upon chocolate before it's ready to serve! With four chocolate ingredients (out of seven!), you know you're going to get the most extreme chocolate flavor you can imagine—and what is more appealing than that? ☻ Serves 8

> 2 (4-serving) packages JELL-O sugar-free instant chocolate pudding mix
> 1⅓ cups Carnation Nonfat Dry Milk Powder
> 2½ cups water
> 1 (6-ounce) Keebler chocolate piecrust
> 1 cup Cool Whip Free
> 1 tablespoon Hershey's Lite Chocolate Syrup
> 1 tablespoon (¼ ounce) mini chocolate chips

In a large bowl, combine dry pudding mixes and dry milk powder. Add water. Mix well using a wire whisk. Spread pudding mixture evenly into piecrust. Refrigerate for 5 minutes. Meanwhile, in a small bowl, gently combine Cool Whip Free and chocolate syrup. Evenly spread topping mixture over set filling. Sprinkle chocolate chips evenly over top. Refrigerate for at least 30 minutes. Cut into 8 servings.

Each serving equals:

HE: ½ Skim Milk • ½ Bread • 1 Slider • 19 Optional Calories

209 Calories • 5 gm Fat • 6 gm Protein • 35 gm Carbohydrate • 502 mg Sodium • 140 mg Calcium • 1 gm Fiber

DIABETIC: 1½ Starch/Carbohydrate • ½ Skim Milk • ½ Fat

Bavarian Chocolate Mint Pie

There's something so fresh and delicious about the blend of chocolate and mint flavors. The chocolate is deep and rich, the mint is cool and light, and together they promise a party of flavors that just never ends!   ❤   Serves 8

2 (4-serving) packages JELL-O sugar-free instant chocolate pudding mix
1⅓ cups Carnation Nonfat Dry Milk Powder
2½ cups water
½ teaspoon mint extract
1 cup Cool Whip Lite ☆
1 (6-ounce) Keebler shortbread piecrust

In a large bowl, combine dry pudding mixes and dry milk powder. Add water and mint extract. Mix well using a wire whisk. Blend in ½ cup Cool Whip Lite. Spread pudding mixture into piecrust. Refrigerate for at least 30 minutes. Cut into 8 servings. When serving, top each piece with 1 tablespoon Cool Whip Lite.

Each serving equals:

HE: ½ Skim Milk • ½ Bread • 1 Slider • 15 Optional Calories

198 Calories • 6 gm Fat • 6 gm Protein • 30 gm Carbohydrate • 527 mg Sodium • 139 mg Calcium • 1 gm Fiber

DIABETIC: 1½ Starch/Carbohydrate • 1 Fat

Lemon-Chocolate Ambrosia Cheesecake

In the old myths, ambrosia was the only food good enough for the gods on Mount Olympus. I stirred so much delectable flavor into this cheesecake that it's downright heavenly—hence the name! If you've never imagined blending chocolate and lemon together, I bet this luscious treat will please you more than you know.

❂ Serves 8

> 2 (8-ounce) packages Philadelphia fat-free cream cheese
> 1 (4-serving) package JELL-O sugar-free instant vanilla pudding mix
> 1 (4-serving) package JELL-O sugar-free lemon gelatin
> 1 cup Diet Mountain Dew
> ¼ cup Cool Whip Free
> 1 teaspoon coconut extract
> 2 tablespoons (½ ounce) mini chocolate chips
> 1 (6-ounce) Keebler chocolate piecrust
> 2 (2½-inch) chocolate graham crackers, made into crumbs
> 2 tablespoons flaked coconut

In a large bowl, stir cream cheese with a spoon until soft. Add dry pudding mix, dry gelatin, and Diet Mountain Dew. Mix well using a wire whisk. Blend in Cool Whip Free and coconut extract. Gently stir in chocolate chips. Spread mixture evenly into piecrust. Evenly sprinkle graham cracker crumbs and coconut over top. Refrigerate for at least 30 minutes. Cut into 8 servings.

HINT: A self-seal sandwich bag works great for crushing graham crackers.

Each serving equals:

HE: 1 Protein • ½ Bread • 1 Slider • 11 Optional Calories

186 Calories • 6 gm Fat • 10 gm Protein • 23 gm Carbohydrate • 645 mg Sodium • 2 mg Calcium • 1 gm Fiber

DIABETIC: 1½ Starch/Carbohydrate • 1 Meat • 1 Fat

Glory Days Cheesecake Pie

What's more American and old-fashioned than an apple pie? I can't think of anything—can you? But what could be both American and as exciting as the new century promises to be? Maybe this richly apple-flavored cheesecake!

◐ Serves 8

> 2 (8-ounce) packages Philadelphia fat-free cream cheese
> 1 (4-serving) package JELL-O sugar-free instant vanilla pudding mix
> ⅔ cup Carnation Nonfat Dry Milk Powder
> 1 cup unsweetened apple juice
> 1 teaspoon apple pie spice
> ¼ cup Cool Whip Free
> ½ cup raisins
> 1 (6-ounce) Keebler graham cracker piecrust
> 2 tablespoons + 2 teaspoons apple butter

In a large bowl, stir cream cheese with a spoon until soft. Add dry pudding mix, dry milk powder, and apple juice. Mix well using a wire whisk. Blend in apple pie spice, Cool Whip Free, and raisins. Spread mixture into piecrust. Refrigerate for at least 30 minutes. Cut into 8 servings. When serving, top each piece with 1 teaspoon apple butter.

HINT: To plump up raisins without "cooking," place in a glass measuring cup and microwave on HIGH for 20 seconds.

Each serving equals:

HE: 1 Protein • ¾ Fruit • ½ Bread • ¼ Skim Milk • ¾ Slider • 14 Optional Calories

217 Calories • 5 gm Fat • 9 gm Protein • 34 gm Carbohydrate • 637 mg Sodium • 76 mg Calcium • 1 gm Fiber

DIABETIC: 1 Meat • 1 Fruit • 1 Starch • 1 Fat

Making Healthy
Exchanges Work
"for You

You're now ready to begin a wonderful journey to better health. In the preceding pages, you've discovered the remarkable variety of good food available to you when you begin eating the Healthy Exchanges way. You've stocked your pantry and learned many of my food preparation "secrets" that will point you on the way to delicious success.

But before I let you go, I'd like to share a few tips that I've learned while traveling toward healthier eating habits. It took me a long time to learn how to eat *smarter*. In fact, I'm still working on it. But I am getting better. For years, I could *inhale* a five-course meal in five minutes flat—and still make room for a second helping of dessert!

Now I follow certain signposts on the road that help me stay on the right path. I hope these ideas will help point you in the right direction as well.

1. Eat slowly so your brain has time to catch up with your tummy. Cut and chew each bite slowly. Try putting your fork down between bites. Stop eating as soon as you feel full. Crumple your napkin and throw it on top of your plate so you don't continue to eat when you are no longer hungry.

2. Smaller plates may help you feel more satisfied by your food portions *and* limit the amount you can put on the plate.

3. Watch portion size. If you are *truly* hungry, you can always add more food to your plate once you've finished your initial serving. But remember to count the additional food accordingly.

4. Always eat at your dining-room or kitchen table. You deserve better than nibbling from an open refrigerator or over the sink. Make an attractive

place setting, even if you're eating alone. Feed your eyes as well as your stomach. By always eating at a table, you will become much more aware of your true food intake. For some reason, many of us conveniently "forget" the food we swallow while standing over the stove or munching in the car or on the run.

5. Avoid doing anything else while you are eating. If you read the paper or watch television while you eat, it's easy to consume too much food without realizing it, because you are concentrating on something else besides what you're eating. Then, when you look down at your plate and see that it's empty, you wonder where all the food went and why you still feel hungry.

Day by day, as you travel the path to good health, it will become easier to make the right choices, to eat *smarter*. But don't ever fool yourself into thinking that you'll be able to put your eating habits on cruise control and forget about them. Making a commitment to eat good healthy food and sticking to it takes some effort. But with all the good-tasting recipes in this Healthy Exchanges cookbook, just think how well you're going to eat—and enjoy it—from now on!

Healthy Lean *Bon Appétit!*

Index of Recipes